Tottel's Managing Business Transfers

Tupe and takeovers, mergers and outsourcing

edited by Murray Fairclough

Second edition

Tottel
publishing

Tottel Publishing Ltd, Maxwelton House, 41–43 Boltro Road, Haywards Heath, West Sussex, RH16 1BJ

© Tottel Publishing Ltd 2006

A CIP Catalogue record for this book is available from the British Library.

ISBN 1 84592 305 7

ISBN 978 1 84592 305 7

Typeset by Kerry Press Ltd, Luton, Beds

Printed and bound in Great Britain by Athenaeum Press Ltd, Gateshead, Tyne & Wear

About the author

Murray Fairclough

Murray is the Director of Legal Services for Abbey Protection Group Limited.

He is a graduate of Nottingham Law School and of the University of Leicester where he received a Masters degree in Employment Law and Industrial Relations. In 1998, he was awarded a Doctorate by the University of Leicester for his research into Civil Legal Aid and the Legal Expenses Insurance Industry.

Previously, he was head of employment law for the Legal Protection Group Limited before becoming senior Employment Law Associate with International law firm Sonnenshein.

He is also a published author and has contributed many articles and commentary to the national press, radio and trade journals.

Murray is a practising barrister and a member of the Employment Law Bar Association and the Employment Lawyers' Association.

Contents

Table of Cases

xiii

Table of Statutes

Table of Statutory Instruments

Table of European Legislation

1. Introduction: the Law on Transfer of Undertakings

What are the TUPE regulations for?

Why the law on transfer of undertakings is important [1.1]

The *Transfer of Undertakings* (*Protection of Employment*) *Regulations 1981* (*SI 1981/1794*) as revoked by the 2006 regulations (TUPE) were originally enacted to comply with the EU Acquired Rights Directive 1977 (77/187/EEC) ('the Directive'). The Directive formed part of a package of measures designed to encourage the restructuring and reorganisation of European businesses. In the Directive, the EU addresses the needs of employees where the business in which they work is taken over by another. The Directive is intended to provide benefits to employees to counterbalance those given to businesses and at the same time to minimise employees' objections to restructuring by guaranteeing them unchanged and continuous employment rights. When it was introduced, contracting out or the subcontracting of services between businesses was unusual. Today it is a very common form of restructuring. The contracting out of services comes within the remit of the Directive and it is in this area that many of today's transfer-related problems arise.

The original Acquired Rights Directive 1977

Interpretation of the Directive [1.2]

The interpretation of any EU document is far from easy. Directives and other EU documents are issued in all the languages of the member states and no single language version has predominance.

Because a literal interpretation is ruled out the European Court takes what is described as a 'purposive' interpretation of a Directive. The 'purpose' is set out in the preamble to a Directive. A Directive and any relevant national law is then interpreted to achieve the purpose. This is a legitimate way to interpret the law and in the UK it is known as the 'mischief rule', albeit used infrequently.

One objective in the preamble to the Acquired Rights Directive 1977 is to harmonise the legal protection provided by the member states to produce a level playing field for conducting business. The objective that has played the most important part in interpreting the Directive is the one providing that:

> 'it is necessary to provide for the protection of employees in the event of a change of employer, in particular, to ensure that their rights are safeguarded.'

This puts employee protection at the forefront of the purposive interpretation.

Content [1.3]

The Directive is brief and its contents are summarised as follows:

- Article 1 in the Directive applies to the transfer of an undertaking, business or part of a business, but does not apply to seagoing vessels.

- Article 2 defines transferor and transferee and representatives of employees.

- Article 3 provides for the transfer of employment rights and obligations from the outgoing to the incoming employer. Collective agreements also transfer but company pension schemes do not.

- Article 4 protects employees against dismissals and substantial changes to employment terms where this is connected with the transfer.

- Article 5 provides for the transfer of employee representatives where the transferring unit remains an autonomous unit after the transfer.

- Article 6 requires, before the transfer takes place, both the transferor and transferee to consult staff who may be affected by the transfer.

- Article 7 permits member states to introduce more favourable laws.

- Articles 8 and 9 deal with the timescale for national enactment and reporting to the European Commission.

Incorporation into national law [1.4]

Member states are given a period of time in which to incorporate a Directive into national law. The period is specified in the actual Directive and for employment Directives is usually two years. If incorporation has not taken place within a reasonable time after the specified date, the European Commission will take enforcement proceedings against that state. The UK was late and lacking in enthusiasm when it incorporated the first Acquired Rights Directive in 1981 instead of 1979.

There is a new sanction introduced in the Amsterdam Treaty which allows the state to be fined for non-enforcement. How this will apply and be enforced in practice is unclear.

Enforcement

By the European Commission [1.5]

In the event a state fails to incorporate a Directive by the set date, or does so inadequately, it may be taken to the European Court by the Commission. Alternatively, another member state can commence similar proceedings.

By individuals [1.6]

Generally, individuals cannot enforce Directives. There is, however, a limited public sector exception.

Case study

Facts

In *Marshall v Southampton and South West Hampshire Area Health Authority (Teaching) [1986] IRLR 140 ECJ*, Mrs Marshall claimed sex discrimination against her employer. Her claim was successful. However, it was argued her award of compensation was subject to the 'cap' placed on such claims under current UK law. Mrs Marshall successfully claimed the UK was in breach of its obligations in not implementing the Directive.

Findings

The European Court held that a member state could not take advantage of its own failure to incorporate a Directive into national law. This meant that a person with a direct claim against the state, or an emanation of the state, which is based on a Directive which either has not been incorporated at all or which has been incorporated in an inadequate way, can sue the state for breach of that Directive. This allows employees in the public sector, who obviously have direct employment claims against the state, to enforce employment Directives, including the Acquired Rights Directive 1977, in full.

There are two conditions:

1. The employee must be employed in the public sector.
2. A Directive provision must be sufficiently clear to be enforced without the need for further explanatory legislation. ➡

The latter seems to have caused few problems for the Directive, but the same cannot be said of the public sector requirement. The European Court defined the 'public sector' in *Foster v British Gas [1990] IRLR 353 ECJ*, another sex discrimination claim, as including a body:

> '... whatever its legal form, which has been made responsible, pursuant to a measure adopted by the state, for providing a public service under the control of the state and has for that purpose special powers beyond those which result from the normal rules applicable in relations between individuals.'

The House of Lords subsequently found that British Gas, although a privatised statutory corporation engaged in commercial activities, was in the public sector. The court went further in *Griffin v South West Water Services Ltd [1995] IRLR 15 Ch D* and specified the three requirements for the public sector:

1. The organisation must be entrusted with the provision of a service by the state.

2. The provision of the service must be controlled by the state.

3. The organisation must have powers over and above those in a normal contractual relationship.

The third requirement may not be essential where the undertaking is not commercial.

Case study

Facts

In *NUT v Governing Body of St Mary's Church of England (Aided) Junior School [1997] IRLR 242 CA*, two schools, one a state school and one a voluntary aided school, were closed in April 1993 and replaced by one new voluntary aided school. There was no prior consultation with the staff and three employees were dismissed. At the time of the transfer the UK version of the Directive, TUPE, excluded from its operation organisations that were not in the nature of a commercial venture, but the Directive itself contained no such restriction. The union and some staff decided to bring a claim based not on TUPE but on the Directive itself. To succeed they had to prove the staff were employed in the public sector. ➡

4

> ### Findings
>
> The Court of Appeal found that employees of a voluntary aided school were employed in the public sector. As far as the first two requirements were concerned, the school governors had chosen to be subject to the state system and, while in that system, the governors were a public body charged by the state with running the school under regulations issued by the state. The court decided the third requirement was not always applicable as not all public sector bodies had contractual relationships – schools certainly did not. The union's claim of failure to consult and the employee's claims of unfair dismissal could proceed to be heard.

It is far more difficult for a private sector employee to seek redress where a Directive has not been incorporated or is inadequately incorporated. Although the European Court has decided that an employee can sue the defaulting state for damages, cases show that this is not an easy task. Once again, a Directive must be clear and unambiguous. In addition, a Directive must be intended to protect the individual and the individual must prove that he has suffered loss as a result of the state's failure to act.

The courts [1.7]

The procedure for bringing a claim based on a failure to incorporate a Directive is to bring the action before the national courts where it is subject to the same procedural rules as national claims, except where these would make it difficult or impossible to bring the claim.

Preliminary hearings [1.8]

National courts may refer questions relating to the interpretation of European law to the European Court for clarification and this applies not only to European law but also to national law, such as TUPE, which is based on European law or is alleged to be the means whereby the requirements of European law are met. The court does not determine the dispute between the parties, it only interprets European law, leaving the national court to make its decision on the facts. These are preliminary hearings. Most TUPE cases referred to the European Court are for preliminary hearings.

The parties themselves cannot refer the question. Their only option is to appeal against the decision. This may result in the case going to every level – tribunal, Employment Appeal Tribunal, Court of Appeal and House of Lords – before being referred to the European Court, causing substantial delay and cost. It is in the interests of both parties that unclear legal points are referred early. Lower courts and tribunals now frequently exercise the right of referral.

Effect of the decision [1.9]

Decisions of the European Court are binding in all member states and override national law. For this reason, any member state has a right of representation in any case, regardless of the country of origin. The UK exercises this right frequently in TUPE cases.

Application [1.10]

The Acquired Rights Directive 1977 applies throughout the European Economic Area (EEA) – the EU plus the European Free Trade Association. It applies to all transfers of undertakings within the EEA, whether the employer is resident or domiciled in the EEA or not.

Example

Two Californian companies, Color Pictures Inc., a film studio, and Distribution House Inc., a distributor of films and videos, merge under an agreement reached in Los Angeles and subject to Californian law. They decide to combine their separate London offices and harmonise the terms and conditions of employment of their employees at those offices. The merger is a transfer of an undertaking and as a result the Directive and TUPE will apply to the two London offices. As a result, Color Pictures and Distribution House should have consulted their respective staff before the transfer. It is unlikely that they will be able to harmonise terms without incurring liabilities for breaching the statutory consultation requirements.

Although all states must comply with the Directive they do not do so in identical ways. It is the relevant legislation of the place where the undertaking is situated which will apply, for example if a UK company disposes of an undertaking in France then the French version will apply. So employers seeking to dispose of or acquire undertakings situated elsewhere in the EEA would be prudent to seek local advice.

The Transfer of Undertakings (Protection of Employment) Regulations 1981 as revoked by the Transfer of Undertakings (Protection of Employment) Regulations 2006   [1.11]

The regulations adhere closely to the Directive. Initially, they were more restrictive than the Directive, for example in requiring the undertaking to be of a commercial nature, in needing assets to transfer and in restricting consultation to the representatives of recognised trade unions. These restrictions and defects had to be removed.

Content   [1.12]

Broadly, the regulations provide that:

- Employees employed in the undertaking prior to the transfer will transfer along with the undertaking on their current terms and conditions (with the exception of pensions) to the new employer.

- Any dismissal connected with the transfer will automatically be unfair unless it can be shown that there was an economic, technical or organisational (ETO) reason for the dismissal entailing a change in the nature of the workforce.

- The new employer will be responsible for all the existing civil legal liabilities in relation to the transferred employees.

- The employee cannot contract out of his TUPE rights.

- Union recognition will transfer so long as the transferred unit remains an identifiable separate unit.

- Collective agreements transfer.

- There must be consultation with recognised unions or elected representatives prior to the transfer.

- Failure to consult will result in a protective award.

- TUPE claims must be made in the employment tribunals.

Interpretation   [1.13]

National law based on European law must be interpreted to comply with European law, including decisions of the European Court. TUPE must be interpreted to comply with the Directive. This means interpretation must be on a purposive and not a literal basis. The initial interpretation of both TUPE and the Directive is made by the tribunals and courts. Referral is only made to the

European Court where the tribunal or court thinks it is necessary. Even where a party thinks there is a difficulty in the meaning of the Directive, if the tribunal or court concludes that it is clear there can be no referral.

When the Directive and TUPE were drafted it was not possible to foresee all the various ways in which business could be restructured. Therefore, the Directive and TUPE have had to be applied to sets of facts that were not envisaged when they were drafted. The results have been neither clear nor satisfactory. The major area of confusion was, and still is, contracting for services. At first it was not clear whether they fell within the ambit of the Directive. Once it was determined they did, the next problem was to decide whether a transfer had taken place.

Case study

Facts

In the case of *Suzen v Zehnacker Gebaudereinigung GmbH Krankenhausserv-ice and Lefarth GmbH [1997] IRLR 255*, Mrs Suzen worked for a company that had the contract to clean the school. The contract came to an end and was awarded to another company and Mrs Suzen's employers dismissed her. She sought a declaration that her contract had not been terminated by the notice of dismissal and that she was employed by the new contractor by virtue of the German legislation enacting the Directive.

Findings

The European Court of Justice held there could, generally, be no transfer of a service contract unless a substantial majority of the employees transferred from one business to another. The decision caused great confusion. In effect, it created a circular argument. In order to see if there is a transfer of an undertaking (in which case the staff transfer) it first has to be shown that the majority of the staff transferred. In recent years there has been a withdrawal from the *Suzen* approach and it has been regarded as too narrow. In *RCO Support Services and Aintree Hospital Trust v Unison [2000] IRLR 401 CA*, it was stated that the transference of workers is only one relevant factor and it should not be singled out to the exclusion of all other circumstances.

The new Acquired Rights Directive [1.14]

A new replacement Acquired Rights Directive (98/50/EC) ('1998 Directive') was agreed in 1998 when the UK held the Presidency of the Council of

Ministers. Although it failed to deal with the pressing issues, it does take account of European Court decisions and the changing circumstances of the internal market.

The main points in the 1998 Directive are as follows:

- It clarifies the definition of a transfer of an undertaking to include:

  'a transfer of an economic entity which retains its identity, meaning an organised grouping of resources which has the objective of pursuing an economic activity, whether or not that activity is central or ancillary.'

  This makes it clear that the 1998 Directive covers contracting out of services and the transfer of minor activities subsidiary to an organisation's main activity.

- It applies to public and private undertakings, even if not operating for gain. The public sector and charities are included.

- It does not apply to the transfer of purely administrative functions between public authorities.

- The definition of an employee is widened to cover anyone protected as an *employee under national law.* Employees engaged under contracts with few hours or under fixed term or temporary contracts are included.

- As in the original Directive, member states may make the liability for claims existing at the time of the transfer joint and several between the transferor and the transferee.

- It permits member states to provide for the transfer of pension rights.

- The transferor would be obliged to notify the transferee of all rights and obligations relating to transferring staff of which he knows or ought to know at the time of transfer. Failure to do so will not affect the transfer or the transfer of the undisclosed rights.

- Collectively agreed terms will continue to apply after the transfer although member states have the right to limit this to one year.

- In bankruptcy and other insolvency situations the strict rules governing the transfer of liability need not apply. This is to enable viable parts of an organisation to continue and to preserve employment. This provision allows for the 'hiving down' of a business in order to salvage some of its parts. The transferred employee would only have entitlement to employment debts under the national employment protection provisions. There would also be the power to transfer on new terms 'in a situation of serious economic crisis' or in an insolvency under court supervision and for representatives and employers to agree new terms.

- If the transferred business retains its autonomy after the transfer, the 1998

Directive provides for the protection of the status and functions of any employee representatives in that unit as at the date of transfer. This will not apply if by law or agreement there is a 'reconstitution' of the representation. If autonomy is not preserved then there must be national arrangements to ensure that employees who were represented prior to the transfer are represented until new arrangements are made.

- The information which must be supplied to the representatives for consultation purposes must be given in good time before the transfer is carried out and, in any event, before the employees are directly affected by the transfer as regards their conditions of work and employment.

The 1998 Directive should have been incorporated into UK law in June 2001. This was delayed and not implemented until April 2006 under the *Transfer of Undertakings (Protection of Employment) Regulations 2006*.

Consultation on the new Transfer of Undertakings Regulations 2006 [1.15]

Although the initial response of both courts and the Government was to restrict and limit the application of TUPE, the advent of privatisation, compulsory competitive tendering and contracting out led to TUPE being recognised as not entirely detrimental. Transfers were certainly easier to promote to employees and unions if they could see their terms and rights were preserved. The current Government warmed to TUPE and in *Staff Transfers in the Public Sector: Statement of Practice* (January 2000) the Government declared that, as far as the transfer of administrative duties in the public sector was concerned, unless there was a good reason to the contrary they should be subject to the TUPE principals. This is now embodied within a formal Code of Practice and effective from Spring 2003.

In addition, although the transfer of company pensions was excluded from both the Directive and TUPE, it has become common for the provision of pensions by the transferee to be dealt with by a term in a privatisation agreement and in any public sector contracting out of services. In local government an agreement has been reached with private sector employers and unions which allows employees transferred to the private sector to retain their membership of the local authority pension scheme. So, in practice, in the public sector the application of TUPE is being widened both to the transfers covered and to the effect of the transfer on terms and conditions.

Perhaps it is not surprising that although the Government did not press for a more far reaching Directive, it has adopted quite a different attitude to the new TUPE regulations of 2006, extending TUPE by law to areas outside the ambit of the Directive along the lines already adopted in the public sector. The purpose of the various extensions is either to simplify the law or to ensure that employees receive the same protection regardless of whether they are in the public or private sector.

The Transfer of Undertakings (Protection of Employment) Regulations 2006 – the new regulations [1.16]

- Revoke the *Transfer of Undertakings (Protection of Employment) Regulations 1981* and contain revised wording as well as reflecting developments in case law since 1981.

- Adopt the 1998 Directive's new definition of a transfer of an undertaking as a transfer of an undertaking business or part of a business as occurring when an economic entity retains its identity after the transfer. Ancillary activities will be covered (see **CHAPTER 2 – WHAT IS AN UNDERTAKING?**).

- Although purely administrative transfers are excluded from the 1998 Directive, the 2006 regulations provide similar protection to transfers in the public sector that might otherwise not be covered (see **CHAPTER 2**).

- Apply TUPE more comprehensively to service operations involving labour-intensive services, such as office cleaning, catering, security-guarding and refuse collection. This will tackle the problems resulting from the decision in *Suzen v Zehnacker Gebaudereinigung GmbH Krankenhausservice and Lefarth GmbH*. Contracting-out, re-tendering or bringing service contracts back in house are subject to the new TUPE regulations.

- Must be considered in conjunction with the *Pensions Act 2004*.

- Through legal obligations placed on the transferor the new employer will be better informed of the ongoing employment rights of the employees he takes on.

- Clarify the circumstances in which employers can lawfully make transfer-related dismissals.

- Give the employer limited power to change employment terms after the transfer in circumstances where the employer would be justified in dismissing the employee for an ETO reason entailing a change in the workforce.

- Introduce new flexibility into the regulations' application in relation to the transfer of insolvent businesses to promote a 'rescue' culture.

- Provide for the transfer of representation rights.

- Although the Government rejected a general application of the joint and several liability rule, it has accepted it in respect of failure to comply with collective consultation obligations and protective awards and Employer's Liability Compulsory Insurance.

As a result of the new regulations there should be some far reaching changes to the 1981 TUPE regulations. The effect of these changes and steps that might be taken to prepare for them will be considered later in this book.

Key points and new developments [1.17]

- The origin of the TUPE regulations is the Acquired Rights Directive 1977.

- Both TUPE and the Directive must be interpreted in such a way as to achieve the purpose of the Directive. A literal interpretation cannot be used.

- The European Court is the final decision making body on questions of European law and national law based on European law.

- Employees in the public sector can bring claims directly, based on the Directive. Employees in the private sector can only sue the state for damages for its failure to incorporate a Directive, or to do so properly.

- The UK was forced to introduce new TUPE regulations to meet the requirements of the 1998 Directive. The new 2006 regulations represent a widening of the ambit and effect of a transfer of an undertaking. They became law in April 2006.

Questions and answers [1.18]

Question

We have just acquired a company and there are some duplicate roles with our core business. Does TUPE affect how we integrate this into our core business?

Answer

Yes. The transferred employees terms and conditions of employment (including their job descriptions) are protected by the TUPE regulations. Harmonisation of roles will have to be considered over a period of time post transfer. Integration and the possibility of job losses will have to be a properly considered exercise involving the employees of both companies, full consultation with all employees concerned and consideration of suitable alternative employment within the merged company as an alternative to compulsory redundancy. ➡

Question

Why do the UK courts have to follow cases arising in Germany, France and other EU countries?

Answer

It is the European Court that finally decides on the meaning and application of European law. Whenever a national law like the TUPE regulations is based on European law, such as the Acquired Rights Directive 1977, national law has to be interpreted in accordance with European law and it is the European Court whose decision is final. The decisions of the European Court are binding on UK courts and tribunals.

The UK courts are not bound by the decisions of other national courts, even when they are giving their interpretation of the Directive, although their views may be helpful and are quoted in legal proceedings.

Question

What is meant by 'taking a purposive interpretation'?

Answer

The UK courts, being mindful that Parliament and not they make the law, have, historically, taken a literal interpretation of the law and this was their first approach to TUPE. But as Directives are enacted in several different languages, all of equal priority, a literal interpretation is impossible. The European Court has therefore adopted a purposive interpretation. It first identifies the purpose for which a Directive was enacted, relying heavily on the preamble to a Directive, and then interprets a Directive and national law to achieve that purpose.

2. What is an Undertaking?

The definition

The *Transfer of Undertakings Regulations 2006 (SI 2006/246)* (TUPE) do not apply to every situation where work is transferred from one business to another. The regulations are restricted in their application and only apply to 'undertakings, or parts of undertakings'. An undertaking is defined as 'trade or business'. The definition in the EU Acquired Rights Directive 1977 (77/187/EEC) ('the Directive') is neater but in essence the same, restricting its coverage to 'an undertaking, business or part of a business'.

Both these definitions lack clarity and it has now become common practice, following a series of European Court decisions in 1998, to refer instead to 'an economic entity' rather than an 'undertaking'. In these cases, an economic entity is described as:

> 'an organised economic grouping of persons and assets which enabled an economic activity to be pursued to achieve specific objectives.'

This better describes what type of unit comes within the ambit of TUPE and the Directive. In the same year, the new Acquired Rights Directive 1998 (98/50/EC) ('1998 Directive') adopted this 'economic entity' description and added it to the original definition of an undertaking.

The 1998 Directive now provides that:

> 'This [1998] Directive shall apply to any transfer of an undertaking, business or part of an undertaking or business to another employer as a result of a legal transfer or merger . . . There is a transfer within the meaning of this [1998] Directive where there is a transfer of an economic entity which retains its identity, meaning an organised grouping of resources which has the objective of pursuing an economic activity, whether or not that activity is central or ancillary.'

This definition is adopted in the 2006 regulations (*regulation 3*).

However, even this new definition is not entirely clear as, like its predecessor, it combines both the definition of an economic entity with that of the transfer of an undertaking. The definition of a transfer requires the economic entity to be identified before the act of transfer and then, in order to prove that a transfer has occurred, it must be identified again after the transfer. As a result, in many legal decisions the definition of the economic entity is inextricably linked with the question of whether a transfer has taken place.

Case study

Facts

A notable exception to the above is the case of *Cheeseman and ors v R Brewer Contracts Ltd [2001] IRLR 144 EAT*. 'B' won a maintenance contract from the local Council that had previously been performed by 'O'. O had used the council's offices and equipment and 14 of its staff to perform the contract. B received neither tangible nor intangible assets from O or from the council. O's employees were dismissed and they subsequently brought claims against B on the grounds there had been a transfer of an undertaking.

Findings

The Employment Appeal Tribunal (EAT) found that the employment tribunal had erred in finding that there was no transfer of an undertaking when the maintenance contract was taken on by B because the existing workforce had not also been taken over by B. The overriding emphasis given to the retention of the workforce by the tribunal conflicted with the European Court's view that all factors have to be taken into account with none to be considered in isolation. The EAT stated that although it was not always easy to do, cases have to be examined in order to separate the issues surrounding the definition of an undertaking or economic entity from those relating to the existence or otherwise of a transfer. In reality, there are three separate stages:

1. The identification of the economic entity or undertaking, business or part of a business.

2. The transfer of the economic entity from one employer to another.

3. The identification of that economic entity after the transfer.

This chapter is concerned with the first stage. **CHAPTER 3 – WHAT IS A TRANSFER?** and **CHAPTER 4 – HAS A TRANSFER TAKEN PLACE?** deal with stages two and three.

Identifying an undertaking or economic entity [2.2]

It is not possible to produce a list of elements that, if present, can be guaranteed to amount to an economic entity. Overtime, different elements have been added by the courts and the emphasis on them has changed.

The earliest list (known by practitioners as 'the shopping list'), and this is just a list of factors to be considered and not a list of requirements to be met, is in *Spijkers v Gebroeders Benedik Abbatoir CV [1986] ECR 1119 ECJ*.

'1. The type of business or undertaking concerned.

2. Whether the business's tangible assets, such as buildings and moveable property, are transferred.

3. The value of the intangible assets at the time of transfer.

4. Whether or not the majority of the employees are taken over by the new employer.

5. Whether or not its customers are transferred.

6. The degree of similarity between the activities carried on before and after the transfer.

7. The period, if any, for which those activities are suspended.'

Ignoring 6 and 7, which relate to the question whether the economic entity transferred, this list can be reduced to three main components:

1. Activity – the business itself.

2. Assets – tangible, intangible and customers.

3. Staff.

Later additions included a need for:

- staff to be dedicated to the activity;

- stability;

- structure and autonomy; and

- an economic objective.

None of these elements will, on their own, amount to an economic entity, but then neither are all of them essential. The importance attached to the various elements will also depend on the nature of the activity. If the activity is staff intensive, as in cleaning and other service activities, then the need for dedicated staff will be critical and the lack of assets of little importance. In other activities, for example running a helicopter transport service, the helicopters may be of greater importance than the staff. It is important to take a holistic view.

The *Spijkers* test was affirmed once more in *McCormack v Scottish Coal Co Ltd [2005] CSIH 68 IH*.

Case study

Facts

In *Francisco Hernandez Vidal SA v Gomez Perez [1999] IRLR 132 ECJ*, the European Court of Justice was considering the importance of the 'activity'. The case concerned a cleaning contract that, having been put out to contract, was later taken back in-house.

Findings

The court held that:

> 'the mere fact that the maintenance work carried out by the cleaning firm and the work carried out itself by the undertaking which owns the premises is similar, does not justify the conclusion that there has been the transfer of an economic entity between the two undertakings. Such an entity cannot be reduced to the activity entrusted to it. Its identity also emerges from other factors, such as its workforce, its management staff, the way in which its work is organised, its operating methods, or indeed, where appropriate, the operational resources available to it.'

Case study

In *Fairhurst Ward Abbotts Ltd v Botes Building Ltd [2004] EWCA Civ 83, CA*, the identification issue was explored further.

Facts

The Court of Appeal considered whether TUPE applied to a change of contractor where, upon re-tender, a contract for the provision of services was split into Areas 1 and 2 and a new company took over the provision of the services in respect of one of those areas. ➡

Findings

Mummery LJ accepted that, if it is possible to identify part of an undertaking as a discrete economic entity before a transfer takes place, an applicant will find it easier to show both that the part transferred retains its identity in the hands of the transferee and that he or she was employed in the part transferred immediately before the transfer. However, it is nevertheless possible, depending upon the facts of the case, for the transfer to occur where the transferred part only becomes an identifiable entity upon the transfer taking place.

The Court held that, in this case, a stable economic entity had existed in the hands of B Ltd prior to the transfer. The fact that this entity had been divided into two upon the transfer did not preclude the tribunal from finding that TUPE applied to the transfer of one of those two parts.

Economic activity: the business itself [2.3]

Although the European Court has now made it clear in several cases, not least the important case of *Suzen v Zehnacker Gebaudereinigung GmbH Krankenhausservice and Lefarth GmbH [1997] IRLR 255 ECJ* (see **1.13**), that an activity on its own does not make an economic entity, the UK courts had been adopting an approach prior to *Suzen* in which little other than the activity was taken into account. This approach led to the finding that a transfer had occurred whenever a similar activity could be identified before and after the transfer. If great importance is placed on the activity alone then, especially when services are contracted out, there is an almost inevitable post transfer identification of the same activity and so the same undertaking. If refuse collection is contracted out, then after the transfer the activity of refuse collection is easy to identify. If the other elements are ignored then the decision will be that a transfer has occurred. These pre-*Suzen* UK cases are unreliable guides to the definition of an economic entity.

However, it is still important to identify the economic activity because the nature of this activity will influence the importance of the other elements.

Assets: tangible, intangible and customers [2.4]

Assets can come in many forms. They may be tangible assets, such as land, equipment, stock, or intangible assets, such as goodwill, customers or contracts. The existence and transfer of assets alone are insufficient to identify an economic entity. There needs to be some activity and an economic objective. This has led employers to claim that only assets and nothing else were being transferred. These claims do not always succeed.

Case study

Facts

In *Premier Motors (Medway) Ltd v Total Oil Great Britain Ltd [1983] IRLR 471 EAT*, a petrol station was sold to *Total*. This appeared to be a simple sale of land. However, the price was based on the profitability of the petrol station.

Findings

The price model meant that goodwill transferred along with the property and this was sufficient to make the transfer one of an economic entity. This type of 'captive' or 'hidden' goodwill can turn an asset sale into the sale of a business caught by the regulations.

If goodwill forms part of the transferred unit, it is a strong indicator that it is an economic entity. Another good example of this is *Kerry Foods Ltd v Creber [2000] IRLR 10 EAT*. Kerry bought the business name and the goodwill attached to St Luke's Sausages. It did not buy the factory or equipment nor did it employ any of the transferor's staff. Nonetheless, what it bought was held to be an economic entity.

Some businesses have no assets or very minimal assets. If this is the nature of the business then the lack of assets will not prevent it from being an economic entity under the TUPE regulations.

Case study

Facts

In *Süzen v Zehnacker Gebäudereinigung GmbH Krankenhausservice and Lefarth GmbH*, one employer lost a contract for cleaning a school. The new contractor did not employ any of the old contractor's staff or take over any equipment. The failure to transfer equipment was not critical, but the failure to take staff was.

Findings

The European Court stated that although it might be normal for an economic entity to have assets, companies in the service industries might➡

---

only have minimal assets. It also considered that the assets might be the 'skills, knowledge and experience of the staff.' In labour–intensive sectors, a group of workers engaged in a joint activity on a permanent basis might constitute an economic entity. Such an entity is capable of maintaining its identity after it has been transferred where the new employer does not merely pursue the activity in question, but also takes over a major part, in terms of numbers and skills, of the employees specially assigned by the predecessor to that task. In those circumstances, the new employer takes over a body of assets enabling him to carry on the activities of the transferor undertaking on a regular basis.

The other extreme is the asset intensive business. Here the entity may be incomplete without the assets.

Case study

Facts

In *Oy Liikenne Ab v Liskojärvi and Juntunen [2001] IRLR 171 ECJ*, a licence to operate a bus route in Helsinki transferred from one operator to another.

Findings

The buses were found to be an essential component of the business. The court concluded that if, as was the case, they did not transfer to the new operator the business did not transfer to him either.

In conclusion, an economic entity will normally have assets, although they are not essential. The need for and importance of assets will depend on the nature of the business.

Staff [2.5]

The purpose of TUPE is to protect staff in the event of a transfer of the economic entity in which they are employed to a new employer. So there must be staff for the TUPE regulations to operate. It is not enough to have staff working in the transferring unit. The staff must be dedicated staff assigned to that unit. A distinction has to be made between losing part of a business and losing a customer. The loss of a customer to a competing organisation may have a major impact, but it is not a transfer of part of the business to the competitor.

Case study

Facts

In *Eidesund v Stavanger Catering A/S [1996] IRLR 684 EFTA Ct.*, Eidesund was employed as a catering worker by Scandinavian Service Partner on Philips Petroleum's Eko Alpha North Sea oil rig. His employer lost the contract to Stavanger.

Findings

The EFTA Court confirmed that a change of contractor could involve the transfer of an undertaking. For this to occur, staff would have to be assigned to the contract. If, in practice, the contract was performed by the allocation of whichever staff happened to be available, then what transferred would not be an undertaking. The court explained that:

> 'for a service provider's business activity to be considered a separate economic activity it must be distinguishable from his other service activities, and normally have employees mostly assigned to that unit. The supply of services, or goods, to one among several customers would normally not qualify as a distinct part of the supplier's business within the meaning of the Directive. Correspondingly, the loss of one customer to a competing company would normally not qualify as a transfer of a business within the meaning of the Directive.'

Case study

Facts

In *Swanton v Computacentre (UK) Ltd (12 November 2004, unreported) EAT*, IBM contracted out the computer maintenance service it provided for Lloyds TSB to SCC Ltd. The contractor assigned eight employees exclusively to the contract, some of whom were based at Lloyds TSB sites. The contract was terminated. C Ltd successfully tendered for the new contract. It decided not to employ any of the eight SCC employees. The SCC employees brought claims of unfair dismissal. ➡

Findings

The EAT held there was no relevant transfer under the 1981 TUPE Regulations. Although the service provided remained identical, the new contractor's allocation of staff to the performance of the contract differed so significantly that it could not be said that the economic entity retained its identity in the hands of the new contractor.

Comment: the new regulations (*regulation 3*) are intended to catch such situations. It now seems likely the employees in SCC Ltd would be protected.

Although the existence of staff is essential, the number can be small. The European Court has referred to the need for the entity to have 'one or more' employees.

Case study

Facts

In *Schmidt v Spar-und Leihkasse der Fruheren Amter Bordesholm, Kiel und Cronshagen [1994] IRLR 302 ECJ*, Chrystal Schmidt was employed as the sole cleaner in a bank. The bank decided to offer the cleaning contract to the company that cleaned its other branches.

Findings

The European Court decided that one employee would suffice to create an economic entity capable of transfer under the regulations. The court held that Ms Schmidt transferred to the cleaning company.

In staff intensive units the staff may well be more important than the assets. In *Francisco Hernandez Vidal SA v Gomez Perez*, the European Court, reviewing three cases involving the transfer of cleaning contracts, stated that such entities may not:

> 'have significant assets, tangible or intangible. Indeed, in certain sectors, such as cleaning, these assets are often reduced to their most basic and the activity is essentially based on manpower. Thus, an organised grouping of wage earners who are specifically and permanently assigned to a common task may, in the absence of other factors of production, amount to an economic entity.'

Stability [2.6]

Stability is a difficult concept. It was introduced by the European Court in *Rygaard (Ledernes Hovdorganisation acting on behalf of Ole Rygaard) v Dansk Arbejdsgiverforening, acting on behalf of Stro Molle Akustik A/S [1996] IRLR 51 ECJ.*

Case study

Facts

Pedersen had a contract with SAS Partners to construct part of a canteen. Having run into financial difficulties, Pedersen asked for the contract to be completed by Stro Molle. Stro Molle then successfully bid for the remainder of the contract. Pedersen transferred a small amount of timber to Stro Molle and agreed to transfer two apprentices to Stro Molle for a period of three months. It gave three months' notice to Rygaard, instructing him to work for Stro Molle during his notice. Rygaard was dismissed by Stro Molle when his notice expired. Rygaard claimed that an undertaking had transferred to Stro Molle.

Findings

Rygaard's claim failed. The European Court held that an economic entity needed to have stability and what transferred to Stro Molle lacked stability. The court took into account:

- the short length of the remainder of the contract;

- the fact that the contract was for only one project and there was no indication of continuing business;

- only minimal assets were included in the agreement; and

- only a few staff transferred for a very short time.

Theoretically, this case raises several problems. Does it mean that a one off project or contract can never be an undertaking or economic entity? Would it have made a difference if the transfer had occurred at the beginning rather than at the end of the contract? How relevant are the length of the contract and the length of the transferred part of the contract?

But, in practice, *Rygaard* seems to have caused few difficulties. Stability is always listed as one of the requirements of an economic entity, but no case ➡

---

other than *Rygaard* itself seems to have turned on that sole point. Also, there does seem to be an attempt to limit its scope. In *Oy Liikenne Ab v Liskojärvi and Juntunen*, the European Court limited *Rygaard* to a 'specific works contract' and in *Cheeseman and ors v R Brewer Contracts Ltd*, its effect was limited to building contracts. In *Allen v Amalgamated Construction Co Ltd [2000] IRLR 119 ECJ*, *Rygaard* was distinguished. In *Rygaard*, the transfer was with the view to completion of a contract, whereas in *Allen* the whole of the work was transferred.

Structure and autonomy [2.7]

Structure and autonomy is also a relatively recent addition to the 'shopping list' for consideration. It first appears in *Sanchez Hidalgo v Ascociacion de Servicios Asser [1999] IRLR 136 ECJ* and in *Francisco Hernandez Vidal SA v Gomez Perez* in which the European Court asserted the need for the economic entity to be structured and autonomous. Both these cases are concerned with several different claims dealing with similar points of law. *Hidalgo* deals with bringing back in-house a home help service and the re-tendering of a surveillance contract at an Army depot. The *Vidal* case relates to three cleaning contracts that were terminated to allow the organisations to bring the contracts back in-house. In *Vidal*, the court advised that the entity 'must be sufficiently structured and autonomous'.

Hidalgo goes much further. It requires the entity to have some freedom of action in organising its activity and the way the service is delivered, even though the organisation contracting out the service will have a considerable say in the way in which the functions are performed. The court is obviously trying to draw a distinction between workers working in an economic entity separately organised by the contractor, and workers supplied to the organisation with the intention for them to be under the organisation's own control.

Example

An IT consultancy asks an agency to supply ten IT engineers to work on a maintenance contract it has just obtained from a bank. The engineers are employed by the agency but their work is entirely structured and organised by the consultancy, not by the agency. Although the engineers are working together on the same project, this is not an economic entity because the agency does not provide any structure and has no autonomy over it.

However, what if the consultancy had given the agency a three-year contract to undertake the consultancy's recruitment activities and to provide it with temporary staff when they were needed? If the agency➡

---

dedicated particular employees to these tasks and these tasks formed the major part of their work, it could amount to an economic entity in relation to the recruitment and temporary work contract. If there were no assigned employees and the duties were spread between the available agency staff, even though someone had prime responsibility for them, there would no longer be an economic entity because no employees were dedicated to the contract.

Economic objective [2.8]

The courts have given little guidance on this requirement. However, we do know it does not mean that the entity has to have the objective of making a profit. In *Dr Sophie Redmond Stichting v Bartol [1992] IRLR 366 ECJ*, a case in which a local authority transferred funding from one charity to another, the European Court had little difficulty in concluding that a charity could be an economic entity. The UK had originally provided that only undertakings of a commercial nature were covered by TUPE and, as a result of this case, had to amend the regulations in 1993 to remove the requirement of commerciality.

It is also settled law that being in the public sector does not automatically bar a unit from being an economic entity. A transfer of one grant maintained school to another grant maintained school could be a transfer of an economic entity (*NUT v Governing Body of St Mary's Church of England (Aided) Junior School [1997] IRLR 242 CA*).

Specific issues

The public sector [2.9]

In the UK, the original version of TUPE included a provision excluding the transfer of 'any part of an undertaking which is not in the nature of a commercial venture'. This raised particular problems in relation to both privatisation and the contracting out of public services.

The Directive itself did not limit its application to commercial undertakings and TUPE was amended in 1993 and the commerciality requirement removed. Once amended it was quite clear that the public sector, as a whole, could not avoid the TUPE regulations. Moreover, the 1998 Directive confirms that it applies to 'public or private undertakings engaged in economic activity whether or not they are operating for gain.'

Parts of the public sector are still not covered and are excluded under the 1998 Directive. These are the purely administrative functions. This exclusion stems from the European Court's decision in *Henke v Gemeinde Scheirke and Verwaltungsgemeinschaft 'Brocken' [1996] IRLR 701 ECJ.*

Case study

Facts

In *Henke*, the facts relate to a reorganisation of German municipalities. It was decided to combine several municipalities in the region, including Gemeinde Scheirke, into one larger municipality, Verwaltungsgemeinschaft 'Brocken'. Mrs Henke was employed as secretary to the mayor in Gemeinde Scheirke. Although offered a post in Brocken she turned it down because she would have been unable to cope with her childcare duties. She was dismissed. She claimed her contract had transferred to Brocken.

Findings

Mrs Henke's claim failed. The European Court decided after looking at various language versions of the Acquired Rights Directive 1977 that it only applied to economic activities. If, therefore, an organisation had purely public sector administrative duties with only minimal economic activities the Directive, and in the UK TUPE, would not apply.

This decision seems to drive a coach and horses through the protection given to public sector employees but, as with *Rygaard (Ledernes Hovdorganisation acting on behalf of Ole Rygaard) v Dansk Arbejdsgiverforening, acting on behalf of Stro Molle Akustik A/S* (see **2.6**), its effect has been quite limited. First, the European Court itself has shown reluctance to extend the application of *Henke*. In *Mayeur v Association Promotion de L' Information Messine (APIM) [2000] IRLR 783 ECJ*, French courts had interpreted the provisions bringing the Directive into French law as excluding transfers to public sector organisations that only performed administrative duties. This applied even when the undertaking being transferred was a commercial undertaking transferring from the private sector. APIM was a non-profit-making organisation providing publicity and information for the city of Metz. As such it was a stable economic entity carrying out publicity services for Metz. It was then transferred to Metz itself and Mayeur was dismissed. The European Court held that *Henke* was restricted to the reorganisation of public administration or the transfer of administrative functions between public administrative authorities and that in other instances the Directive applied. It did not matter that APIM was not a profit-making organisation, nor did it matter what its legal status was nor how it was funded. The transfer was not excluded from the operation of the Directive because the transferee only performed public duties. The activities of the transferee are irrelevant, it is what is transferring that counts.

In *Collina and Chiappero v Telecom Italia SPA [2000] IRLR 788 ECJ*, it was claimed that the transfer in its entirety of the state telecommunications service to a private law company fell within the administrative duties provision of *Henke*. The European Court rejected this outright. It was a transfer of an undertaking. It was a fact that the telecommunications service was managed by a public administrative body, however, running such a service consisted of more than administrative duties. The service was an economic entity. Again, the fact that the entity had no profit motive and was in the public sector did not matter.

The second limitation on *Henke* stems from the changed attitude of the Government towards TUPE itself. Eventually it was realised that TUPE could play a useful part in the transfer even of administrative functions. By guaranteeing a transfer of employment terms and rights it lessened both union and individual opposition to change. Also, it is inherently inequitable that employees in parts of the public sector should be afforded inferior protection than that afforded to other employees.

Initially, the Government's approach was to deal with the matter on an ad hoc basis by including a version of TUPE in the authorising legislation, as in the creation of NHS Trusts under the *National Health Service and Community Care Act 1990*. Here, *sections 6* and *7* ensured the employees transferred to the new trust on the same or not less favourable terms and conditions along with the health authority's rights, powers, duties and liabilities under the employment contract. Protection was also specifically provided in the privatisation of the dockyards under the *Dockyard Services Act 1986* – although following *Mayeur* and *Collina* this may well have been a transfer of an economic entity.

A uniform approach has now been adopted in the UK. In *Staff Transfers in the Public Sector: Statement of Practice* (January 2000) (now a formal Code of Practice with effect from Spring 2003), the Government pointed out that there could well be TUPE transfers between:

- local government and civil service departments and agencies;
- local government and Non-Departmental Public Bodies (NDPB);
- local government and the NHS;
- the NHS and civil service departments and agencies;
- the NHS and NDPBs; and
- the NDPBs and civil service departments and agencies.

It was accepted that some transfers and reorganisations in the public sector would not be transfers covered by TUPE, for example when the transfer concerned a reorganisation of purely administrative functions within the civil service or between the civil service and public bodies. The Government has outlined its intention not only to treat all transfers from the public to the private sector in public private partnerships as subject to the principles of TUPE, but also reorganisations and transfers from one part of the public sector to another and reorganisations within the civil service where TUPE cannot apply because there is no change of employer. The Government will apply TUPE to these transfers unless there is a good reason to do otherwise. Coverage will be achieved either by an express provision in any relevant legislation relating to the transfer or by using *section 38* of the *Employment Relations Act 1999* which empowers the Secretary of State to issue regulations applying the TUPE principles to non-TUPE transfers. This regulatory power was used in *The Transfer of Undertakings (Protection of Employment) (Rent Officer Service) Regulations 1999 (SI 1999/2511)*. In all other cases, where neither legislation nor *section 38* can be used, the principles of TUPE will be applied.

The Government reiterated and expanded this approach in the consultation document on the proposed new TUPE regulations. It proposed that government departments should use separate legislative measures or regulations under *section 38* for those parts of the public sector within their area of responsibility or, as a last resort, should apply the Code of Practice.

Administrative duties in the private sector [2.10]

Henke and subsequent cases make it quite clear that the administrative duties exclusion only applies in the public sector. However, in the private sector, if the unit to be transferred only performs administrative duties it may not be an economic entity. In 1981, at the time of the 'Big Bang', Barclays Bank reorganised. It transferred employees' contracts of employment from one subsidiary to another. It was decided that there was no transfer of a business. A similar decision could be reached in respect of pure administrative duties.

Charities [2.11]

There was, initially, considerable uncertainty as to whether charities were covered, the question being complicated in the UK by the requirement of commerciality.

Case study

The matter was settled beyond all doubt in *Dr Sophie Redmond Stichting v Bartol*. ➡

Facts

Sophie Redmond was a charitable foundation offering help and social activities to drug addicts and their families, especially to those from Dutch Surinan and the Netherlands Antilles. Premises and funding were provided by the Groningen local authority. Groningen decided to transfer both funding and premises to Sigma, another charitable foundation that offered similar but not identical services.

Findings

The European Court decided that Sophie Redmond's activities amounted to an undertaking. It had an activity, assets and dedicated staff. The lack of a profit motive did not matter. Charities are covered by the Directive and the TUPE regulations.

Contracts for services [2.12]

It is possible for a contract, particularly a contract for services, to be a separate economic entity from the organisation benefiting from the contract. This is so even if, to an outsider, the contractor's activities seem to be fully integrated into those of the organisation. The whole question is whether contract activity and organisation meets the requirements for an economic entity. This was a major part of the European Court decisions in *Sanchez Hidalgo v Ascociacion de Servicios Asser* and *Francisco Hernandez Vidal SA v Gomez Perez*. It does not mean that every service contract is an economic entity – whether or not there are dedicated staff. Dedicated staff may indicate the contract is an economic entity. If no staff are dedicated to the contract it is still possible for such service contracts to be regarded as economic entities. Whether the unit is an economic entity is a question for the national courts, initially being decided by the employment tribunal.

The 2006 regulations have provided some clarity and certainty. Under *regulation 3*, where a '*service provision change*' takes place and '*prior to the change there are employees assigned to an organised grouping the principle purpose of which is to carry out the service activities in question on behalf of the client concerned*'; then TUPE will apply. Such service provision changes are expressly regarded as 'relevant transfers' under the new regulations.

It is not only a lack of dedicated staff that could cause difficulties. There is also the problem set out in *Rygaard (Ledernes Hovdorganisation acting on behalf of Ole Rygaard) v Dansk Arbejdsgiverforening, acting on behalf of Stro Molle Akustik A/S of* the one-off contract where there is no expectation of continued need. In *Rygaard* the court was prepared to regard such situations as an exception to the application of TUPE.

Peripheral activities [2.13]

At first, the tribunals, influenced by the use of the words 'undertaking' and 'business' in the definitions section, concluded this referred to the main objective of the organisation. For example, catering, cleaning and maintenance were peripheral to the main activity and so were not subject to TUPE. The European Court decided that peripheral activities were not excluded.

Case study

Facts

In *Rask & Christiansen v ISS Kantineservice A/S [1993] IRLR133 ECJ*, Philips contracted out the running of its canteen to ISS. Philips provided the premises, essential services, equipment and disposables and ISS provided the staff. It had been suggested that the business remained that of Philips and it was only the management of that business which had been contracted out. It was further suggested that the service contracted out was not a service to the business, but to the businesses' staff.

Findings

The European Court had little difficulty in concluding that the Directive applied to a contract for the provision of services and that, in turn, this covered contracts to provide services to staff.

The 1998 Directive is quite specific on this point ensuring that it is of no matter whether the activity is 'central or ancillary'.

Regulation 3 of the 2006 regulations goes even further. In order to avoid the uncertainty over whether the service contract is a legal entity and whether that economic entity has transferred to the new employer, the new regulations extend the scope of existing legislation to include 'service provision changes'. This includes contracts to perform service activities, either directly or through an intermediary, '*where the arrangement consists in practice of more than a single contract made in contemplation of a specific task*'. The *Rygaard* exception remains and the extended application only applies to circumstances in which a continuing need is envisaged.

Example

Company A provides its staff with a canteen service. The service is contracted out to a catering company. This service contract is now covered under (*regulation 3*) of the 2006 regulations as a 'service provision change'.

The company has two manufacturing bases. In one it makes dolls and in the other computerised toys. The doll-manufacturing site is due to be redeveloped for housing and must be vacated in ten months' time on 31 December. On that date it has decided to cease doll manufacturing completely. In order to persuade the staff to stay until closure, the company decide to bring in a free lunchtime sandwich service to be operated by a small local firm. The ten-month contract with the local firm is not covered by the new extended 2006 regulations because there is no expectation of a continued service need. It is a one-off contract (as in *Rygaard*).

Part of a business   **[2.14]**

The whole undertaking or business does not have to transfer, it is enough that part of it does. Nor does that part have to operate as a separate part before the transfer takes place.

Case study

Facts

In *CWW Logistics Ltd v (1) Ronald (2) Digital Equipment (Scotland) Ltd [1999] IDS 633 EAT*, Ronald was employed as a packer in Stage 3 of Digital's manufacturing process. Stage 3 was contracted out to CWW and Ronald was made redundant. He claimed that his employment had transferred to CWW under TUPE.

Findings

The decision dealt with several points. The first being whether Stage 3 could be a separate economic entity. It was found that it was. In particular, it found that Ronald and his colleagues were dedicated to Stage 3 work. So it follows that there would not be a separate entity if there were no ➡

> dedicated staff. The part of the undertaking must meet the requirements of the definition of a separate entity.

There is no reason why an organisation should not split part of its activities into a separate unit and dispose of it or contract it out. Or why an organisation with national coverage should not divide an activity into regions and dispose or contract out those regions. There seems to be no requirement that they should actually have operated as a separate business separately beforehand. Indeed, the phrase 'part of a business' implies that this is not necessary. But the part will need to have an activity, assets where appropriate and dedicated staff. The latter point is the difficult one. If there is to be a TUPE transfer staff will need to be assigned to that part.

Key points and new developments [2.15]

- The first stage in a transfer of an undertaking is to identify the undertaking, business or part of a business, also known as the economic entity.

- There is no mandatory list of requirements for an economic entity, but the tribunals pay regard to an activity, the existence of assets, dedicated staff, stability, organisation and economic objective. Depending on the nature of the business, one element may be more important than the others.

- A profit element is not necessary; charities and the public sector are covered.

- Transfers of purely administrative duties between public bodies are excluded.

- A contract for services can constitute an economic entity.

- Under *regulation 3* of the new regulations, where a 'service provision change' takes place and '*prior to the change there are employees assigned to an organised grouping the principle purpose of which is to carry out the service activities in question on behalf of the client concerned*'; then TUPE will apply. Such service provision changes are expressly regarded as 'relevant transfers' under the new regulations.

- The unit may consist of only part of the business.

The new Acquired Rights Directive 1998 [2.16]

The 1998 Directive makes it clear that peripheral and ancillary activities can be economic entities and that the public sector is included. The 1998 Directive will:

> 'apply to any transfer of an undertaking, business or part of an undertaking or business to another employer as a result of a legal

transfer or merger . . . There is a transfer within the meaning of this [1998] Directive where there is a transfer of an economic entity which retains its identity, meaning an organised grouping of resources which has the objective of pursuing an economic activity, whether or not that activity is central or ancillary.'

This definition is now enshrined within *regulation 3* of the 2006 regulations with effect from April 6 2006.

Questions and answers [2.17]

Question

We want to change our contract cleaning company as it is just not performing. We have found a new contractor but someone has told us that we have to take all the former cleaners into the new contract because of TUPE. Is this true?

Answer

No. Your current contractor is the employer of the cleaners you currently use. Subject to the terms of your commercial contract with your current contractor you can serve notice of termination. You are then free to engage the new contractor. There may be an issue of a relevant transfer for the outgoing and incoming contractor, particularly where the cleaners concerned are dedicated to cleaning your premises. The *Spijkers v Gebroeders Benedik Abbatoir CV* test (the 'shopping list' (see **2.2**)) will need to be applied between the contractors, as will *regulation 3* of the 2006 regulations regarding 'service provision change'. To ensure you get a change of cleaners, inform the incoming contractor that in no circumstances do you want the same individuals cleaning your premises.

Question

What is the difference between undertaking or business and an economic entity?

Answer

The Acquired Rights Directive 1977, on which the TUPE regulations are based, requires the transferring unit to be 'an undertaking, business or part of a business'. This was included in TUPE alongside a requirement that➡

the undertaking or business had to be of a commercial nature. This latter requirement was withdrawn in 1993 because it breached the Directive. The definition is not entirely helpful so the European Court began to refer instead to an 'economic entity' that is 'an organised economic grouping of persons and assets which enabled an economic activity to be pursued to achieve specific objectives'. This gives a far better idea of the type of unit concerned.

When the new Acquired Rights Directive was finally agreed in 1998, it had taken on board the concept of the 'economic entity' and added to their existing definition so giving us:

> 'an undertaking, business or part of an undertaking or business . . .meaning an organised grouping of resources which has the objective of pursuing an economic activity, whether or not that activity is central or ancillary.'

As a result, undertakings and businesses are the same as economic entities.

Question

How do you identify an economic entity?

Answer

It is not easy. There is no mandatory list of components, only a so-called 'shopping list' of items to be taken into account. Key requirements are:

• a specified activity; and

• staff assigned to that activity.

There will usually be assets, but they are not essential, and there may be no assets or only minimal assets in staff intensive entities, such as cleaning and catering contracts.

Question

If an organisation contracts out some of its services, such as maintenance and security, is that covered by TUPE?

Answer

The UK assumed at first that these ancillary activities were outside TUPE, but had to change its views following early decisions of the European➡

Court holding that the contracting out of such services (such as an employees catering facility) was the transfer of an economic entity. The 2006 regulations expressly seek to include such situations and service contract changes within its definition of 'relevant transfer' (*regulation 3*). Exceptions are very limited and the law is now much clearer.

Question

Can an organisation that is designed to be non-profit making be an economic entity?

Answer

Yes it can. There was originally some doubt about both charities and the public sector. In *Dr Sophie Redmond Stichting v Bartol*, the European Court decided that charitable work could be an economic entity and in *Collina and Chiappero v Telecom Italia SPA* it decided the fact that a service (in this case telecommunications) was run by the state did not prevent it from being an economic entity. It followed that when it was privatised it was subject to the Acquired Rights Directive 1977.

Question

Can only a part of the business be transferred?

Answer

If that part can be a separate economic activity then it can be an economic entity and transferred under TUPE. Where the unit operated as a unit prior to the transfer there is unlikely to be any problem. However, where the entity did not operate separately before the transfer there can be difficulties. This is because the need for staff to be assigned to the entity and for assets may not be fulfilled. The remedy is to assign assets and staff before the transfer takes place.

3. What is a Transfer?

The requirements   [3.1]

For a transfer to exist in law, it is not enough for the control of a business entity to move to another organisation or person. The move must involve a change of employer and must occur as the result of a relevant transfer. This chapter only considers the meaning of 'relevant transfer', that is to say the manner of the transfer. Whether there is a transfer under TUPE (*Transfer of Undertakings (Protection of Employment) Regulations 2006 (SI 2006/246)*) will also depend on whether an economic entity exists (see **CHAPTER 2 – WHAT IS AN UNDERTAKING?**) and whether that entity can be identified after the transfer (see **CHAPTER 4 – HAS A TRANSFER TAKEN PLACE?**).

Change of employer   [3.2]

TUPE only applies where there is:

> 'a transfer from one person to another of an undertaking situated immediately before the transfer in the UK or a part of one which is so situated.'

There are two common situations where this critical change of employer does not occur:

1. Transfers within the organisation.
2. Acquisitions by share transfer.

Transfers within the organisation   [3.3]

Where work is reorganised and transferred from one department to another in the same organisation, there is no TUPE transfer because there is no change of employer. However, although the employees transferred may not have protection under TUPE, depending on their contract terms and the nature of the reorganisation, they may have remedies for breach of contract, unfair dismissal and redundancy. The new 2006 regulations make no changes to internal transfers in the private sector. They will not be covered by TUPE.

Transfers within the public sector   [3.4]

There are two circumstances that may prevent a transfer within the public sector. The first is that an entity only concerned with the administration of public duties is not an economic entity. The second is that even if the unit is an economic entity, if the transfer is within the civil service there is no change of employer, all civil servants being employed by the Crown. If the transfer is within the public sector but to another legal entity, for example from the civil service to the NHS, then there is a change of employer.

Transfers within public administration are not addressed by the new 2006 regulations but instead by applying the policy *Staff Transfers in the Public Sector* and, where appropriate and subject to prior consultation with interested parties, ensuring that TUPE-equivalent protections are afforded to affected employees.

Alternatively, it will provide that the principles will apply in any enabling legislation or it will use *section 38* of the *Employment Relations Act 1999* (*ERA 1999*) that allows the Secretary of State to apply statutory employment protection to additional categories of workers. *Section 38* enables the Secretary of State to apply TUPE, or similar provisions, to circumstances in which TUPE does not actually apply, for example to internal civil service transfers. A good example of this application is *The Transfer of Undertakings* (*Protection of Employment*) (*Rent Officer Service*) *Regulations 1999* (*SI 1999/2511*).

Share transfers [3.5]

Rather than buy the business activity the acquirer may choose to buy the shares of the company conducting the business, or at least sufficient shares to obtain a controlling interest in the company. In such circumstances, there is no change of employer. Even though the new shareholders may appoint a new board of directors and take the business in a completely different direction, there is no change of employer. The employees remain employed by the same company. Even if the company name is changed, they remain employed by the same company. This means, for example, that the company is not bound by the restrictive provisions in TUPE on changing contract terms and it can vary the contracts in the normal way.

> ### *Case study*
>
> #### *Facts*
>
> In *Brookes v Borough Care Services Ltd and CLS Care Services Ltd [1998] IRLR 636 EAT*, Wigan Borough Council set up a company, Borough Care Services Ltd, and transferred its care homes and staff to it. The council then decided to transfer the homes to the voluntary sector. CLS was interested in acquiring the homes under a TUPE transfer but knew it would have to make changes to the way they were run, including➡

employment terms, if the homes were to be put on a sound financial footing. The decision of *Wilson v St Helens Borough Council [1996] IRLR 320 EAT* was published before the transfer occurred in *Brookes*. This case decided that a consensual variation of employment terms was ineffective in the event of a TUPE transfer. It followed that CLS would not be able to agree new terms with the workforce. It therefore abandoned the TUPE option and instead took a transfer of the shares in Borough Care. All but one of the Borough Care directors resigned and were replaced by CLS nominees, thus giving CLS control of Borough Care. The staff claimed the transfer of shares to CLS was in reality a TUPE transfer and, as a result, there could be no change to their employment terms.

Findings

The employees' claim centred on two main points:

1. The transfer was a sham. In reality it was a TUPE transfer to CLS and there had been a change of ownership. This part of the employees' claim was rejected by the Employment Appeal Tribunal (EAT). The EAT held that:

    *   Wigan still had care agreements with Borough Care;

    *   the homes were still owned by Borough Care;

    *   the staff were still employed by Borough Care;

    *   CLS had its own staff;

    *   CLS had lent money to Borough Care;

    *   they were separately registered for VAT; and

    *   each had its own spheres of operation.

    The EAT concluded it was not a sham.

2. Borough Care and CLS were a single operating unit and that, although the two were separate companies, the EAT should look behind the technical corporate structure (the 'corporate veil') and accept that CLS was the real employer. The EAT refused to do this. It held that 'the corporate veil has, on rare occasions, been pierced – but not here.'

The EAT also carefully examined both the EU Acquired Rights Directive 1977 (77/187/EEC) ('the Directive') and TUPE. It was clear to them that a change of employer was essential. The preamble to the Directive referred to protection in the event of a change of employer. Articles 1, 2 and 3 all refer to a change of employer as does *regulation 3* of the 1981 ➡

TUPE regulations with the wording 'transfer from one person to another'. The EAT concluded that there was no intention to include share transfers in TUPE and they were not, in fact, covered.

Clearly, employers who wish to retain the normal power to change contract terms in accordance with the contract provisions or with the agreement of the employees should consider whether a share transfer is a viable option.

Relevant transfer [3.6]

Regulation 3(2) of the 1981 TUPE regulations defined a relevant transfer as a transfer 'whether affected by sale or some other disposition or by operation of law'. This seemed wider than the Directive which requires the transfer to be by way of a 'legal transfer or merger'. Both definitions were to be given a very wide interpretation by the European and the UK courts.

Sales and mergers [3.7]

Sales and mergers are mentioned in the definitions and obviously qualify as relevant transfers. However, the sale of shares in a company, rather than the sale of the business or part of the business run by the company, is not a transfer because there is no change of employer (see *Brookes v Borough Care Services Ltd and CLS Care Services Ltd* (**3.5**)). A merger, whether by the absorption of one company by another or by the combination of both companies into a brand new company, will always be a transfer. This is because, whether by absorption or by combination, the final company is a new legal entity quite separate from its component merging parts.

> *Example*
>
> Alpha Co Ltd and Beta Co Ltd both manufacture floor tiles. Alpha wishes to acquire Beta's business. It could achieve this in various ways:
>
> * It could buy the floor tile manufacturing business. Beta Co Ltd would continue to exist and all other assets and all debts would remain with Beta. There would be a TUPE transfer of the tile manufacturing business. Therefore, the staff would transfer to Alpha on the same terms and conditions and could take advantage of the special protective conditions which apply under TUPE to the dismissal of staff and the variation of terms.
> * Alpha Co Ltd could buy the shares in Beta Co Ltd. Beta Co Ltd would continue to exist as a separate company but would now be a subsidiary of Alpha Co Ltd and would operate along lines determined➡

by Alpha. This would not be a TUPE transfer as there is no change of employer. Beta would be able to change terms in the way permitted under its employment contracts or by law and could, in fact, start to bring terms into line with those of Alpha. Alpha would acquire all the Beta staff on their existing terms but without the special TUPE protection.

- Alpha could merge with Beta, retaining the name 'Alpha Co Ltd'. However, as the new Alpha is a combination of both Alpha and Beta, it is a new legal entity. So there would be a TUPE transfer in respect of both companies and the staff of both would be entitled to TUPE protection.

- The effect is the same if both companies merge into a company with a new name – Cappa Co Ltd. Again, there is a change of employer and TUPE applies.

Mergers and transfers within a group of companies will also be TUPE transfers. The European Court has refused to consider a group of companies, even when engaged in similar activities, to be one business or undertaking. It has stuck strictly with the legal entities and held that subsidiaries are separate organisations. As a result, when rationalisation results in the merger of subsidiaries or the transfer of work from one company in the group to another, it will be a TUPE transfer.

Case study

Facts

In *Allen v Amalgamated Construction Co Ltd [2000] IRLR 119 ECJ*, Amalgamated Construction (Amalgamated) and A.M. Mining Services Limited (AMS) were both subsidiaries of AMCO. Amalgamated undertook tunnel driving work for RJB Mining and AMS undertook maintenance and shaft filling and other work incidental to tunnel driving for the same company. At one site, Amalgamated subcontracted certain work to AMS. There was no break in the work in the transfer to AMS and Amalgamated staff transferred to AMS on less advantageous terms. Subsequently, Amalgamated resumed responsibility for the transferred work and the transferred staff returned to Amalgamated not on the original Amalgamated terms, but on the less advantageous AMS terms. The transferred staff claimed that two transfers had taken place under TUPE and therefore they were entitled to the original Amalgamated terms. ➡

Findings

The European Court of Justice (ECJ) held that TUPE applied whenever there was a change of employer. It was irrelevant that the two employers were part of the same group and administered centrally. If an economic entity is identifiable and can be shown to have transferred to the fellow subsidiary then TUPE will apply. The ECJ refused to be swayed by the fact that Amalgamated regularly worked for RJB and regularly subcontracted that work to AMS or that Amalgamated and AMS' work frequently overlapped. They were two separate companies and so were distinct legal entities. Transfers of work and staff between them were, therefore, TUPE transfers.

Asset sales [3.8]

The relevant transfer has to be the transfer of an economic entity. If all that transfers is assets then there is no relevant transfer. This makes it tempting to try to dress up a TUPE transfer as nothing more than a simple transfer of assets, but as the courts and tribunals look beyond the form to see what is actually being transferred this sleight of hand is impossible to achieve.

Case study

Facts

Melon v Hector Powe Ltd [1981] 1 All ER 313 HL is a redundancy case but the issues are the same as under the TUPE regulations. Under the *Redundancy Payments Act 1965*, when there was a change in ownership of all or part of a business and the otherwise redundant employees were taken on by the new owner on terms not less favourable than before, the employees were not entitled to redundancy pay. In this case, Hector Powe, who manufactured men's suits, sold one of its factories to Executex. The agreement provided that Executex would complete the work in hand and Hector Powe would provide work on a subcontract basis for around six months. During that period, about 70% of Executex work was from Hector Powe.

Findings

The House of Lords drew a distinction between the transfer of physical assets and the transfer of a business. A business transfer has to be the transfer of a going concern from one set of hands to another. If assets transfer to a new owner to use as he wills, this is not a transfer of a business. ➡

> This was the transfer of a factory for Executex to do with as it willed. The orders given to Executex were to tide it over until it was established; it was not the transfer of a business to Executex.

Land and leases [3.9]

Sales of farms, public houses, petrol stations etc may take the form of a sale or lease of land. On the surface this looks like an asset sale which avoids TUPE. However, this may not be the case. The sale of a freehold or the creation or transfer of a lease is a sale or disposition and so it must be a relevant transfer. The agreement then has to be scrutinised to see whether it is a document transferring just land or whether it is also transferring a business. If it is transferring nothing more than an interest in land then it will not be a relevant transfer. If goodwill is transferred the transfer will be of an economic entity. This is where 'captive goodwill' comes into play. Captive goodwill is not expressed in the transfer documentation but is implicit in the deal.

Case study

Facts

In *Premier Motors (Medway) Ltd v Total Oil Great Britain Ltd [1983] IRLR 417 EAT*, the sale appeared to involve nothing more than land on which two petrol stations stood.

Findings

The EAT held that the price of the land was linked to the profitability of the petrol stations and so included captive goodwill. This captive goodwill was sufficient to convert a land sale into one of an economic entity. The following three European Court cases illustrate this point.

In *Foreningen AF Arbedjsldere I Danmark v Daddy's Dance Hall A/S ECJ [1988] IRLR 315 IRLIB 355*, Palads Teatret had granted Irma Catering a non-transferable lease on its restaurants and bars. The lease was not renewed but a new lease was granted to Daddy's Dance Hall, which took over the restaurants and bars running them without any interruption to the business. On these facts, the court held that there was a transfer of an undertaking.

In *Landsorganisationen I Danmark v Ny Molle Kro ECJ [1989] IRLR 37*, the lease of a tavern was forfeited for breach. The lessor then took over and ran the café herself. Again, this was held to be another transfer. ➡

In *Daddy's Dancehall* and *Ny Molle Kro* there was only one stage in the transfer. In the next case there were two stages.

In *P Bork International A/S v Foringen AF Arbejdsledere and other cases ECJ [1989] IRLR 41*, Bork leased a beechwood veneer factory from OFT. Bork terminated its lease, dismissed its staff and ceased business on 22 December 1981. OFT took over the main elements of the undertaking and then sold the factory on 30 December to Junckers Industrier A/S. This was a transfer of an undertaking:

> 'when the lessee in his capacity as employer loses this capacity at the end of a lease and a third party subsequently acquires this capacity under a contract of sale concluded with the owner, the resulting transaction could fall within the scope of the Directive as defined in Article 1(1). The fact that, in such a case, the transfer takes place in two stages inasmuch as the undertaking is initially retransferred by the lessee to the owner who then transfers it to the new owner, does not preclude the application of the Directive . . .'.

Control of the business operation [3.10]

A transfer can take place without any formality. Whenever another person or organisation takes control of an economic entity and runs it for his own benefit, a transfer has occurred. This means the transfer may have taken place before the formalities are completed.

The two cases that best illustrate this both involve small organisations where a prospective purchaser starts to operate the business whilst negotiating the final deal. Then the deal fails and the owner resumes control. There are two transfers: one to the prospective purchaser and the second from the prospective purchase back to the owner.

Case study

Facts

In *Berg v Besselsen [1989] IRLR 447 ECJ*, Besselsen owned a bar/discotheque. This business transferred to Manshanden and Tweehuijzen (M and T) by payment in instalments and ownership would only transfer when payment was complete. Meanwhile, M and T could take over the business and run it for their own profit during the payment period. The sale agreement terminated for breach and the business reverted to Besselsen. ➡

Findings

The European Court held that a change of ownership was not essential. It was sufficient for the transferee to operate the business for his own benefit. A transfer had taken place when M and T operated the business for their own benefit and another when the business transferred back to Besselsen. The European Court insisted that an economic not contractual approach be applied to the question of transfer.

Case study

Facts

In *Dabell v Vale Industrial Services (Nottingham) Ltd [1988] IRLR 439 CA*, Nofotec Company was interested in buying the shares in Vale, a manufacturer of labelling machines. It wanted Vale to join the Nofotec Group but it turned out that Vale was technically insolvent. In principle, it was agreed that Nofotec would take over Vale's business and assume liability for Vale's debts. In addition, Nofotec would take on Vale's managing director as a consultant. Before the agreement was completed, Vale's orders were transferred to Nofotec and Vale's machinery and staff moved to Nofotec's site.

Findings

The EAT held that there could be no transfer to Nofotec because there was no formal written agreement. The Court of Appeal disagreed with this finding. It held that no formal agreement is necessary to achieve a change in the ownership of a business.

A similar situation arises where a company becomes insolvent and the directors decide to continue to operate the business in their personal capacity. The EAT held this to be a relevant transfer in *Charlton and Charlton v Charlton Thermosystems Ltd [1995] IRLR EAT*.

Service contracts   [3.11]

The initial view of the UK tribunals was that activities ancillary to the main contract were not covered by TUPE. In addition, it was also thought that a change of contractor following a re-tendering exercise could not be covered by TUPE. This belief was founded on the assumption that for a relevant transfer to exist there would have to be a direct contract between the two contractors.

As a result of these two views, contracting out a service to a subcontractor, changing contractors and bringing the service back in-house were generally held not to be transfers of undertakings.

These early beliefs were soon laid to rest by the European Court.

Case study

Facts

In *Rask & Christiansen v ISS Kantineservice A/S [1993] IRLR 133 ECJ*, the management of a canteen for staff was contracted out.

Findings

The European Court decided that ancillary service contracts were economic entities and contracting them *out* for the first time to a subcontractor was a relevant transfer.

In the similar case of *Sanchez Hidalgo v Ascociacion de Servicios Asser [1999] IRLR 136 ECJ*, the court held that bringing a service *back* in-house was also covered by the regulations. In both cases, there would be a contractual relationship between the transferring employer (the contractor) and the acquiring employer (the erstwhile client). But when a contractor is changed following re-tendering, each contractor will have a contract with the client, but rarely with each other. If such a contract exists, it will be very helpful in proving the existence of a relevant transfer but it is not essential.

In certain circumstances, a transfer can be achieved through the decision of the client. In *Dr Sophie Redmond Stichting v Bartol [1992] IRLR 366 ECJ*, the European Court decided there was no need for a contract between the transferring employer and the incoming employer. Therefore, when a local authority transferred funding and premises from one charity to another, this was a relevant transfer despite the lack of a contractual nexus between the charities.

Case law is now supported by *regulation 3* of the new 2006 regulations.

Contracting out services [3.12]

The contracting out of services, re-tendering for services and bringing services back in-house are now intended to be covered by the extended new 2006 regulations. There are very few exceptions to *regulation 3* of the new regulations which deal with 'service provision changes'. Under the new regulations the party responsible for the carrying out of the service activities before the change shall be treated as the transferor and the party responsible for the carrying out of the service activities after the change will be treated as the transferee. Even before the new regulations came into force, in most cases, service provision changes fell within the scope of the *Acquired Rights Directive* and of the 1981 TUPE regulations. (See also **CHAPTER 2**).

The 2006 regulations have provided some clarity and certainty. Under *regulation 3*, where a 'service provision change' takes place and 'prior to the change there are employees assigned to an organised grouping the principle purpose of which is to carry out the service activities in question on behalf of the client concerned'; then TUPE will apply. Such service provision changes are expressly regarded as 'relevant transfers' under the new regulations.

Example

Facilities management

Facilities management is where the client employer contracts out the management of various services, such as cleaning, maintenance, security etc, to a contractor to manage. The facilities management contractor then contracts out the various services to specialist subcontractors and manages their effective delivery. When the client first enters into a facilities management contract, having previously had all the services performed in-house, the transfer from client employer to subcontractor will probably be a relevant transfer. There does not have to be a contract between the client employer and the subcontractor, just a transfer of the economic entity as in the *Sophie Redmond* case above. This view was maintained by the European Court of Justice in *Abler v Sodexho MM Catering Betriebsgesellschaft mbH (C-340/01) [2004] IRLR 168, ECJ*.

When there is a change of facilities management contractor, any change of subcontractor by the new management contractor will be subject to *regulation 3* of the 2006 regulations. It does not matter that the client company had no direct contract with the subcontractor.

Case study

Facts

In *Temco Service Industries SA v Imzilyen [2002] IRLR 214 ECJ*, Volkswagen Bruxelles SA engaged BMV to clean a number of its plants.➡

BMV set up a subsidiary, GMC, to undertake the work. Eventually, BMV lost a re-tendering exercise to Temco and GMC dismissed all but four of the staff working on the contract. Under a legally binding collective agreement, Temco had to take on 75% of GMC's staff and did so. The problem lay with the staff left behind.

Findings

The ECJ decided it did not matter that there was no contract between Volkswagen and GMC. The sole question was whether an economic entity transferred from GMC to Temco. Cleaning was a labour intensive activity so assets would be unimportant. The key issue would be whether the staff transferred were an essential part of the economic activity in terms of their number and skills. It made no difference that Temco had to take staff on under the terms of a collective agreement, especially when the agreement was designed to deal with the same issues as the Directive. It also pointed out that the transfer does not have to take place in one step but can be the result of a series of transactions.

The court finally summed up its decision by stating it was 'sufficient for the subcontractor to be part of the web of contractual relations, even if they are indirect.'

The ECJ went on to point out that the Directive did not allow the new contractor to only take on 75% of the assigned staff – it had to take the lot. In the event that an employee refused to transfer, he could not be forced to do so. If the employee refused, his rights would be subject to national law (see **CHAPTER 5 – TRANSFER OF STAFF**). In the UK, he will have no rights unless his refusal is based on a prospective breach of contract by the new employer (e.g. an offer of less favourable terms).

Case study

Facts

In *Abler* a contractor lost a hospital catering contract. The meals were prepared on the hospital premises using its water, energy and all necessary equipment. Following a dispute the contract was lost to Sodexho. Sodexho refused to accept the situation amounted to a transfer of an undertaking under the *Acquired Rights Directive*. It refused to take on any of the previous contractor's employees. The employees filed claims against Sodexho.   ➡

Findings

The ECJ confirmed the *Acquired Rights Directive* applies to a second generation contracting out of services where the incoming contractor (Sodexho) uses substantial parts of the tangible assets, made available by the contracting authority, which were previously used by the outgoing contractor. This is so irrespective of whether the incoming contractor takes on its predecessor's employees.

Contracting out under compulsory competitive tendering and best-value contracting [3.13]

Compulsory competitive tendering (CCT) ended in January 2000 under the provisions of the *Local Government Act 1999* and in its place came best-value contracting. However, CCT should not be ignored. If services were contracted out under CCT this may well have been a TUPE transfer. If so, then the employees transferred will have retained their contracts terms and continuity of employment and these will carry forward in the event of a subsequent TUPE transfer of the service.

Therefore, whenever as a result of CCT or best-value contracting a service is out sourced, it will be a relevant transfer.

Privatisation [3.14]

Much depends on the way in which privatisation occurs. If the entity converts into a company and the shares are sold to a third party, then the transfer to the company will be a TUPE transfer because it involves both a change of employer and a legal transfer.

Case study

Facts

In *Collina and Chiappero v Telecom Italia SPA [2000] IRLR 788 ECJ*, the transfer of the whole of the Italian state telecommunications system and network transferred to a private company.

Findings

The European Court held this disposition to be a relevant transfer caught by the regulations. ➡

> The sale of shares is not a TUPE transfer because there is no change of employer in a share transfer arrangement.

Management buyouts [3.15]

Management buyouts depend on the way in which the buyout occurs. If sufficient shares transfer to give the management control of the company it is not a TUPE transfer. Conversely, if the management buy part of the business it will be a TUPE transfer.

Franchises and licences [3.16]

The creation of a new franchise or licence will not normally be a TUPE transfer, even when staff may have previously worked for other franchisees or licensees, as there is no existing business to transfer. However, if an existing business converts into a licence or franchise, that will be a transfer.

> ### Case study
>
> *Facts*
>
> In *Journey's Friend Ltd v Hayes (EAT unreported 1984)*, a hotel ran its own gift shop but then granted a licence to Journey's Friend to run it.
>
> *Findings*
>
> The EAT held that this was a valid transfer under the [1981] TUPE regulations.
>
> Generally, the replacement of an existing franchisee or licensee with a new one will be a TUPE transfer.

While there can be no doubt that the transfer of a licence or franchise can be a relevant transfer, there are some early cases where the tribunals questioned whether the transfer was of a business.

> ### Case study
>
> *Facts*
>
> In *Seligman (Robert) Corpn v Baker Times Law Reports 9 February 1989*, a hair salon under the Debenhams' name and in Debenhams' store was transferred from one licensee to another. ➡

Findings

The EAT held that what transferred did not amount to a business. The goodwill belonged to Debenhams and the new licensee obtained assets only. The early decisions were not followed by the courts in later case and this position is unlikely to change. Certainly where the licensee can make a profit from the licence it is difficult to see how it cannot be an economic entity.

Case study

Facts

In *LMC Drains and Metrorod Services Ltd v Waugh [1991] IRLIB 433 IDS 449*, there were three changes of franchisee for a particular region. Waugh had transferred his employment to each consecutive franchisee.

Findings

The EAT held that a transfer had occurred on each occasion. This was despite the considerable control exercised by the franchisor over the operation of the franchise. The goodwill attached to the franchise belonged to the franchisor and a transfer could not occur without the intervention of the franchisor.

Partnerships   [3.17]

In a partnership arrangement, the employees are employed by all the partners. It follows that whenever there is an addition to the partners or a partner leaves the employer changes. This will also occur where a sole trader becomes a partnership or vice versa; the change will be a relevant transfer.

Some other disposition   [3.18]

'Some other disposition' is a wide 'catch all' phrase and was utilised in *Vaux Breweries v Tutty [1996] IDS 571 EAT.*

> ## Case study
>
> ### Facts
>
> In *Vaux Breweries*, a social club, which purchased a considerable amount of beer from the brewery, became insolvent. The brewery took over and ran the club for a couple of months until it could be sold.
>
> ### Findings
>
> The EAT held that this was a transfer by some other disposition to the brewery.

Key points and new developments   [3.19]

For a transfer to exist in law the following must be considered:

- There must be a change of employer.

- Share transfers do not involve a change of employer. As such, they are not caught by the TUPE regulations.

- Mergers are relevant transfers because they involve a change of employer.

- Mergers and transfers of businesses within a group of companies will be relevant transfers.

- Changes of licensee and franchisee will probably be relevant transfers.

- A formal document or agreement is not necessary. A transfer will occur whenever a new organisation comes in to operate a business for its own benefit.

The new TUPE regulations 2006   [3.20]

The new 2006 regulations do not address internal civil service transfers. Instead, the Government proposes to apply the principles of TUPE, or to use *section 38* of the *ERA 1999*, which allows the Government to extend TUPE to situations which would otherwise not be subject to TUPE.

In the private sector the 2006 regulations (*regulation 3*) aim to provide certainty and they intend to apply TUPE to all contracting out, contracting in and re-tendering exercises.

Questions and answers [3.21]

Question

Is the sale of shares in a company a transfer of the business of that company to the new shareholders?

Answer

No. The staff are employed by the company. The company is a separate legal entity from the shareholders. Although it is common to describe the shareholders as the owners of the business operated by the company, in reality they are not. The business belongs to the company and the staff remain employed by the same company after the sale and transfer of the shares. The company may operate in a different way after the new shareholders take control but the employer does not change. Without a change of employer there can be no transfer under TUPE.

Question

If two subsidiaries merge, is that a TUPE transfer?

Answer

Yes it is. The European Court refused to recognise a group of companies as one economic entity even when the companies within the group were doing the same kind of work. Each subsidiary will be a separate economic entity or will consist of several economic entities. A merger of two subsidiaries will be a transfer of an economic entity. A rationalisation of work between subsidiaries with work moving from one to another can also be a transfer of an economic entity.

Question

If an organisation contracts out a non-core activity, such as catering or cleaning, is that a TUPE transfer? Is a change of contractor following a re-tendering exercise a TUPE transfer? ➡

Answer

Yes it is. Ancillary activities have been recognised as economic entities by the European Court. This view was adopted by the Acquired Rights Directive 1977 by it specifically including ancillary activities. The agreement to outsource the catering service would be a transfer of the economic entity to the new contractor. This position is now supported by the new 2006 regulations (*regulation 3*). The situation is slightly more complicated when the 'client' organisation decides to change contractor. In such circumstances, there is no contract between the two contractors. The European Court decided that such an agreement is not necessary. The transfer may be created by the decision of a third party, such as the client. What is important is the movement of the economic entity from one employer to another.

Question

A company decides to buy a small business with the price depending on turnover. The accounts are in a mess. The purchasing company moves into the business and re-brands it as part of their group, leaving the accountants to work out the price. On full examination, the accounts show the business is in serious financial difficulties and the prospective purchaser withdraws. Is there a transfer to the prospective purchasing company?

Answer

Not only is there a transfer to the company there is also a second transfer back to the original owners. No formality is required for a transfer. It is a question of fact. Whenever one employer runs an economic entity belonging to another employer for his own benefit, then the economic entity transfers to him. Here, once the deal fell through, the prospective purchaser no longer ran the business and it reverted to the original owner.

4. Has a Transfer Taken Place?

Same economic entity [4.1]

The third and final stage of a transfer under the *Transfer of Undertakings (Protection of Employment) Regulations 2006 (SI 2006/246)* (TUPE) is to identify the same economic entity after the transfer has occurred. This is often the most difficult stage.

Temporary or permanent identification? [4.2]

In order for the economic entity to have transferred, it must still be identifiable after the transfer. It may be identifiable for only a short period before it is absorbed into the acquiring employer's (the transferee) activities, completely changed or even shut down. What is important is that immediately after the transfer the entity was identifiable in the hands of the transferee. Permanent or long-term identification is not necessary.

Example

Company A buys a public house. After running it for one week it is shut down with a view to turning it into a restaurant and café. That will be a transfer of an undertaking. What transferred was the business of the public house. The fact that it was intended to be and subsequently became a restaurant and café does not affect this.

Case study

Facts

In *Farmer v Danzas (UK) Ltd [1994] IDS Brief 530 EAT*, Farmer was employed by his own company and supplied lorries and drivers to Danzas. Danzas offered employment as a manager to Farmer and took on all Farmer's staff. The staff continued to do the same work. Danzas also acquired certain equipment from Farmer's company. Farmer himself, however, was dismissed after five months. The issue was whether he had sufficient continuity of employment to support a claim of unfair dismissal. If there had been a TUPE transfer, he could add his earlier, pre-transfer➡

employment to that with Danzas and would have the necessary continuity of employment to support an unfair dismissal claim. If there was no TUPE transfer his five months' service with Danzas would not be sufficient to bring the claim.

Findings

The Employment Appeal Tribunal (EAT) was satisfied that there was an economic entity which was capable of transfer. Danzas then argued that, because it had incorporated the Farmer business into its own business immediately after the transfer, Farmer's business had not retained its identity and therefore there was no transfer. This was rejected by the EAT which stated that as the intention of many transferees is to integrate their acquisition this would defeat the purpose of the EU Acquired Rights Directive 1977 (77/187/EEC) ('the Directive'). The EAT also said that it was what the transferee obtained which mattered, not what he did with it immediately afterwards. The EAT held that there was a transfer and Farmer had enough continuity to bring an unfair dismissal claim.

Identifying the economic entity post transfer   [4.3]

This involves checking all the items identified as forming part of the economic entity and then identifying them once again after the transfer.

Case study

Facts

In *Convy and ors v Saltire Press Ltd and anor [2000] IDS 675 EAT*, Convy was employed by AQ, a printing company in the Mirror Group, which only printed tabloids and which was non-profit making. The work was transferred to Saltire Press which also printed broadsheets and magazines and inserted fliers for clients including companies in the Mirror Group. This work required different skills from the work done with AQ. Only some employees were offered work with Saltire. The rest sought redundancy. If there had been a transfer under TUPE then Saltire would be liable to make redundancy payments, but if there was no transfer the responsibility would lie with AQ.

Findings

The EAT found the work at AQ was an economic entity. There was an identifiable process, carried out in a particular way on particular machines ➡

> by particular people. Although the entity was capable of a TUPE transfer there was, in fact, no TUPE transfer because the entity could not be identified after the transfer. After the transfer the work done, machines used and clients were different. Because there was no TUPE transfer the redundant employees could not bring a claim against Saltire but had to claim against AQ.

The European Court provides guidance in *Spijkers v Gebroeders Benedik Abbatiors CV [1986] CMLR 296* in order to undertake the identification process to see whether a protected transfer has occurred. In this case, the court stated it was necessary:

> 'to consider all the factual circumstances characterising the transaction in question including:
>
> - The type of business or undertaking concerned.
>
> - Whether the business's tangible assets, such as buildings and moveable property, are transferred.
>
> - The value of the intangible assets at the time of transfer.
>
> - Whether or not the majority of the employees are taken over by the new employer.
>
> - Whether or not its customers are transferred.
>
> - The degree of similarity between the activities carried on before and after the transfer.
>
> - The period, if any, for which those activities are suspended.'

None of these on their own are sufficient to indicate a transfer, nor do all have to be shown to have transferred. This is not a mandatory list but a list of items to be considered. The importance of one item against another will depend on the nature of the business. If the business is staff intensive then the transfer of staff will be important. If assets are a major element and they do not transfer, there may be no transfer.

The *Spijkers* test was affirmed once more in *McCormack v Scottish Coal Co Ltd [2005] CSIH 68 IH*.

The type of business or undertaking concerned [4.4]

This refers to the identified pre-transfer economic entity and is precisely what must be identified post transfer. Once the type of business or undertaking existing before the transfer has been identified, it will enable the activity to be identified and the key requirements of the business.

Although a business is more than its activity and it must include, in addition, an organised structure, resources, assets and dedicated staff, unless the activity transfers there can be no transfer of an economic activity and the activity must be the same activity.

The need for similarity of activity [4.5]

If the new owner never operates the old business but instead runs a different one then the original economic activity cannot be identified after the transfer and TUPE will not apply. This causes little difficulty when the business really is different. For example, if the public house referred to in **4.2** was bought and immediately run not as a public house but as an antiques arcade, the business would not be identifiable after the transfer and TUPE would not apply. Unfortunately, the facts are not usually that simple. Frequently, the difference between the business activity pre and post transfer is one of degree.

Case study

Facts

In *Crook v H Fairman Ltd EAT [1990] IDS 412*, the owner of a dress shop sold the lease to Fairman and sold all the stock to the public in a final sale. The owner then paid off all the staff and gave them their P45s. Fairman opened a different type of dress shop that was far more up market and had a different logo. Although at first the old staff were taken on, they were dismissed seven months later with one week's notice on the grounds that they were unsuitable for the new business.

Findings

The EAT held this was not the transfer of an economic entity, only the lease transferred. Each business had a separate identity. The new shop post transfer was a different type of dress shop aimed at a different type of customer. The business image was different. The new business was a different business from the old one.

Case study

A similar decision was reached in *Mathieson and Cheyne v United News Shops Ltd [1995] IDS Brief 541 EAT*. ➡

Facts

Mathieson and Cheyne had been employed in a shop run by an NHS Trust in a portacabin. Following redevelopment, shop units were built and United News Shops won the concession. Whereas the old shop had mainly sold newspapers, magazines, confectionery and flowers, the new one did not sell flowers but stocked a wider range of goods, including clothes, toys, music, electrical goods and sandwiches. The shop opened longer hours and, unlike the old one, paid a commercial rent and used marketing skills to make a profit.

Findings

Although the new shop served the same clientele as the old one and still sold most of the goods of the old shop, the tribunal decided it was a different business. It found too many differences between the two shops – hours, stock and commercial attitude – for the business to be the same. The EAT held that the tribunal had correctly applied the guidelines in *Spijkers v Gebroeders Benedik Abattoir CV* and other European Court of Justice (ECJ) decisions so there had been no misdirection of law. The EAT upheld the decision but stated that it might not itself have reached the same conclusion.

Below are conflicting cases that demonstrate how difficult the issue of similarity of activity can be in practice.

Case study

Unison v East Sussex Health Authority and Eastbourne Hospitals NHS Trust [1994] IT (unreported).

Facts

The care of long stay elderly patients transferred out of one hospital environment into three separate newly built units. Here patients would live in better domestic surroundings, have greater control over their lives and would be attended by senior consultants and their own GPs rather than living in large 'Nightingale' wards where they had to get up, eat etc at the same time. The premises were different and the type and standard of care would differ. ➡

Findings

The tribunal held that there was a transfer of an undertaking. There was the same economic activity before and after the transfer.

Case study

Playle v Churchill Insurance Ltd [1999] IDS 651 EAT.

Facts

There was a transaction between CGA Group Ltd and CGA Direct (Insurance Brokers) Ltd (CGA) and Churchill. Under this transaction, customers of CGA were transferred to Churchill. CGA and Churchill conducted their businesses in different ways. CGA consisted of an insurance company that was not licensed to trade as an insurance firm, a firm of insurance brokers and an offshore reinsurance vehicle. The risk was shared between CGA and the third party insurer through reinsurance. Churchill was a licensed insurance company operating an insurance business.

Findings

The tribunal decided that there had been no transfer because of the dissimilarities between the operations. The EAT sent the case to another tribunal for reconsideration. It gave guidance in the following terms:

- the tribunal should start by looking at what was transferred;
- the tribunal should concentrate on what was similar, not what was different;
- that the parties had contracted on the basis that it was a transfer; and
- Churchill had informed CGA clients that it was business as usual and that it, Churchill, had taken over the business.

The EAT believed there could be sufficient similarity between the activities if the tribunal knew what to look for.

The only conclusion that can be drawn from all these cases is that whenever there is more than a minor change in the activity, it will be difficult to be certain in advance that sufficient similarity exists. Similarity will depend on the facts and is largely a matter for the tribunal. In *Playle*, the tribunal was instructed to concentrate on the similarity, not the differences.

The importance of assets and stability [4.6]

Assets may be tangible, such as buildings and moveable property, or intangible assets, such as contracts, customers or goodwill. As with the business activity, the mere transfer of assets will not be a transfer of an undertaking. In *Crook v H Fairman*, the transfer of a lease and no more was not the transfer of an undertaking. However, when the incoming lessee decides to undertake the same type of activity as the previous lessee then there is always the possibility of the transfer of 'captive goodwill'. In *Premier Motors (Medway) Ltd v Total Oil Great Britain Ltd [1983] IRLR 471 EAT* (see **2.4** and **3.9**) and *Litster v Forth Dry Dock and Engineering Co Ltd [1989] ICR 341*, it was pointed out that goodwill could attach to land and transfer to the new lessee or freeholder even when goodwill was not an express element of a sale agreement. The transfer of goodwill or customers is indicative of a transfer of an undertaking. In *Playle*, the fact that the customers had transferred helped to persuade the EAT that a transfer had occurred.

The mere fact that the incoming employer finishes off an existing contract on behalf of the transferring employer, or the transferring employer enters into a contract for work to be done by the incoming employer in order to help the incoming employer to get on his business feet, will not amount to a transfer of assets sufficient to ensure that a transfer has occurred. In *Melon v Hector Powe Ltd [1981] 1 All ER 313 HL* (see **3.8**), the House of Lords said that for a business to transfer there had to be a transfer of a 'going concern' and, in that case, completing a contract on behalf of the transferor and being given work by the transferor to tide a company over until it was established was not enough to show that a transfer had occurred.

Then there is the *Rygaard (Ledernes Hovdorganisation acting on behalf of Ole Rygaard) v Dansk Arbejdsgiverforening, acting on behalf of Stro Molle Akustik A/S [1996] IRLR 51 ECJ* effect (see **CHAPTER 2 – WHAT IS AN UNDERTAKING?**). In *Rygaard*, the European Court decided that only stable businesses could be transferred. To be stable the business has to have an expectation of continuing or future work. In *Rygaard*, the transfer consisted of the end of a carpentry contract. There was no expectation of future work so the business was unstable and could not transfer. The end of the carpentry contract was not a sufficient asset.

Where the economic entity is asset intensive and the assets are crucial, then unless the assets transfer there will be no TUPE transfer. This happened in *Oy Liikenne Ab v Pekka Liskojarvi and Pentti Juntunen 2001 IRLR 171 ECJ* (see **CHAPTER 2**) where the European Court held that there was no transfer of the contract to operate buses because no buses were transferred from the outgoing to the incoming contractor. Bus services are asset intensive so there was no transfer without the buses, even though most staff took up employment (albeit on different terms) with the new employer and some of the uniforms were transferred to the new employer.

This may be a case in which to redress an imbalance whereby the European Court has emphasised too much the asset transfer. In *Suzen v Zehnacker Gebaudereinigung GmbH Krankenhausservice and Lefarth GmbH [1997] IRLR 255 ECJ* (see **4.7**), the balance is redressed in favour of the need for a transfer of staff. *Spijkers v Gebroeders Benedik Abattoir CV* points to a more holistic approach in which assets, staff and activity are all taken into account. In addition, there is a feeling that the aspect of the staff transfer in *Oy Liikenne* was given insufficient consideration.

Case study

An extreme example of the transfer of assets clinching the transfer is *Kerry Foods Ltd v Creber [2000] IRLR 10 EAT*.

Facts

WH Luke & Sons manufactured sausages. The company was in financial difficulties and receivers were appointed. Nineteen employees were dismissed on the 27 January and ten more on the 31 January. A sale of the brand name and goodwill having been made to Kerry, the remaining employees were dismissed by the receiver 50 minutes before the Kerry deal was complete.

Findings

This was held to be a transfer of an undertaking. Kerry ensured that Luke's factory could not be used for sausage manufacture and continued to manufacture the same sausages for the same clients at its own factory under the same brand name. Kerry obtained the recipe, the customers, the brand name and the goodwill. In other words, it obtained the business.

Much will depend on the definition of 'assets'. In many service contracts the contractor is given a licence to use the client's premises and facilities. The Appeal Court in *Betts v Brintel Helicopters Ltd [1997] IRLR 361 CA* (see **4.7**) refused to accept that the right to land helicopters on oil rigs and to use Shell's facilities were assets that could be transferred. Tribunals have not always been so narrow in their interpretation of assets and have accepted that a licence to occupy premises could be a transferred asset.

It is not essential that there should be a transfer of assets. Some businesses, particularly some service businesses, will have few assets but many staff. The European Court in *Merckx and Neuhys v Ford Motors Co Belgium SA [1996] IRLR 467 ECJ* rejected the need for a transfer of tangible assets but, in that case, the transferor did write a letter of recommendation to existing customers and that could be a transfer of intangible assets. In a staff intensive business there may be no assets to transfer or the skills and experience of the staff may be the assets (see *Suzen* below on the transfer of staff).

The transfer of staff [4.7]

Spijkers v Gebroeders Benedik Abattoir CV lists as one of the factors to be taken into consideration whether the majority of the staff transferred. This raises a circular argument.

- In order to see if employees transfer with the business there has to be a TUPE transfer.

- For a TUPE transfer to exist, the majority of the staff must transfer with the business.

- To consider whether the staff transfer with the business, you have to establish whether the majority of the staff have transferred.

Much of this problem is theoretical because *Spijkers* does not make the transfer of a majority of the staff a mandatory requirement – just a matter to be taken into account. It is not difficult to envisage a situation where the transfer of a majority of staff could be critical under *Spijkers*. If it was not clear whether there was a TUPE transfer but the majority of staff transferred then that, in itself, could clinch the decision making it a TUPE transfer.

Placing emphasis on the need for a transfer of the majority of staff creates a loophole that could allow one or both parties to decide whether or not TUPE will apply simply by agreeing or deciding to limit the number of employees who transfer.

Case study

Facts

In *Rotsart de Hertaing v (1) Bendoit S/A in liquidation (2) IGC Housing Services S/A [1997] IRLR 127 ECJ*, the parties tried to do just that. They agreed that a particular individual, Mrs Hertaing, should not transfer. ➡

Findings

The ECJ held that, under the Directive, any person still employed on the day of the transfer transferred to the new employer whether he wanted them or not. She was employed on the transfer date so her transfer was automatic and neither employer could prevent it. The parties could not, by agreement, prevent the application of the Directive.

The decision in *Suzen v Zehnacker Gebaudereinigung GmbH Krankenhausservice and Lefarth GmbH* signalled a change of approach to the interpretation of the Directive and introduced a high degree of uncertainty into the question of a transfer. Until the decision in *Suzen*, UK decisions had paid little attention to the transfer of staff but had instead concentrated on the transfer of an activity. This extreme concentration on the importance of the transfer of an activity and ignoring of the need for a transfer of staff was about to change.

Case study

Facts

In *Suzen*, a contractor lost a contract for cleaning a school and made the eight staff employed on that contract redundant. The new contractor refused to take on any of those staff. There was no doubt the school cleaning contract was an economic entity:

- there was an activity – cleaning the school;

- there were assets – the cleaning materials and equipment;

- there was a dedicated staff compliment – the eight cleaners; and

- there was stability – there was an expectation of future work.

All the requirements for an entity were present.

Findings

The European Court decided that only the activity had transferred. The new contractor did not take a transfer of assets nor did he take on a majority of the staff. There was no transfer of an undertaking.

On the issue of assets the European Court, whilst emphasising the general need for some transfer of assets, accepted that in service industries either the assets may be minimal or the assets could lie in the skills and knowledge of the staff or the staff themselves could be seen as an➡

'organised body of assets' (*Oy Liikenne Ab v Liskojarvi and Juntunen*). The conclusion, therefore, was that in a staff intensive business there can be a transfer even if no assets (in the normal sense of the word) transfer. In a staff intensive business, the major part of the staff assigned to the entity, in terms of numbers and skills, must transfer for there to be a valid transfer of an undertaking.

After *Suzen*, incoming contractors were frequently reluctant to take on the outgoing contractor's staff, so breaking the TUPE chain. This had unfortunate results for the first contractors to lose their service contracts after *Suzen*. Because UK decisions had overly concentrated on the transfer of an activity (until this case), there had been an automatic assumption that a transfer of an activity was indeed a transfer of an undertaking. Typically, the incoming contractor took over all the staff from the outgoing contractor. The very fact that all the staff transferred was sufficient to make the transfer a TUPE transfer even under the *Suzen* rules. The contractor was not concerned about redundancy and other rights should he lose the contract because the staff and their redundancy rights would transfer in their entirety to the new contractor.

After *Suzen*, the new contractor could refuse to take the staff and this prevented a TUPE transfer occurring. The outgoing employer, who now had excess staff, might have to make them redundant. If the original employer who had first contracted out the service had given the staff generous redundancy terms, as is not uncommon in the public sector, these terms would have transferred from one contractor to the next as each re-tendering would have been a TUPE transfer. Any contractor caught in a situation where he would have to meet redundancy payments would face a major cost that, not having been foreseen, would not have been taken into account when negotiating the contract price. It was also feared that, in future, contractors might include the redundancy costs in the price. The client would then have to 'pay' at least an element of the redundancy costs in each contract. A possible result would be that if the existing contractor kept winning the re-tendering exercise, the client would pay for the risk of a redundancy that did not in the event arise.

Initially, *Suzen* was followed slavishly.

Case study

The first major UK case after *Suzen* was *Betts v Brintel Helicopters Ltd*.

Facts

Shell had three helicopter contracts with Brintel. On re-tendering one was lost to KLM. KLM refused to on take any of Brintel's staff. ➡

> ## Findings
>
> The Court of Appeal decided that the helicopter transport contract was an economic entity. It consisted of Brintel's helicopters, premises, infrastructure and staff. But all that transferred was the activity of the helicopter service. The staff, helicopters and premises did not transfer. This did not amount to a transfer of an undertaking. The court said that several earlier cases would have to be reconsidered in the light of *Suzen*.

The ECJ continued its restrictive definition of a transfer in *Francisco Hernandez Vidal SA v Gomez Perez [1999] IRLR 132 ECJ* (see **CHAPTER 2**) when cleaning which had previously been contracted out and recontracted was brought back in-house, and in *Sanchez Hidalgo v Association de Servicios Aser and Sociedad Cooperative Minerva [1999] IRLR 136 ECJ* (see **3.11**) which concerned the re-tendering of a home help contract. In both cases, the ECJ held that these service contracts could be economic entities and their transfer to a new employer could be subject to the Directive, but it would depend on the facts – not just what transferred but also the nature of the entity. It reiterated that the fact that the new service 'is similar does not justify the conclusion that the transfer of such an entity has occurred'.

In *Suzen*, the court referred to the need for 'a major part, in terms of numbers and skills' to transfer. This, plus the reference to the staff's skill and knowledge as assets, raises interesting questions about the number of staff who have to transfer. If those with the key skills and experience transfer does it matter that they do not constitute a majority? Or, in a reverse case, if the essential skilled staff did not transfer but a majority of the total number of staff did transfer, would there be a TUPE transfer? Logically, given the need for the transfer of a going concern or if the skills and knowledge of the staff are to be treated as assets, the staff transferring should be assessed not on numbers but on skills. Although it was only an aside in its decision in *Temco Service Industries SA v Imzilyen [2002] IRLR 214 ECJ* (see **3.12**), the European Court referred to the transferred staff having to be 'an essential part, in terms of their number and their skills of the staff . . .assigned to the performance of the contract'. However, the tribunals seem to prefer simple mathematical calculations. But there was one case in which they almost had to deal with the question.

> ## Case study
>
> ### Facts
>
> In *Whitewater Leisure Management Ltd v Barnes [2000] IDS 662 EAT*, Whitewater managed a leisure centre on behalf of a local authority. Six of the key management staff also had duties in other parts of Whitewater. ➡

When the management of the centre was taken back in-house by the authority these managers did not transfer. There was also a team of 14 core staff and seven of those did not transfer. The majority of the other staff – part-timers and casuals – did not transfer.

Findings

The EAT decided that there was no transfer because following *Suzen*, a majority of the total staff did not transfer. The EAT also noted the fact that not only did the key staff not transfer, but they had considerable duties elsewhere within the organisation. In the EAT's view this severely affected the stability of the organisation and brought *Rygaard (Ledernes Hovdorganisation acting on behalf of Ole Rygaard) v Dansk Arbejdsgiverforening, acting on behalf of Stro Molle Akustik A/S* into play. If the failure of key staff, or those with skills and experience, to transfer is to be taken into account this could have repercussions in re-tendering. Towards the end of the contract, the current contractor may well put his better managers into the contract in order to retain it, but may be unwilling to see his well-trained and best staff transfer to a new contractor in the event of the contract being lost.

The UK approach to the transfer of staff [4.8]

Although in *Suzen* the court came down heavily on the need for a transfer of a majority of staff, it did reiterate the holistic list in *Spijkers v Gebroeders Benedik Abattoir CV* and accepted that there could be transfers without the transfer of assets and without the transfer of a majority of the staff, although the majority of staff would need to transfer in a staff intensive business. This and the decision of the European Court that it is for the national court to decide, on the facts, whether a transfer has occurred, eventually allowed the UK courts and tribunals to take a different approach from *Suzen*.

Case study

Facts

In *ECM v Cox [1999] IRLB 623 CA*, Axial had a contract to carry cars for VAG. To this end it had dedicated a fleet of vehicles and staff to carry cars. It lost this contract to ECM. ECM at first intended to take on the Axial staff but, realising that the staff were unhappy and might make unfair dismissal claims against ECM, decided, relying on *Suzen*, to avoid a transfer of an undertaking by not employing any of Axial's staff. ➡

Findings

The Court of Appeal confirmed that the controlling decision on whether or not there has been a TUPE transfer is *Spijkers* and the decision in *Suzen* in no way affected the correctness of *Spijkers*. Therefore, the question is whether the entity retains its identity after the transfer. The tribunal first checked to see if there was an economic entity and decided that there was. It was 'the VAG contract itself and the activities which surrounded that VAG contract.' The work done by the Axial staff was predominantly that of the VAG contract, other work being minimal. Without the VAG contract they had no job, indeed they were made redundant and so they were assigned to the contract. The next step was to see if the economic entity could be identified after the transfer. The way in which ECM undertook the VAG work did differ from that of Axial. But, having considered all the factors in *Spijkers*, the tribunal decided that there had been a transfer. This was not the loss of one contract with one customer, or just for one location, and did not depend solely on similarity of services.

Key findings in the decision were:

1. *Spijkers* and *Schmidt v Spar-und Leihkasse der Fruheren Amter Bordesholm, Kiel und Cronshagen [1994] IRLR 302 EC* were not overruled by *Suzen*.

2. National courts have to determine the facts and see if there is a transfer.

3. National courts have to take all the factors in *Spijkers* into account.

4. *Suzen* decided that:

   • for an entity to transfer its operation must continue;

   • all the facts characterising the transfer had to be considered;

   • the similarity of service provided by the two contractors was not enough – regard must be had to workforce, management, operating methods and resources;

   • the mere loss of a contract does not indicate a transfer – it might just be the loss of a customer; and

   • the fact that a majority of the staff are taken over is a fact to be taken into account as well as the similarity of services and type of undertaking.

The European Court has not had to deal with the deliberate avoidance point raised in *ECM*. The nearest it has come to this problem is in the *Rotsart de Hertaing v (1) Bendoit S/A in liquidation (2) IGC Housing Services S/A* case where it held that the two employers could not enter into an agreement to prevent the transference of an employee. The existence of a transfer and the transfer of an employee were not issues for the employers to determine. Logically, if the two employers cannot prevent a transfer then one employer should not be able to do so. *ECM* does ameliorate the circular argument.

The EAT and the Court of Appeal have now each had a further review of the *ECM* decision and have attempted to reconcile it with *Suzen*. The EAT review was in *Cheeseman and ors v R Brewer Contracts Ltd [2001] IRLR 144 EAT* (see **CHAPTER 2**). While accepting the *Suzen* decision that in a staff intensive business, generally, there could be no transfer if the majority of the staff did not transfer, the EAT said that *Suzen* has to be seen in its proper context. *Suzen* did not overrule the holistic list approach in *Spijkers* and *Schmidt* so even in staff intensive businesses the other *Spijkers* factors have to be taken into account. As far as the transfer of staff is concerned the EAT accepted the *Suzen* approach – but only as a first step. Before concluding that because the staff had not transferred there is no TUPE transfer, the tribunal must first check the reason why the staff had not transferred. The second step is to apply *ECM*. If the reason why the incoming employer is refusing to accept a transfer of staff is to avoid a transfer caught by the TUPE regulations, then the fact that the staff have not transferred will not prevent the existence of a transfer. The staff (or the liability for them) will transfer in any event.

Case study

Facts

This approach was confirmed in *ADI (UK) Ltd v Willer [2001] IRLR 542 CA*. ADI had a security contract with a shopping centre in Shrewsbury. The centre made certain facilities, including CCTV and a room, available to ADI. ADI terminated the contract. The replacement contractor considered taking on some staff but eventually did not because he could not reach agreement with them on overtime. Having accepted there was an economic entity, the question was whether it had transferred.

Findings

The court decided that with a service entity such as this it would be far more likely that specifically and permanently assigned staff would constitute the entity rather than assets, so the critical question became 'did ➡

the staff transfer?' The majority of the court applied the *ECM* two-step approach reproducing it as two questions:

1. Would there have been a transfer if the majority of staff had been taken over by the new employer?

2. Was the reason why they were not taken on to avoid TUPE?

If the answer to both questions is 'yes' then TUPE applies.

The authority of *ADI* is diminished as the dissenting judge rigidly applied *Suzen*. He held that if the majority of the staff did not transfer there could be no TUPE transfer.

Case study

The Court of Appeal has had another look at the question in *RCO Support Services Ltd v UNISON [2002] CA unreported (case no A1/2000/2569)*.

Facts

This case concerns the transfer of whole wards plus theatres, equipment and medical staff from one Liverpool hospital, Walton, to another, Fazakerley. The questions related to the cleaning and catering staff. Cleaning at Walton had been contracted out to Initial Services. RCO were the cleaning contractors at Fazakerley. Clearly there was an economic entity. The activity was defined and there was no doubt that the cleaners were assigned to the wards and theatres. However, none of the 26 cleaners and three supervisors from Walton were taken on by RCO. RCO would have been quite willing to take them on but only if the cleaners resigned first, which they would not do. The catering staff at Walton were directly employed by the Trust, but at Fazakerley catering was contracted out to RCO. Six chefs transferred but remained Trust employees, six support staff were redeployed within the Trust and three made redundant. RCO offered to employ the redundant staff and one was taken on. Some catering-related assets transferred. In two entities that were obviously staff intensive, only one employee transferred.

Findings

On these facts the tribunal, the EAT and the Court of Appeal found there had been transfers of undertakings. This result was achieved by returning▶

69

to the holistic approach of *Spijkers v Gebroeders Benedik Abattoir CV* and noting that the European Court has never stated that in a staff intensive entity there can never be a transfer if no staff or assets transfer. Both the tribunal and the EAT had undertaken a thorough assessment of the facts and the authorities. On the facts there was a clear case for ward transfer – the patients would go to the same ward and be treated by the same staff. The training, organisation, standards, cleaning and catering would all be the same. The analysis of the authorities produced no ruling that would prevent a decision in favour of a transfer. The Court of Appeal agreed with this although it also noted that in *Suzen* and subsequent decisions the European Court had set limits to the application of the Directive to contracting out cases. In fact, the court had returned to the old test of the transfer of a 'going concern', a test into which *Spijkers* fits comfortably.

The court also noted and criticised the circular argument that results from the strict interpretation of *Suzen,* following and approving the interpretation of *ECM v Cox* in *ADI.*

Key points to determine the question of the transfer of staff are:

- *Spijkers* should be used as guidance, but not as a mandatory list.

- *Suzen* is a reminder that it is not enough to show the transfer of an activity, the transfer of staff is also relevant and in most staff intensive entities the transfer of staff will be critical.

- *ECM*, as interpreted in *ADI*, requires an investigation as to why staff have not transferred and if the reason is to avoid TUPE, then TUPE will apply.

- Even without the intention to avoid TUPE, using *Spijkers* and the going concern test there may still be a transfer even if no staff move across to the new employer.

Whichever way the problem is approached there is an apparent conflict between *Suzen* on the one hand and *ECM, RCO* and *ADI* on the other. It is probably safe to assume the UK tribunals will follow *ECM, RCO* and *ADI* until this conflict has been properly dealt with by the European Court.

Case study

Gardner's Building Supplies Ltd v Mathieson [2000] EAT (unreported).

Facts

A construction company closed its store and agreed to buy all supplies from Gardner's. To help the storeman it asked Gardner's to take him on.

Findings

The tribunal decided this was more than a transfer of an activity because Gardner's was also acquiring his skills in management. It did not matter that only one employee was being transferred. This allowed Mathieson to include his employment with the construction company in his continuity of employment. The EAT also confirmed that whether there is a transfer is a mix of fact and law and mostly a matter for the tribunal.

Case study

Argyll Training Ltd v (1) Sinclair and (2) Argyll and the Islands Enterprise Ltd [2000] IRLR 630 EAT.

Facts

Ms Sinclair was employed by BEST who had a training contract with Argyll and the Islands Enterprise Ltd (AIEL). The training contract was lost to Argyll Training Ltd (ATL) who took over the training contracts for the individuals but not Ms Sinclair, AIEL's only employee.

Findings

The EAT concluded that a transfer had taken place following the reasoning in *RCO*, even though no staff transferred and it is questionable whether any assets transferred. It is not clear whether the training contracts with the individual students could be assets. The EAT concluded that the definition of 'undertaking' in EU law is so ambiguous that it could not say that the tribunal had made an error. The tribunal also avoided *Rygaard (Ledernes Hovdorganisation acting on behalf of Ole Rygaard) v Dansk Arbejdsgiverforening, acting on behalf of Stro Molle Akustik A/S*, which had said there had to be stability and raised the question whether one training contract met the stability requirement. The EAT stated that it was difficult to see what *Rygaard* meant and restricted it to construction contracts. ➡

There is an added twist in this case. The training requirement did not pass directly from BEST to ATL but transferred on a temporary basis to AIEL before being allotted to ATL. The EAT decided that AIEL did not have any liability under TUPE because it undertook no material activity during the short period between the two contracts.

Gaps: temporary closure of the undertaking [4.9]

If the transfer occurs during a period of temporary closure of the undertaking this will raise questions as to whether the undertaking has actually transferred. In *Landsorganisationen I Danmark v Ny Molle Kro [1989] IRLR 37 ECJ* (see **3.9**), the European Court emphasised that the question remained 'did the undertaking retain its identity?' A tavern was leased to a Mrs Larsen. The trade was seasonal and the tavern closed over the winter. In October, during the closed season, the lease was forfeited for breach. At this point no staff were employed by Mrs Larsen. The lessor then opened the tavern herself the following March. It was decided that the tavern retained its identity; it was of no importance whether staff were employed during the closed season. Despite the time gap, there was a transfer of an undertaking. This meant the lessor was bound by the legally binding pay agreement Mrs Larsen had contracted with the union.

In this case there was only a temporary interruption in the activity. If the activity closed permanently the result would be different.

Example

Company A decides to give up its licence to run a café in a museum and, at the same time, the museum decides it no longer wants to have a café on site. In these circumstances, the original café business simply ceases to exist. Six months later, Company B applies to the museum for a licence to run a café. Over the last six months the museum has lost more revenue than it thought it would from the closure of the original café. The museum reverses its decision for sound business reasons and grants a new licence to Company B. This does not constitute a continuation of the original licensee's business.

Identification through an accumulation of factors [4.10]

The transfer results not from an agreement to take over a business but from the fact that the business has transferred. Normally, there will be an agreement to transfer or a decision to replace one contractor with another, but that is not the only way a transfer can occur.

Case study

Facts

In *P Bork International A/S v Foreningen AF Arbedjdsledere and other cases ECJ [1989] IRLR 41*, Bork leased a veneer factory from Orehoved Trae-og Finerindustri A/S (OTF). Bork, in financial difficulties, terminated the lease and terminated the contracts of the employees, ceasing operation on 22 December 1981. Junckers Industrier bought the veneer factory from OTF on 30 December, taking possession on 4 January 1982. On 8 January, it bought the stock, spare parts, tools, auxiliary material and furniture from Bork. It also took on over half of Bork's employees, but without the agreement of Bork.

Findings

The European Court held that an undertaking could transfer back to the original owner and then, shortly afterwards, be transferred to a new owner, but it is for the national court to decide whether the undertaking has remained intact during the transfers.

Agreeing the transfer is a TUPE transfer   [4.11]

In *Playle v Churchill Insurance Ltd*, the EAT drew the tribunal's attention to the fact that the transferor and transferee had contracted on the basis that the transfer was subject to TUPE. So, although the parties cannot themselves decide if the transfer will or won't be subject to the TUPE regulations, the tribunal will take note of their intentions and where the issue is not clear it could tip the balance. Certainly, if one effect of deciding the transfer is covered by TUPE is that the incoming employer takes over the majority of the staff, then the agreement to abide by TUPE could become a self-fulfilling prophecy.

Could the parties agree to treat a transfer that clearly falls outside the ambit of TUPE and the Directive as a TUPE transfer and give enforceable rights to the employees? This is now a possibility following the enactment of the *Contracts (Rights of Third Parties) Act 1999 (C(RTP)A 1999)*. Generally, the only persons who can enforce a contract are the parties to it. If a transferor and transferee were to agree that the employees should have the benefit of TUPE, even though TUPE did not apply to the transfer, the employees would have the power to enforce the terms intended to benefit them. Only the transferor can implement this and he would probably be reluctant to do so. The *C(RTP)A 1999* allows the parties to give third parties enforcement rights. The Act requires agreement:

- to expressly provide that the third party (the employees transferring) can enforce a term or terms in the contract; and

- to identify the individual or group of third parties (those transferring employees) who will be entitled to enforce the term. These do not have to be limited to those who would have been covered had it been a TUPE transfer, a wider, or indeed smaller group, could be identified.

In addition, the terms to be enforced will need to be identified. These could be all the TUPE terms or only some of them.

If the employees are to have enforcement rights the agreement must be clear:

- the terms should be in writing;

- the benefits of TUPE should be expressed as applying to the transfer; and

- the third parties empowered to enforce the rights should be identified.

The employees would not have TUPE rights as such; they could not bring claims directly based on TUPE. Instead, they would bring a breach of contract claim or seek to enforce a contract term. The content of the terms being enforced would be the same as in TUPE. Claims for breach of contract can be brought before employment tribunals, but the contract must have ended and the claim brought within three months of termination. Tribunals cannot award damages in excess of £25,000. Claims can be brought in the ordinary courts even though the contract has not ended. The limitation period is six years in England and Wales and five years in Scotland.

The Act also covers terms that 'purport to confer a benefit'. If there is no intention to confer enforceable benefits the parties can contract out of the Act. Indeed, it is more common to see terms excluding the Act than terms conferring enforcement rights. The power to do so now exists.

Key points and new developments [4.12]

- For a transfer to exist in law, the economic entity must still be identifiable after the transfer.

- The economic entity does not have to remain in a permanently identifiable state. The period of post transfer identification can be short.

- The list in *Spijkers v Gebroeders Benedik Abattoir CV* together with the question 'has the transferor been put in charge of a going concern?' are useful guidance.

- If the entity is staff intensive then generally there will be no transfer unless the majority of staff transfer to the new business.

- It is also possible for there to be a transfer under the TUPE regulations without staff transferring if the tribunal decides on a holistic basis that the entity has transferred.

- If the transferor refuses to take the transferee's staff into employment in order to avoid a transfer then TUPE will still apply.

- A transfer of assets alone is not a transfer of an undertaking. This is often difficult to prove, especially where the price contains an explicit or implicit element for goodwill.

Questions and answers [4.13]

Question

If the acquiring employer completely incorporates the transferred business into his own business so that it is completely unidentifiable, does that mean that TUPE will not apply?

Answer

No. Many transferees absorb the new business into their own immediately they acquire it. All that is needed is that the business is identifiable immediately after the transfer. See *Farmer v Danzas (UK) Ltd*.

Question

In the case of an activity, such as cleaning, catering or security, which is very staff intensive and has few assets, can there be a transfer if, following a re-tendering exercise, the new contractor does not take on any of the staff?

Answer

Yes and no. ➡

In the case of *Suzen v Zehnacker Gebaudereinigung GmbH Krankenhausserv-ice and Lefarth GmbH*, the contractor who won a cleaning contract refused to take on any of the outgoing contractor's staff. The European Court decided that, in a staff intensive and asset light entity, there need be no assets but the staff would be a key element in the entity and the majority would have to transfer for the transfer to be covered by the Acquired Rights Directive 1977. So, in that particular case there was no transfer. It did not say that a transfer of the majority of the staff was mandatory and relied on the guidance in *Spijkers* which makes a transfer of the majority of staff an item for consideration, but no more. The UK courts have decided that even in staff intensive businesses there can be a transfer even if no staff move across. This arises in two different situations. The first is where, looking at the business as a whole, it is possible to say that the business has transferred because of other factors – transfer of customers, similarity, organisation, work etc (*RCO Support Services Ltd v UNISON*). The second is where the refusal to take the staff is a deliberate ploy to prevent the operation of TUPE.

Question

If the transferee decides to run the business differently, will that prevent the operation of TUPE?

Answer

Not necessarily. The question is not 'is the manner of performance different?' but rather 'is the business different?' Particularly in contracting new contractors who will be very keen to show that they can do the job better, if not cheaper, and this will usually entail changes in the way work is done. However, this does not indicate a different business.

It is all a question of degree and without a doubt a major change in performance could mean that the original business has not transferred, as in *Mathieson and Cheyne v United News Shops Ltd* where the replacement hospital shop sold a wider range of goods to a wider clientele than the small shop it replaced. A view followed by the EAT in *Swanton v Computacentre (UK) Ltd (12 November 2004, unreported) EAT*. Showing sufficient dissimilarity is far from easy especially as in *Playle v Churchill Insurance Ltd* where the tribunal was told to concentrate on what is similar.

Question

How important is it to show that assets have transferred? ➡

Answer

Generally, one would expect assets of some kind, tangible or intangible, to transfer. Where the assets are a key element of the business then, if they do not transfer, there may be no transfer of an undertaking. This occurred in the *Oy Liikenne Ab v Pekka Liskojarvi and Pentti Juntunen* case which concerned the transfer of a licence to run a bus service. The buses did not transfer. It is not possible to run a bus service without buses so the court concluded that there was no transfer of an undertaking

Many service contracts require few assets but may staff. In these staff intensive businesses the assets are of little importance and their absence from the transfer will not prevent a transfer of an undertaking from taking place.

Question

If a contractor engages a subcontractor to do all or part of the contract work and the contractor loses the work to a new contractor who will do the whole job himself without using subcontractors, is there a transfer of an undertaking from the subcontractor to the new contractor?

Answer

Assuming the work is the same and the other conditions for an economic entity are present the answer would appear to be yes. In *Temco Service Industries SA v Imzilyen*, the European Court held that a transfer could take place through more than one transaction and there need be no contract between the transferee and the client organisation that entered into the contract with the original contractor.

The contracting out of services, re-tendering for services and bringing services back in-house are now intended to be covered by the extended new 2006 regulations. There are very few exceptions to *regulation 3* of the new regulations which deal with 'service provision changes'. Under the new regulations the party responsible for the carrying out of the service activities before the change shall be treated as the transferor and the party responsible for the carrying out of the service activities after the change will be treated as the transferee. Even before the new regulations came into force, in most cases, service provision changes fell within the scope of the *Acquired Rights Directive* and of the 1981 TUPE regulations (see also **CHAPTER 2**).

5. Transfer of Staff

Common law – statutory protection [5.1]

The background to the concept of transferring staff lies in common law where it has long been established that there is no inherent right to transfer employees from one employer to another. In *Nokes v Doncaster Collieries Ltd [1940] 3 All ER 549 HL*, even the amalgamation of two companies under the *Companies Act 1929* did not have the effect of transferring the employees of the two old companies to the new merged company, even though the rest of the business did transfer. What is more, unless due notice to terminate the contract has been given, to enforce a transfer amounts to a breach of contract.

This situation was reduced to one of historical interest only with the arrival of the EU Acquired Rights Directive 1977 (77/187/EEC) ('the Directive') and the *Transfer of Undertakings (Protection of Employment) Regulations 1981 (SI 1981/1794)* (TUPE) and now the 2006 TUPE regulations (*SI 2006/246*). When there is a transfer of an economic activity both the business and the employees now transfer to the new employer. *Regulation 4(1)* of the 2006 TUPE regulations ensures that:

> 'a relevant transfer shall not operate so as to terminate the contract of employment of any person employed by the transferor and assigned to the organising grouping of resources or employees that is subject to the relevant transfer, but any such contract shall have effect after the transfer as if originally made between the person so employed and the transferee.'

In short, TUPE transfers the employees automatically on their current terms and conditions and there is no breach of contract. In effect, the position that existed in common law has been reversed.

In order to transfer, the employees have to be employed in the economic entity immediately before the transfer and to have been assigned to the part transferring.

Employed immediately before the transfer [5.2]

The Directive only applies to employees employed on 'the date of transfer' (Article 3(1)). This, on the face of it, appears to exclude anyone not so employed on that day. The wording of the TUPE regulations is more ambiguous in that it refers to 'a person so employed immediately before the transfer'. Both make it necessary to identify when the transfer takes place.

Where there is a formal agreement and the transfer takes place both legally and in practice on an agreed date the situation is clear and TUPE applies. However, it is by no means unusual in practice for legal documentation and the formal transfer of ownership to take place after the practical transfer has been effected. On occasion, the proposed transferee may run the business for his own benefit before terms have finally been agreed. In *Berg v Besselsen [1989] IRLR 447 ECJ* and *Dabell v Vale Industrial Services (Nottingham) Ltd [1988] IRLR 439 CA* (for full details see **CHAPTER 2 – WHAT IS AN UNDERTAKING?**), both the European Court and the Court of Appeal decided that the point of transfer was the point where the incoming transferee started to run the undertaking for his own benefit. In neither case was the transfer permanent.

In *Berg*, the legal title to the business would only transfer when payment was complete. The transferee was to pay in instalments and when he failed to meet the payments the sale was terminated for breach. In *Vale*, the transferee took control of the business while the final terms were being negotiated. No final agreement was reached so the transferor resumed control. In both these cases there were two points of transfer; one to the prospective new owner and one back to the original employer. At no stage was there any formal or legal transfer of ownership. The European Court confirmed that a change in ownership was not a necessary element of a transfer and the Court of Appeal confirmed that a transfer could take place without a formal agreement. It comes down to the basic question of 'who is obtaining the economic advantages from the business'. In both *Berg* and *Vale* there were two points of transfer as discussed above. In this type of transfer the actual date of the transfer may not be entirely clear.

Example

Apex Ltd has contracted out its IT services for three years to Better Solutions Ltd. Better Solutions Ltd terminates the contract with Apex without notice. Needing an immediate replacement service, Apex asks IT Contractors Ltd to take over the service. It does so on 1 May but the new contract is only formally signed on 24 June. In these circumstances, the transfer date would be 1 May and any staff employed on or immediately before that date would transfer to IT Contractors Ltd.

Case study

In several cases the courts have considered whether the transfer has to take place at an identified point of time or can take place over a period of time. These cases were recently reviewed in *Celtic Ltd v Astley ECJ, 26.5.05 (C-478/03)*. ➡

Facts

The question in Astley was how long the period could be. Briefly, in 1990, the Department of Employment transferred its training activities to the Training and Enterprise Councils (TECs). Civil servants were seconded under three-year contracts to TECs. At the end of three years they could choose to join TECs or stay in the civil service. Some remained on a second secondment and transferred to TECs in 1996. The secondees claimed they transferred to TECs under TUPE and that they could therefore count their period of employment in the civil service in their continuity of employment. They argued the transfer took place from 1990 until the final secondment in 1996.

Findings

The ECJ held a transfer of an undertaking does not take place in stages. It can only occur on a particular date, namely when the transferee assumes responsibility for carrying on the business unit transferred. Workers employed on that date will be entitled to the employment protection conferred by the *Acquired Rights Directive*.

The ECJ considered how the date is to be identified. In its view, the 'date of transfer' was when there was a change in the legal or natural person who is responsible for carrying on the business and who continues or resumes the operation of the unit in question, retaining its identity. The ECJ therefore concluded that the date of a transfer was 'the date on which responsibility as employer for carrying on the business of the unit in question moves from the transferor to the transferee'.

Comment: the concept of 'responsibility' is potentially open to a wide range of interpretations, particularly in complex cases such as *Celtic* where a reorganisation or privatisation of a business has occurred. It is possible future courts and tribunals will struggle in the determination of this issue.

Dismissal before the transfer [5.3]

On the face of it if the employee was dismissed before the transfer he should be outside the protection of the TUPE regulations. This is not necessarily the case. If an employee has been dismissed before the transfer, even if that dismissal was on the date of the transfer and only a very short time before the transfer, there is no actual transfer of employment to the incoming employer. The employee does not become the employee of the new employer. Instead, all his employment liabilities transfer to the new employer.

Case study

Facts

In *Litster v Forth Dry Dock and Engineering Co Ltd [1989] IRLR 161 HL*, the employees were dismissed at 11 am and the business was transferred to the new owners at 2 pm.

Findings

The House of Lords decided that a dismissed employee could not transfer to the incoming employer under [1981] TUPE regulations. That said, the regulations do provide that anything done by the transferring employer will be deemed to have been done by the acquiring employer, so the liability for the transferring employer's act of dismissal becomes the liability of the acquiring employer. The dismissed employee does not transfer.

This position is now supported by *regulation 4(3)* of the new 2006 regulations to the effect that the transferee inherits liabilities towards those employees who would have transferred had they not been unfairly dismissed by the transferor prior to the transfer for a transfer-related reason.

In *Wendelboe v LJ Music AP S [1985] ECR 475 ECJ*, the European Court of Justice (ECJ) decided that an employee who was not employed on the date of transfer could not transfer. The court did not decide that those employed on the date of the transfer must transfer across.

These cases seem to supply unscrupulous employers with an opportunity to avoid problems and take on staff free from their current contract terms by the simple device of ensuring they were dismissed prior to the actual transfer. Such action is doomed to failure since this 'loophole' has been sealed by the ECJ and the new 2006 regulations.

Case study

P Bork International A/S v Foringen AF Arbejdsledere I Danmark ECJ [1989] IRLR 4. ➡

Facts

A number of employees were dismissed by the transferor prior to the transfer of a business and subsequently some were taken on by the transferee (see **4.10** for the full facts of this case).

Findings

The European Court decided that employees who had been dismissed prior to the transfer but who had subsequently been taken on by the incoming employer could rely on Article 4(1) of the Directive that provides that the transfer itself will not be grounds for dismissal. The court held that employees whose contracts had been terminated before the transfer in breach of Article 4(1):

> 'must be considered as still employed by the undertaking on the date of the transfer with the consequences, in particular, that the obligations of an employer towards them are fully transferred from the transferor to the transferee . . .'.

It follows that although there was a gap between the termination of employment with Bork and the new employment with Junkers Industrier, the dismissal had been caused by the transfer and so employment liabilities transferred to Junkers.

A similar decision was made on similar facts by the European Court in the more recent case of *Jules Dethier Equipment SA v Dassy and Sovram Sprl (in liquidation) [1998] IRLR 266.*

The UK version of Article 4(1) is to be found in *regulation 7* of the 2006 TUPE regulations. *Regulation 7* makes every dismissal connected with the transfer automatically unfair. There is only one defence to a transfer-related dismissal, namely for the employer to show that the dismissal was for an economic, technical or organisational (ETO) reason requiring a change in the nature of the workforce. If the employer can prove there was an ETO reason, that will be a valid ground for the dismissal and provided a proper dismissal process has been followed, the dismissal will be fair.

Dismissals to prevent the transfer of employees will be connected with the transfer and in normal circumstances it will be difficult to show that there is an ETO reason. If there is a dismissal connected with the transfer and but for the dismissal the employee would have remained in employment and transferred to the incoming employer, then the liability in respect of the dismissal (and indeed any other claims which the employee may have) transfer to the incoming employer. It is the incoming employer who has to meet any claims for unfair dismissal, breach of contract, redundancy, discrimination, unpaid wages etc. The transferee may have avoided taking on the staff but they get all the liabilities in connection with the dismissal.

In *Litster v Forth Dry Dock and Engineering Co Ltd* (see above), the dismissal was effected at 11 am and the transfer took place at 2 pm. The House of Lords looked at the purpose of the Directive (to protect staff in these situations) and interpreted the statute to achieve this objective. It decided that employment did not transfer because the staff had been dismissed. The Lords used *regulation 8* (of the 1981 regulations – now *regulation 7* of the 2006 regulations) and found the dismissal was related to the transfer and therefore was automatically unfair. The liability for the dismissal transferred to the new employer.

In cases such as this the Lords proposed the following procedure to establish the transfer of liability:

• It must first be decided whether the dismissal was for a reason connected with the transfer. This would make it automatically unfair under *regulation 8* (now *regulation 7*).

• Then the tribunal must decide whether, but for the dismissal, the employee would have been employed immediately before the transfer.

• If the answer to the second point above is 'yes', then liability will transfer to the incoming employer.

• If there was an ETO reason at the time of dismissal then all existing liability will remain with the outgoing employer. A valid ETO reason is a good defence to automatic unfair dismissal under *regulation 8* (now *regulation 7*) and no liability will transfer to the acquiring employer.

In *Wilson v St Helens Borough Council and Meade and Baxendale v British Fuels Ltd [1998] IRLR 706 HL*, the Lords confirmed that employees dismissed immediately before the transfer did not transfer into the employment of the acquiring employer, although their rights and liabilities will under *Litster* and now also under regulation 4 of the new regulations.

The employee resigns [5.4]

If the employee resigns before the transfer he will not transfer. A resignation is voluntary and therefore the employee will not have any rights under the TUPE regulations as he will have chosen not to transfer (see *Hay v George Hanson (Building Contractors) Ltd [1996] IRLR 427 EAT* (**5.12**)). If, however, his resignation is caused by a breach of contract by the transferring employer he will be able to bring an unfair dismissal claim against him and, if related to the transfer, the dismissal will be automatically unfair.

Series transfers [5.5]

Before the TUPE regulations existed, employers occasionally used a device known as 'hiving down' to transfer a business to a new owner without all the employees or to limit the transferring employees' continuity of employment.

First, the assets were transferred to a wholly owned subsidiary leaving the employees employed by a company of no value. The subsidiary was then acquired by, or assets sold to, a new owner. The new owner then engaged only those employees he needed and they had no continuity of employment. The remaining employees might be unable to obtain recompense against their employer and seek to rely upon the statutory insolvency protection now to be found in the *Employment Rights Act 1996 (ERA 1996)*.

Regulation 3 of the 2006 TUPE regulations ensures that such a device will not operate to avoid TUPE and provides that a transfer may take place as a result of a series of two or more transactions. *Regulation 4* further provides that where a transfer is achieved by a series of transactions, the employees employed immediately before each transaction are protected. The transfer is treated as completed at the time of the last transaction.

Hiving down is not completely outlawed. It is permitted in limited circumstances, in insolvency and receiverships under *regulation 9*. This device can now only be used by receivers and liquidators so that saleable parts of the failing enterprise can be sold and the employment of some employees preserved.

Regulation 4 will only help to preserve employment if the tribunals take a generous view in deciding what amounts to a series of transactions.

Case study

Longden and Paisley v Ferrari Ltd and Kennedy International Ltd [1994] IRLR 157 EAT.

Facts

Ferrari was in the hands of administrative receivers and planning to dismiss all the staff. Kennedy considered purchasing Ferrari and in order to preserve the business during negotiations provided money to keep it going. Kennedy also indicated the staff that it thought it essential to keep the business alive. The next day Mrs Longden, who was not on the list of➡

---

essential employees, was dismissed. Eight days later Kennedy purchased an option on Ferrari and five days after that it purchased the business by an asset sale from the receivers.

Findings

The Employment Appeal Tribunal (EAT) held this was not a series of transactions effecting the transfer to Kennedy. It was 'effected' by the one simple transaction of an asset sale. The liability for Mrs Longden remained with Ferrari. She could not bring an unfair dismissal claim under *regulation 8* (now *regulation* 7 of the 2006 regulations) against Ferrari because her dismissal was caused by the financial difficulties of Ferrari, not the sale, and so was not connected to the transfer. The prospective sale caused the retention of staff who would otherwise have been dismissed, not the dismissal of those whom Kennedy did not consider essential.

Employed in the transferred economic entity   [5.6]

In order for an employee's employment to transfer to the incoming employer, he employee must not only meet the temporal requirement of being actually employed at the point of transfer, but must also meet the substantial requirement of being employed in the economic entity. This is a question of fact for the tribunal and is relatively simple if the employee has been formally assigned to the entity. Where there is no formal assignment then the tribunal must make a decision based on the facts. The most difficult decisions concern employees with work responsibilities in more than one part of the organisation. In the rare instances where the employee has separate and independent contracts for his different work, it might be possible to treat him as having separate assignments for each contract.

Example

A delivery driver who works Monday to Friday, 9 am to 5 pm, has a separate part-time contract with the company as a security guard working from 10 pm to 6 am over Saturday night and Sunday morning. If the company were to contract out the security work the driver will transfer to the contractor for his security duties while remaining a driver with the company. This is because he has two separate contracts of employment.

Most employees do not have separate contracts and the development of multi-skilling is increasing the number of employees whose duties and working time are dispersed throughout the organisation.

The first European Court decision on the extent to which the employee must be engaged in the economic entity, *Botzen v Rotterdamshe Droogdok Maatschappi BV [1985] ECR 519 ECJ*, has caused some confusion. The decision of the court is quite clear. It insists that for there to be an employment relationship capable of transfer the employee must be assigned to the part transferred. It is a simple question of assignment. The Advocate General, Sir Gordon Slynn, advised the court that the employee had to be wholly engaged in the economic entity with any additional duties being minimal. This is not the correct test. Rather unhelpfully the first UK case, *Anderson v Kluwer Publishing Ltd COIT 15068/85*, took a different approach by looking a the percentage of time the employee spent in the different units and concluded that 80% in one unit was sufficient time for the employee to transfer when that unit transferred.

Case study

The percentage test has been rejected by the Court of Appeal in *Jones and anor v Darlows Estate Agency [1999] IRLB 613 CA*.

Facts

Jones and Kingston worked for Cornerstone Estate Agents and were based in the regional office for Wales and the West of England. When Cornerstone transferred its Welsh branches to Darlows, Cornerstone withheld Jones and Kingston from the transfer as it still required them. Shortly afterwards, Cornerstone went into receivership and Jones and Kingston were made redundant. They claimed they had been unfairly dismissed and that because they spent the larger proportion of their time in the Welsh branch, they had transferred with that branch to Darlows.

Findings

The tribunal found that they were assigned to the whole of Wales and West of England region and had not been specifically assigned to either. They had worked wherever they were most needed and that happened to be Wales. It could well have been the West of England. They had not been assigned to Wales and did not transfer to Darlows. The Court of Appeal agreed with this finding.

However, in the absence of a clear express assignment, the assignment test is not an easy one. Without an express assignment the tribunal will have to base the decision on the facts of the case.

The fact that the contract contains a mobility clause may not prevent the employee from being assigned to his current unit.

> ## *Case study*
>
> ### *Facts*
>
> In *Securicor Guarding Ltd v Fraser Security Services Ltd [1996] IDS Brief 572/15 EAT*, security guards worked on one site but had a mobility clause in their contracts which would allow them to be assigned to a different site.
>
> ### *Findings*
>
> The EAT decided the guards were assigned to their current site until such time as Securicor relocated them. When Securicor lost the contract to Fraser, the staff, not having been relocated, should have transferred to Fraser. They did not do so because Fraser offered them employment on different terms. Although they eventually accepted casual work with Securicor, liability for their dismissal lay with Fraser.

In *Duncan Web Offset (Maidstone) Ltd v Cooper [1995] IRLR 633 EAT*, it was accepted that an employee could be assigned to an economic entity even though he did not spend the whole of his working time there. The EAT suggested a tribunal should take into account:

- the amount of time spent on the various duties;
- the value of the work to each part;
- the apportionment of the employment cost; and
- the contract terms.

Such a wide remit is not always easy to apply. In reliance on this guidance, the EAT decided that a purchasing manager with group responsibilities but who was largely involved in the daily business of the unit, the head of HR who spent 80% of his time in the unit, and an employee working four days in the unit and one day elsewhere were all assigned to the unit transferred and thus became the responsibility of the acquiring employer.

It would appear that where there is no express assignment, the amount of time spent in various parts of the business may be taken into account, but it is not conclusive and there is no 80% rule.

The approach taken by the ECJ in *Botzen* and the EAT in *Duncan Web* are now supported further by *regulation 4* of the new 2006 regulations which is intended to incorporate into statute well-established developments in case law that are considered to be the correct interpretation of the *Acquired Rights Directive*.

The *Botzen* test was applied in *Securiplan v Bademosi EAT, 9.5.03 (1128/02)*.

Case study

Facts

B worked for 21 years as a security officer at a Cable & Wireless (C & W) site for which B's employer provided security services. B sustained an accident at work in 2002 and could no longer fulfil his duties at the C & W site. His employer relocated him. The contract at the second site was abruptly terminated and the contract for security awarded elsewhere. B brought a number of claims against S Ltd. S Ltd denied liability claiming the employment had transferred to the winner of the security contract at the second site, albeit the assignment to the second site was intended to be temporary.

Findings

The EAT upheld the tribunal's decision that B did not transfer under TUPE to the winner of the contract on the second site. It found the placement of B in the second site was always on the understanding that it was temporary until he was well enough to resume duties with C & W. The EAT took into account the very long period B had worked at the C & W site prior to injury.

This case is a reminder that tribunals assessing the issue of assignment are to take a commonsense view of the facts behind an individual pattern of employment. Therefore, the artificial use of temporary assignments to shift employees in and out of certain parts of the undertaking – a method practised by what the EAT described as 'unsavoury' employers – would be a risky ploy to adopt.

Case study

Facts

The unlucky employees are those with very widespread duties, as in *Hassard v McGrath and NI Housing Executive December [1997] NICA*➡

unreported. Hassard, a joiner, had been working in the general building, plumbing, electrical and change of tenancy departments – 8%, 62%, 17% and 12% of his time, respectively. The work was contracted out to two different employers. One obtained contracts on which Hassard had spent about 73% of his time and the other contract taking up 25% of his time.

Findings

The court followed the decision in *Botzen v Rotterdamshe Droogdok Maatschappi BV.* As he was not solely assigned to any department when it was contracted out he did not transfer to either new contractor. This case differs from the driver with a separate security contract because he had two independent contracts. The question of assignment would not arise in that case.

Lifting the corporate veil – looking behind the corporate structure [5.7]

Groups of companies may have flexible arrangements under which both work and staff may be transferred from one company in the group to another. This raises two questions. First, can the whole group be one organisation? Second, can the tribunals lift the corporate veil and look behind it at the real practical human resource structure? The answer to both questions would appear to be 'no'.

In *Allen v Amalgamated Construction Co Ltd [2000] IRLR 119 ECJ* (see **3.7** for the facts of this case), the European Court insisted that as each company in the group was a separate legal entity the group as a whole could not be treated as one organisation, even if the group was administered centrally.

The courts will only look behind the corporate legal structure (lift the corporate veil) to see who actually controls the company in very rare instances.

Case study

The courts were asked to do so in *Michael Peters Ltd v (1) Farnfield and (2) Michael Peters Group plc [1995] IRLR 190 EAT.*

Facts

Mr Farnfield was the chief executive of Michael Peters Group plc (MPG), the holding company for 25 subsidiaries. MPG and four subsidiaries were➡

located in the same office. Receivers of MPG and the subsidiaries' undertakings were appointed on 22 and 23 August 1990, respectively. They sent Mr Farnfield a letter of dismissal on 27 August 1990 having told him that he would be made redundant. The following day a company referred to as 'CLK', which later turned out to be Michael Peters Ltd, made an offer to purchase just four of the subsidiaries. The receivers accepted this offer on 30 August. By agreement the vendors were the subsidiaries. MPG transferred to CLK some of its assets, such as goodwill, book debts, office equipment and premises.

Findings

The EAT held that Farnfield, whose role encompassed all the companies of the group, was not employed by any of the four subsidiaries that transferred. He was not assigned to the part of the undertaking transferred and did not, therefore, fall within the protection of TUPE. The EAT refused to look behind the companies themselves (to pierce the corporate veil).

Case study

On the other hand, in *Sunley Turriff Holdings Ltd v Thompson [1995] IRLR 184 EAT*, the EAT took a different approach.

Facts

Lilley Construction Ltd had divided its operations into divisions and subsequently into companies that were profit centres. Thompson was employed by Lilley Construction Ltd but also worked for Lilley Construction (Scotland) Ltd. In fact, he was company secretary and chief accountant of both companies. The group was in financial difficulties and in the hands of receivers. The receivers sold the business of Lilley Construction (Scotland) Ltd to Sunley Turriff. When Thompson asked why he was not being transferred the receivers told him he was still employed by Lilley Construction Ltd. The receivers did not adopt his contract but he continued to work for the receivers for around two months until he was made redundant.

Findings

The tribunal concluded that the split between the companies had no particular effect on the activities of the staff or the accounts. Work➡

contracted to and undertaken by the subsidiary was undertaken by Lilley Construction Ltd. The assets and some of the contracts transferred with Lilley Construction (Scotland) Ltd belonged to Lilley Construction Ltd. The EAT concluded that what transferred was not only the business of Lilley Construction (Scotland) Ltd, but also a substantial part of Lilley Construction Ltd. Therefore, Thompson transferred with the business.

Similarly, in *Duncan Web Offset (Maidstone) Ltd v Cooper*, the EAT applied the economic argument in that complicated corporate structures should not be allowed to get in the way of deciding where the employee was assigned to work. The court accepted that he could be employed by one company within the group but assigned to another company in the group. It even considered that he might be employed by an organisation independent from the group or the company, as were a third party acting as employing agent for the organisation for whom he worked.

Turriff, *Duncan Web* and now *regulation 4* of the 2006 regulations require the tribunals to make difficult decisions and after *Allen v Amalgamated Construction Co Ltd* the analysis is likely to be based on form, not on the commercial economic reality.

The acquiring employer does not know the employee works in the unit [5.8]

Case study

Facts

In *TC Cleaning Contractors Ltd v Joy [1996] IDS Brief 574 EAT*, when TC won a cleaning contract the outgoing contractor provided a list of transferring staff. The list did not include Ms Joy because she was absent on sick leave. She was fit to work after the contract had transferred.

Findings

It was held that she transferred under the 1981 TUPE regulations even though the new contractor was not aware of her existence. As long as the employee meets the necessary conditions she will transfer.

The employee is ignorant of the transfer [5.9]

Case study

Facts

In *Secretary of State for Trade and Industry v Cook [1997] IRLR 150 EAT*, Gayton International, a company in financial difficulties, made its staff redundant and told them the business was being taken over by Intro Business Ltd. The employees were not told their employment would transfer. When Gayton could not meet its liabilities the staff sought payment from the Department of Trade and Industry under the insolvency protection provisions.

Findings

The Secretary of State was not liable. The staff transferred even though they were unaware of the transfer so the liability to meet redundancy payments had transferred to Intro Business Ltd.

An earlier EAT decision, *Photostatic Copiers (Southern) Ltd v Okuda [1991] IRLR 11 EAT*, had reached the opposite conclusion. This case has been much criticised and reliance is generally placed on *Cook*.

The employers agree that TUPE will not apply [5.10]

Employers have no right to agree not to apply the TUPE regulations. Such agreement will be ineffective (see *Rotstart de Hertaing v (1) Bendoit S/A in liquidation (2) IGC Housing Services S/A [1997] IRLR 127 ECJ* (**4.7**)).

Employees working abroad [5.11]

A transferred undertaking may have employees who work wholly or mainly abroad. They are still covered by the TUPE regulations and will transfer to the acquiring employer on the same employment terms and conditions. Whether or not an employee working abroad is able to bring a claim under the new regulations will now depend on the normal principles of international law. There may be practical difficulties with regard to enforcement unless they return to the UK.

Employees who do not transfer

Employee refusal [5.12]

Although both the Directive and TUPE state the employee assigned to the unit transfers to the acquiring employer, the employee transfer cannot take place contrary to the employee's wishes. He is free to refuse to transfer.

Case study

The ECJ confirmed this principle in *Katsikas v Konstantinides [1993] IRLR 179 ECJ.*

Facts

Katsikas worked as a cook in a Greek restaurant in Germany. When the restaurant was sold he refused to transfer.

Findings

The court ruled that the Directive did not prevent an individual refusing to transfer. When this occurs, national law governs the employee's rights. German law does give rights to those who refuse to transfer and Katsikas was able to take advantage of them.

In the UK, there was no specific law on this point, although the application of the ordinary rules of unfair dismissal, redundancy and breach of contract would probably have denied him any compensation had he brought a claim in the UK.

Clarification came in *section 33* of the *Trade Union Reform and Employment Rights Act 1993* that amends TUPE to provide that a refusal to transfer will terminate the contract but this will not amount to dismissal by the employer for any purpose. *Regulation 4(7)* of the 2006 TUPE regulations provides that the regulations will not operate to transfer an employee's:

> 'contract of employment and the rights powers duties and liabilities under or in connection with it if the employee informs the transferor or the transferee that he objects to being employed by the transferee.'

Regulation 4(8) of the 2006 regulations provides:

> 'Where an employee so objects, the transfer of the undertaking or part in which he is employed shall operate as to terminate his contract of

93

employment with the transferor but he shall not be treated, for any purpose, as having been dismissed by the transferor.'

The effect of this is to terminate the employment at the time of the transfer and to deny the refusing employee any claim of unfair dismissal, redundancy or breach of contract against either employer. He does not transfer to the acquiring employer and any outstanding legal claims that he might have, such as unpaid wages or discrimination, will remain with the transferring employer.

The EAT has commented that the original regulations in this respect were badly drafted. It had difficulties with 'objects'. An employee might well 'object' to the transfer, but transfers nonetheless. The EAT has decided that the regulations in this respect only apply where the employee refuses to transfer. This refusal does not have to follow any particular form. It does not have to be in writing. The tribunal may draw an inference of refusal from the facts. The employee only has to inform either the transferring or the acquiring employer of his refusal to transfer.

This can put a vociferous objecting employee in a difficult situation as his conduct may give rise to an assumption of refusal. Employers might avoid this by providing a pro forma for the refusing employee to complete.

In summary:

- The employee can inform either the transferring or acquiring employer.

- No particular form is needed – such as it being required in writing – the objection can be oral. Caution is required since strong emotions can be expressed in unfortunate terms and the employee has to be careful how he expresses his objection to the transfer.

- Employment with the transferring employer will terminate automatically at the time of the transfer but the employee will not enter the employment of the acquiring employer. The employee refusing to transfer is not employed by the transferor or transferee at the time of the transfer. He can have no claim against the acquiring employer.

- The termination of his employment is automatic and is not a dismissal by his employer. This means he cannot bring a claim of breach of contract, unfair dismissal or redundancy in respect of the termination of his employment.

- Any earlier claims against the transferring employer, such as unpaid wages, remain valid.

Case study

Hay v George Hanson (Building Contractors) Ltd.

Facts

Hay was employed by Argyll and Bute District Council as a joiner and carpenter. The council contracted out its repair and maintenance services to George Hanson. Hay was not happy about this. He sought alternative employment with the council or redundancy even though Hanson offered continuation of employment. He tried to negotiate the ability to do private work in the Hanson contract, although it was not in his council contract. He took sick leave in the hope of remaining with the council and did not reply to two letters from Hanson in which it alleged he was objecting to the transfer.

Findings

On the facts, the tribunal concluded Hay was refusing to transfer. The EAT upheld this decision.

Refusal to transfer for a valid reason   [5.13]

If the acquiring employer will not allow the employee to transfer to him on his own or better terms but insists on changing those terms to the employee's detriment, then the position is different. The employee can refuse to transfer and retains his legal rights relating to termination. This is because *regulation 4* of the 2006 regulations provides that if the employee refuses to transfer he retains his right to terminate his contract without notice if a substantial change is made in his working conditions to his detriment. No such right will arise if only the identity of his employer changes unless the employee shows that, in all the circumstances, the change is significant and to his detriment. *Regulation 4* of the 2006 regulations is based on a similar provision in Article 4(2) of the Directive.

Regulation 4 is not particularly clear. The first problem encountered by the courts was the relationship between the 1981 *regulations 5(4)(a)* and *5(4)(b)* under which the employee does not transfer and loses his termination rights, and *regulation 5(5)* under which he does not transfer but retains his termination rights. The Court of Appeal decided that *regulation 5(5)* should be given a purposive interpretation and should not be restricted by *regulations 5(4)(a)* or *5(4)(b)*. It held that if an employee refused to transfer then he did not do so and the liabilities attached to him did not transfer to the acquiring employer. If the employee's reason for refusal was a substantial detrimental change in his working conditions, he did not lose his termination rights under *regulation 5(4)(b)* but retained them.

The second problem was the meaning of a 'substantial change in his working conditions'. Did this mean his actual terms and conditions of employment or could it include non-contractual matters? In *Rossiter v Pendragon plc [2002] IRLR 483 CA*, the EAT had decided that the wording of *regulation 5(5)* was sufficiently wide to include a change in non-contractual working conditions. In this case, a reduction in his responsibilities, a change in the commission rate and a decision not to pay holiday pay on the basis of the last twelve months' commission. However, the Court of Appeal did not agree with the EAT. It insisted that the change had to be to the contract terms and not to non-contractual working conditions. The Appeal court held that there was no distinction between constructive dismissal in *section 95(1)(c)* of the *ERA 1996* and *regulation 5(5)*.

Obviously, a change of employer is a change to the employment conditions but to bring a claim on this ground the employee has to discharge a heavy burden of proof. He must show that the change of employer is not just significant but also detrimental to him. The fact that the acquiring employer is under funded and his employment is likely to be at risk will not suffice. Examples are hard to come by. Perhaps it would be held as a substantial and detrimental change if the employee had previously worked for the acquiring employer and had been wrongly or unfairly dismissed by him.

Where there is a substantial and detrimental change neither employee nor rights and liabilities in respect of that employee transfer to the acquiring employer. The employee has to make his claim against the transferring employer, even though the breach is not his fault but the fault of the acquiring employer. This is an interesting reversal of the normal situation. Most TUPE cases under *regulation 5* of the 1981 regulations and now *regulation 4* of the 2006 regulations are concerned with the acquiring employer being made liable for the acts of the transferring employer. In the particular circumstances described above it is the other way around.

The employee has a difficult choice. He can refuse to transfer and bring termination claims against his employer. Or he can transfer and insist on the acquiring employer providing him with his pre-transfer employment terms.

Case study

Humphreys v University of Oxford [2000] IRLR 183 CA.   ➡

Facts

Humphreys was employed by Oxford University but as the result of a TUPE transfer was to work for the Associated Examining Board. Under Oxford's employment terms he had a tenured position and could have remained in employment until the age of 67, but under the Associated Examining Board's terms of employment he had no such rights. This, he argued, involved a detrimental change to his notice terms. He refused to transfer.

Findings

The court held that under *regulation 5(5)* (of the 1981 regulations – now *regulation 4* of the 2006 regulations) an employee who refuses to transfer because of a substantial detrimental change to his terms does not transfer but retains all his rights in respect of termination. The refusal to apply his existing terms was breach of contract by the Associated Examining Board. He could therefore bring a claim against Oxford University for breach of contract and unfair dismissal. The dismissal, being connected with the transfer, would be automatically unfair.

Case study

Merckx and Neuhys v Ford Motors Co Belgium SA [1996] IRLR 467 ECJ.

Facts

Under his pre-transfer contract Merckx was entitled to a salary that was partly related to turnover. His employment was transferred to Novarobel SA, an independent motor dealer. Novarobel refused to guarantee the same level of remuneration.

Findings

This was a sufficiently serious breach to bring Article 4(2) of the Directive into play so the employer (Ford) was to be regarded as liable for the breach.

It must be clear that the terms will change. A fear or expectation of change will not be enough to be a sufficiently serious breach.

Case study

Sita (GB) Ltd v Burton [1997] IRLR 501 EAT.

Facts

Kingston upon Thames Council employed Burton and Pickard. Their work was to be contracted out to Sita. They were fearful their terms of employment would change as a result of statements made during consultation by Sita staff. As a result, they resigned alleging constructive dismissal.

Findings

It was held that the acquiring employer was not liable because it had never been their employer. Nor could the employees sue the transferring employer for breach of mutual trust and confidence based on their fears of what might happen after the transfer. Employees should beware jumping the gun. Burton and Pickard should have transferred and then insisted on the continuance of their pre-transfer terms. The situation would have been different if Sita had insisted upon a change in the terms rather than indicating a possible change.

Retained employees [5.14]

Not every employee who could transfer under TUPE does so. Some staff may be retained in the employment of the transferring employer.

If the staff are to be retained for a short period and are then to transfer it would be sensible to make the arrangement clear. If some staff are to be retained for a short period and transfer at a later date this could be a transfer in two stages allowing both groups of employees to take advantage of the TUPE protection. Another option would be for the staff to transfer under TUPE and be seconded back to the transferring employer for the necessary period. Alternatively, the TUPE transfer could take place in stages, the final stage being the transfer of the retained staff.

The employer may wish to retain some staff, particularly those in whom he has invested training or who are skilled and experienced. If there is a mobility clause in the contract he may use that to transfer the employee to a new position. It must be noted that terms giving the employer the power to change the employee's job, place of work or other contract terms are discretionary terms and the discretion must be exercised with due regard to the implied term of mutual trust and confidence. Breach of that term can result in constructive dismissal. The dismissal would be connected with the transfer and so be automatically unfair under *regulation 7* of the 2006 regulations unless the employer could show there was an ETO reason.

Generally, employees who are retained by the employer are happy with the situation, but this is not always the case. The employee may prefer to transfer where the acquiring company has greater financial stability than his current employer. This was the case in *Jones and anor v Darlows Estate Agency* and *Longden v Ferrari Ltd* (see **5.6**).

One other possible solution could be for the employer to offer the employee new employment within the organisation. There is a danger this might be viewed as a contracting out of the employee's rights under TUPE that is forbidden and rendered void under *regulation 18* of the 2006 regulations. If the employee accepts the variation there is no dismissal and so there can be no question of an unfair dismissal. Also, he will not be employed in the transferring unit when the transfer takes place so he cannot transfer to the new employer. Presumably, in such cases, the employee is happy to be retained and so is unlikely to transfer. The only risk would seem to be where the employee was retained without his consent. If this occurs he could bring a claim under *regulation 18* of the 2006 regulations.

It is not uncommon for organisations in the service industry to seek to retain their skilled and experienced staff rather than lose them to the new contractor. In order to provide adequate information on which a new tender may be made and to ensure a smooth transfer and prevent the replacement of staff by those of a lower calibre, some service contracts contain clauses which require either the notification of changes to staff or even the employee's consent before the substitution can take place.

Example

Stated within the contract are the following provisions:

- Six months prior to the expiry of the contract the contractor will provide the company with the names of all the employees assigned to the contract.

- On the same date the contractor will also inform the company of any employee who will after that date cease to be assigned to the contract due to an agreement or provision already in being on that date.

- And/or from that date until the date of expiry of the contract the contractor will not remove any employee from the contract without➡

---

first obtaining the written consent of the company.

Retaining employment [5.15]

There are many reasons why employees are frequently reluctant to transfer. For example:

- loss of pension rights;
- loss of non-contractual benefits;
- fear that terms will not improve under the new employer (being 'red-circled'); and
- diminished career development opportunities.

These problems are increasingly facing public sector workers who are subjected to public private partnerships (PPPs) and the private finance initiatives (PFIs). To overcome staff and union resistance to PPPs and PFIs, some NHS trusts are experimenting with an arrangement under which the responsibility for the service is transferred but the staff remain in the employment of the Trust. Any new staff will be engaged and employed by the Trust.

If the staff are a key element of the entity then, if they do not transfer, this raises a serious question as to whether there is a TUPE transfer at all following the decision in *Suzen v Zehnacker Gebaudereinigung GmbH Krankenhausservice and Lefarth GmbH [1997] IRLR 255 ECJ*. Even if there is a transfer, staff that at a later date decide to transfer to the service provider may not be protected by TUPE. There will, of course, be the inevitable problems of control over the staff, disciplinary and grievance issues and vicarious liability. It remains to be seen if this is a viable solution.

Fraud [5.16]

In one most unusual case the fraud of the transferor prevented the employee's transfer.

Case study

Facts

In *Carisway Cleaning Consultants Ltd v Richards and Cooper Cleaning Services Ltd [1998] IDS 621 EAT*, allegations were made against a cleaner working on a contract. He was first suspended and then on 10 October ➡

---

his suspension was lifted and he was offered two posts; one permanent and one temporary. He took the permanent post. He was not told until 12 October, after he accepted the new position, that his employer had already lost that cleaning contract and the contract was transferring to the new contractor on 15 October. He did transfer but did not like the new job. He left claiming unfair dismissal but was uncertain which employer to sue. On the facts it should be the new employer. He should transfer. He was assigned to the contract and employed on the contract at the date of transfer and did in fact work for the new employer.

Findings

However, the EAT held that Richards did not transfer. Richards had been given no notice of the transfer and his name was not on the list of transferring employees supplied to the new contractor. The EAT decided this was a fraud on both Richards and the new contractor and that fraud made the apparent transfer void. This is a case where justice was done but the legal basis for the decision has been criticised.

It is not unknown for the outgoing employer to replace existing assigned staff with employees with poor health, attendance or performance records. This is not fraud. Carisway was deliberately concealing information and misleading the parties. Fraud requires proof of fraudulent intent.

The self-employed [5.17]

Article 4(1) of the Directive permits member states to exclude:

> 'specific categories of employees who are not covered by the laws or practice of the member states in respect of protection against dismissal.'

The TUPE regulations define an employee as:

> 'any individual who works for another person whether under a contract of service or apprenticeship or otherwise but does not include anyone who provides services under a contract for services.'

This seems to exclude anyone who is self-employed whether or not they really do have their own business. The wider category of 'worker', which under discrimination legislation, the *National Minimum Wage Act 1998*, the *Working Time Regulations 1998 (SI 1998/1833)* and other statutory protection includes the self-employed who do not run their own business as well as employees, is not recognised under TUPE. Conversely, some individuals who regard themselves as self-employed but are not genuinely running their own business may in fact be employees under the TUPE provisions.

This is a particularly difficult issue in the construction industry where self-employed 'lump' workers may be employees, as in *Lee v (1) Ching and (2) Shun Shing Construction and Engineering Co Ltd [1990] IRLR 236 PC*, or providers of services, as in *Byrne Brothers (Formwork) Ltd v Baird [2002] IRLR 96 EAT*. It will all depend on the facts and circumstances of the case.

Any organisation taking over an economic entity under a TUPE transfer will need to extend due diligence to all the apparently self-employed individuals to see whether or not they are really employees. Unfortunately, there is no simple test for employment. The courts and tribunals use several tests. For example:

- the control test which looks at the extent to which the organisation controls the way in which work is done or factors such as hours, location, pay and discipline;

- the integration test that is concerned with whether the individual is integrated into the organisation;

- the 'is he his own boss' or 'investment test' which looks at the extent to which the individual is free to make his own decisions, has invested in his business and can make more or less money by taking management decisions; and

- the essential elements test – the factors required to create a contract of employment. These include a duty to work and for work and, with some minor exceptions, for the work to be performed personally.

Whether home-workers are employees or self-employed is a question of fact for the tribunal.

Agency workers [5.18]

Agency workers supplied to the transferring employer will not normally transfer to the acquiring employer. They are not engaged by the transferring employer to work in the unit being transferred. However, there is an exception where the agency worker is found to have become the employee of the hiring organisation.

This question will usually arise with agency workers who have worked for the hirer for a long time. It will be necessary to show:

- the agency worker has a contract with the hirer; and
- the contract was one of employment.

The contract does not have to be express, it can be implied from the facts, but length of working with the hirer alone is not sufficient to imply a contract. Once a contract is identified it will be necessary to see if the individual is an employee using the employment tests detailed above.

Workers abroad [5.19]

The 2006 regulations apply fully to those who work wholly or mainly abroad. Whether or not an employee working abroad is able to bring a claim under the new regulations will now depend on the normal principles of international law.

Impossibility [5.20]

Impossibility was mentioned but not dealt with as a specific issue in *Morris Angel and Son Ltd v Hollande [1993] IRLR 169 CA.*

The court questioned whether it was possible to transfer the service contract of a board director from one company to another and whether this was a situation in which the transfer would be impossible and *regulation 4* of the new 2006 regulations would not apply. The court drew no specific conclusions on this point. (See **6.11** for full details of this case.)

Due diligence: avoiding staff transfer problems [5.21]

Knowledge of the persons working in the transferring unit is absolutely critical for the acquiring employer. He needs to be aware of the composition of the workforce and not assume that only the on site workers are employees. Nor is it sensible to rely simply on the statements of the transferring employer. It may not be realised that a particular agency worker or an apparently self-employed worker is in fact legally an employee capable of being transferred. Although the acquiring employer may be able to obtain a warranty or undertaking that the provided list of employees are the only employees engaged in the undertaking, it is still advisable to check the situation thoroughly.

Checklists [5.22]

1. The status of the staff:

    - employees – include employees absent on sick leave, maternity leave or any discretionary leave;

    - the self-employed – check whether they are likely to be regarded as employees by applying the tests described above;

    - agency workers – check whether they may be regarded as having become employees over the passage of time; and

- home-workers – check whether they may be regarded as employees (see above tests).

2. Assignment to the unit:

   - formally assigned;

   - informally assigned; and

   - not assigned.

3. Employed immediately before the transfer:

   - if dismissed was the dismissal related to the transfer?

   - if 'yes' but for the dismissal would the employee have been employed at the time of transfer?

   - is there an ETO reason causing a change in the workforce?

4. Not transferring:

   - has the employee refused to transfer?

   - has this been clearly expressed?

   - was the expression in writing?

   - what is the reason for the refusal?

   - is it because of a substantial and detrimental change to his terms and conditions of employment?

   - is he remaining in the employment of the transferring employer?

The outgoing employer may be willing to give a warranty in respect of the list of employees engaged in the transferring unit. In the case of re-contracting, the unsuccessful contractor has no duty to the new incoming contractor and is unlikely to provide anything more than they are statutorily obliged to do so. Note her *regulation 11* of the 2006 regulations and the duty to provide 'employee liability information' (see later at **6.20**).

Warranty [5.23]

A typical warranty wording would be: *[The organisation] warrants that [the list] is accurate at [date] and that any change to the list will be notified to [transferee] in writing within [number of days] and that no change will be made as from [number of days before transfer].*

If the list is inaccurate it will not mean the omitted employees will not transfer but it will give a right to sue the outgoing employer for breach of his warranty. Sometimes, the warranty is reinforced by an indemnity.

Indemnity [5.24]

A typical indemnity wording is as follows: *[Organisation] agrees to indemnify and hold safe [transferee] against any loss or claim caused by [organisation's] breach of the [above] warranty and against any costs reasonably incurred in respect of such loss or claim for [period of time] from the date of transfer.*

Key points and new developments [5.25]

- Employees engaged in the economic entity immediately before the transfer will transfer to the employment of the acquiring employer.

- According to the ECJ ruling in *Celtic Ltd v Astley and ors ECJ, 26.5.05 (C-478/03)*, a transfer of an undertaking does not take place in stages. It can only occur on a particular date, namely when the transferee assumes responsibility for carrying on the business unit transferred.

- Only those who are employed transfer, the self-employed and agency workers will not transfer unless found to be employees of the transferring organisation.

- The employee will only transfer if assigned to the economic entity being transferred.

- It does not matter that one or both of the employers were unaware the individual was an employee – he will still transfer.

- It does not matter that the employee was unaware that the transfer was taking place – he will still transfer.

- The employers cannot agree that the TUPE regulations will not apply to one or more employees, although the transferring employer may be able to retain staff that would otherwise transfer.

- An employee can refuse to transfer. In this case, his contract will terminate automatically on the transfer and he will have no rights in respect of that termination.

- If the employee's refusal to transfer is because of a substantial change to his detriment in his terms and conditions of employment, he can refuse to transfer and will retain his termination rights against the outgoing employer.

- If the employee is dismissed before the transfer he cannot become an employee of the new employer. But all the rights and liabilities in respect of his employment will transfer to the new employer unless the dismissal was unconnected with the transfer or was due to an ETO reason requiring a change in the workforce – this follows the principles laid down in *Litster* and *regulation 4* of the 2006 regulations.

Questions and answers [5.26]

Question

The transferring employer has forgotten about an employee who had been given two years' unpaid leave of absence to obtain an MBA at an American business school. Although he was formally assigned to the transferring economic entity, the acquiring employer was not aware of his existence and now refuses to employ him. What is the position?

Answer

The student was still an employee at the time of transfer and was assigned to the unit concerned. It does not matter that he had not recently worked in the unit or that the new employer was unaware of his existence. He will still transfer. If the new employer refuses to employ him that will be a dismissal and being connected with the transfer it will be automatically unfair (see *TC Cleaning Contractors Ltd v Joy* (**5.8**)).

Question

A secretary works 45% of her time for the managing director and the other 55% for the HR director. The HR function is currently being outsourced to Independent Consultants Ltd which insist she will not transfer to it under TUPE.

Answer

If the secretary has been assigned to the HR department she will transfer. However, if there is no formal assignment then working for the HR department 55% of her time does not indicate an implied assignment. On the facts it is unlikely she will transfer.

Question

Do agency workers transfer? ➡

Answer

Only employees transfer. Unless, by applying the tests for employment (see **5.17**), the agency worker has become an employee of the transferring employer they will not transfer.

Question

If a transferring employee is offered different terms and conditions by the acquiring employer can he refuse to transfer?

Answer

There is no way an employee can be compelled to transfer. But if he refuses to do so his contract ends automatically on the transfer and he has no rights in respect of the termination of his employment. If his refusal to transfer is based on a substantial detrimental change to his terms and conditions of employment he can refuse to transfer and retain all his termination rights, for example unfair dismissal, breach of contract and redundancy. These rights will be enforceable against the transferring employer.

6. Transfer of Rights and Liabilities

Protection of rights [6.1]

One of the express objectives of the EU Acquired Rights Directive 1977 (77/187/EEC) ('the Directive'), which is clearly stated in its preamble, is:

> 'to provide for the protection of employees in the event of a change of employer, in particular, to ensure that their rights are safeguarded.'

The courts and tribunals have to take this into account when interpreting both the Directive and the *Transfer of Undertakings* (*Protection of Employment*) *Regulations 2006* (*SI 2006/246*) (TUPE). This requirement is of considerable importance in the transfer of rights and liabilities.

The Directive protects employees not only by transferring their employment to the new employer but by also ensuring they transfer across on their existing terms and conditions. Article 3(1) of the Directive deals with both the transfer of employment and the transfer of the rights and obligations of the parties:

> 'The transferor's rights and obligations arising from an employment relationship existing on the date of the transfer . . .shall, by reason of such transfer, be transferred to the transferee.'

The new 2006 TUPE regulations provide for the transfer of employment in *regulation 4* (see **5.1**) and for the transfer of rights and liabilities in *regulation 4(2)* by stating that:

> '(a) All the transferor's rights, powers, duties and liabilities under or in connection with any such contract, shall be transferred by virtue of this regulation to the transferee; and
>
> (b) anything done before the transfer is completed by or in relation to the transferor in respect of that contract or person assigned to that organised grouping of resources or employees shall be deemed to have been done by or in relation to the transferee.'

This is very wide and encompasses not only the terms and conditions of employment but could extend to rights under related contracts 'under or in connection with any such contract.' It also includes things the transferor may have done and things the employee may have done in relation to the contract. If an employee was part way through disciplinary proceedings at the time of the transfer, the transferee could continue the proceedings from the point of transfer and rely on the transferor's investigation and on the statements and actions of the employee.

This wide transfer of rights and liabilities arises in respect of two groups of employees:

• It obviously applies to those whose employment itself transfers.

• It also applies to anyone who was dismissed before the transfer, but who would still have been employed at the transfer but for that dismissal unless that dismissal was unconnected with the dismissal transfer? For example, the dismissal was for gross misconduct or there was an economic, technical or organisational reason for the dismissal. In these cases, the actual employment does not transfer but the rights and liabilities do (see *Litster v Forth Dry Dock and Engineering Co Ltd [1989] IRLR 161 HL* (**5.3**), *regulation 4(3)* of the 2006 regulations and **CHAPTER 8 – AUTOMATIC UNFAIR DISMISSAL**).

Excluded rights and liabilities [6.2]

Certain rights and liabilities do not transfer.

Criminal liabilities do not transfer and are specifically excluded by *regulation 4* of the 2006 TUPE regulations. This will exclude, for example, any criminal liability for breach of the *Working Time Regulations 1998 (SI 1998/1833)* and of the *Health and Safety at Work Act 1974* and its related regulations. But the associate civil liability (for example for failure to provide a safe system of work) will transfer.

Regulation 10 excludes occupational pension schemes. This is receiving an increasingly restrictive interpretation in accordance with the need expressed in the Directive to safeguard the rights of employees. Thus it is restricted to pension rights due on retirement and does not include other benefits that may be wrapped up in the pension scheme (see **CHAPTER 7 – PENSIONS**).

In addition, non-contractual benefits do not transfer.

Non-contractual rights [6.3]

Employees frequently have well founded expectations that their employer will behave in a particular way. An expectation is not a contractual right and does not transfer. Non-binding employment practices do not transfer.

Case study

Ralton and ors v Havering College of Further and Higher Education [2002] IDS 701 EAT.

Facts

In this case, prior to a TUPE transfer, two employees had been employed on fixed-term contracts incorporating the local authority collectively agreed 'silver book' terms and one on a silver book terms indefinite contract. They transferred on those terms to the college in 1992. When the fixed-term contracts expired, they were renewed on the same terms. However, in 1994 all three signed new contracts that did not include the silver book terms.

Being public sector employees they decided to base their claim on the Directive itself rather than on TUPE (see *Marshall v Southampton and South West Hampshire Area Health Authority (Teaching) [1986] IRLR 140 ECJ* (**1.6**)). They relied on the provision in Article 3(1) that rights and obligations arising from the 'employment relationship' transfer and that collective agreements must be observed. They claimed it was part of the relationship and that as long as the silver book existed its provisions had to be in their contracts.

Findings

This was rejected by the Employment Appeal Tribunal (EAT) because all that transferred were rights and obligations existing at the transfer. Although the local authority would probably have continued to include the silver book, it was not legally bound to do so. It was not a right or obligation so it did not transfer. If it had transferred, it would have bound the college to apply the silver book even though the local authority was not bound to do so and, therefore, it would not have been a transfer of the same but of different terms.

As only legally binding terms and conditions transfer the contract terms must be identified. This is not easy to do. In particular, there are problems with discretionary terms, collective agreements and policies and procedures.

Identifying the contractual terms [6.4]

It is sometimes wrongly thought that discretionary terms are not legally enforceable. In fact, they are, but they do give the employer a degree of flexibility.

Case study

French v Barclays Bank plc [1998] IRLR 646 CA.

Facts

The case involved a discretionary loan as part of a relocation package. The bank did not have to offer a loan and it could have offered the loan on any terms. It chose to offer French an interest-free loan. The bank decided to impose a commercial interest rate.

Findings

The Court of Appeal reiterated that a discretionary term was binding. It said the actions of the bank amounted to a breach of contract. The bank had exercised its discretion when it offered the loan and at that point could have included a term allowing it to impose an interest rate but had not done so. French had accepted the offer and so was entitled to an interest-free loan and it was breach of contract to demand interest. It follows that all the discretionary benefits, such as private medical insurance, loans and training allowances, will transfer.

Collective agreements [6.5]

Collective agreements are made between the union and the employer but are frequently intended to regulate the relationship between the employer and his employees. As far as the relationship between the employer and the union is concerned, *regulation 5* of the 2006 TUPE regulations provides that the collective agreement transfers (see **CHAPTER 13 – COLLECTIVE AGREE-MENTS**). This chapter is concerned with the transfer of collectively agreed terms as part of the employment contract. Ascertaining whether the collective agreement is incorporated into the contract is crucial. The following guidelines are a useful starting point:

• If the contract provides that 'you will be employed on terms to be agreed from time to time between the employer and the union' or something similar, then the collectively agreed terms are incorporated and will transfer.

- The courts are beginning to accept that collective agreements may be incorporated by custom. The custom will need to be long standing, reasonable and notorious; it is not always easy to see when the point of incorporation has been reached.

- Where the employer and employee have put into effect the terms of the collective agreement, they are incorporated. Unlike the other two methods of incorporation, this method only leads to the incorporation of the agreement that has been acted upon and not to the incorporation of other or future agreements.

Policies and procedures [6.6]

If policies and procedures are referred to in an offer letter or in the contract of employment, they will be contractual unless there is some statement to show they are not intended to have legal effect. If the employee has only been given written particulars and they are referred to in the written particulars this will be evidence, but not conclusive proof, that the procedure or policy is contractual. As far as policies and procedures are concerned, although, in theory, it is possible to show they are not contractual, in practice it will be exceedingly difficult to do so in the absence of a statement to the effect that they are not legally binding.

As with collective agreements it is possible for a policy or procedure to be incorporated by custom. In *Quinn v Calder Industrial Materials Ltd [1996] IRLR 126 EAT*, it was thought that a published redundancy policy that had been followed automatically by management could, over time, become contractual.

Staff handbook [6.7]

Sometimes employers refer the employee to a staff handbook. If it is not clear which parts of the handbook are incorporated, the court or tribunal will decide. It is quite likely that policies and procedures will be contractual.

Case study

Wandsworth Borough Council v D'Silva [1998] IRLR 193 CA.

Facts

This case concerned a sickness policy contained in a staff handbook. ➡

Findings

Lord Woolf said that he and his colleagues would normally find that a disciplinary procedure was contractual. As such, the court held that the part of a sickness policy that dealt with dismissal was contractual, but not the trigger point for the consideration of action on long-term sickness. The interesting point is that the policy statement was not referred to in any contractual document.

Job descriptions [6.8]

It is also worth checking the position of job descriptions. When first used, they were no more than instructions as to how the job should be performed and the employer was free to change instructions within the parameter of the contract. Employers are now more inclined to include them in the contract, in which case it will be a right that transfers.

The transfer of contract terms [6.9]

Once the transferring terms have been identified they must be applied in the new situation. Sometimes, this can prove difficult or even impossible. In any event, the employee is only entitled to the rights and benefits he had prior to the transfer and not to greater rights. Thus, if the employee is employed on a fixed-term contract it is only the remaining period of that contract which transfers. The employee will have no greater rights to renewal than the legal rights he possessed before the transfer.

Redundancy, disciplinary and grievance procedures [6.10]

Acquiring employers often find they need to reduce staff numbers. Therefore, it is essential to check whether redundancy, retention and retraining schemes are contractual prior to the transfer of the business. With redundancy the main issue is usually whether the redundancy policy is contractual.

Case study

Facts

In *Quinn v Calder Industrial Materials Ltd*, a redundancy policy had been applied on four previous occasions within a particular organisation. It had been applied between 1987 and 1994 whenever a redundancy situation arose. ➡

Findings

The EAT refused to hold that the redundancy policy had become a contractual term. Policies will only stand a chance of becoming terms if they have been drawn to the attention of employees by management or have been followed for a substantial period, and all the other circumstances of the case are taken into account. In this case, the payment of the enhanced redundancy payment followed a decision to make the payment on each occasion.

Case study

Facts

In *Pellow v Pendragon [2000] IDS 634 EAT*, Lex had transferred a garage to Pendragon. There had been a consistent custom and practice over 20 years concerning the payment of redundancy pay. The published policy reserved to management the right to determine on each occasion the amount that would be paid.

Findings

This was sufficient to prevent the custom becoming contractual. So, when Lex transferred the garage to Pendragon, there was no contractual term relating to redundancy. The EAT held that it was no more than a management policy and management was free to determine on each occasion whether an additional payment would be made and, if so, how much.

Sometimes, redundancy benefits are tied up in the pension scheme, especially the right to an early pension when made redundant.

In *Beckmannn v Dynamco Whicheloe MacFarlane Ltd [2002] IRLR 578 ECJ*, the European Court decided that the rule preventing the transfer of pensions related only to pensions narrowly defined as payments made on reaching retirement age. So, the right to an early pension on redundancy was not a right to a retirement pension. It therefore transferred to the acquiring employer. Even if long-term disability benefit, life insurance and private medical insurance are part and parcel of the pension scheme, the benefits will transfer. For greater detail see **CHAPTER 7**.

Sometimes, the transferring employer pays redundancy pay to the employees who are transferring to the acquiring employer under TUPE. There is, in fact, no redundancy so no pay is due. The implications of the payment of redundancy pay are discussed later in **CHAPTER 12 – REDUNDANCY**.

Under *section 3(1)* of the *Employment Rights Act 1996* (*ERA 1996*), employees of employers (together with any associated employer) employing 20 or more staff have to be notified of the steps they should take to appeal against a disciplinary decision, or to raise a grievance, as part of their written particulars. Unless this procedure is stated to have no legal effect it will probably be legally binding. Some changes came into effect under the *Employment Act 2002* (*EA 2002*). *Section 1* of the *EA 2002* applies to all employers regardless of size. A minimum statutory dismissal, disciplinary and grievance procedure, as set out in *Schedule 2*, is written into every contract. If the employer has a more favourable procedure that will still have to be followed. These statutory changes came into effect in October 2004. Whether the employer's procedure is legally binding will be decided in the same way as before. It is important to know if the employer's procedure is legally enforceable for two reasons:

1. There can be a breach of contract claim if it is not followed. There is no service qualification required to commence a breach of contract claim.

2. It is very difficult to change a contract term when the cause is the transfer, but a non-contractual procedure can be changed. The post transfer harmonisation of procedures is easier when they are not contractual.

Restraint clauses [6.11]

Sometimes the literal application of an existing term in the employment environment of the new employer has the effect of changing the term. This frequently occurs with restraint clauses.

Example

Take a simple clause that prevents an employee soliciting work from any person who had been a client of his outgoing employer in the previous twelve months. On transfer, the new employer replaces the outgoing employer with two results:

1. The outgoing employer loses the protection against future solicitation. If he has transferred the complete business there will be no problem, but if he has only sold part of it there could be a problem. This situation is yet to be addressed by the courts.

2. The clause as applied to the new employer may be too wide to be enforceable. The new employer will only need protection in respect of those clients with whom the employee has had contact and not in➡

---

respect of all the clients of the new employer. If the clause is enforced it places a far wider restraint on the employee than he had before.

One court has dealt with the second problem by rewriting the restraint clause so that it was no wider in practice than it was before the transfer.

Case study

Facts

In *Morris Angel and Son Ltd v Hollande [1993] IRLR 169 CA*, Hollande was group managing director with a wide restraint clause in his contract. For the period of one year after the termination, the clause prevented him from procuring orders or doing business with any person, firm or company who had at any time during the one year immediately preceding the termination done business with the group. The business was transferred to a new group which immediately dismissed Hollande. The new group sought an injunction to enforce the restraint clause.

Findings

The Court of Appeal took a purposive, but not literal, view of the TUPE regulations. Although after the transfer the contract is deemed made by the employee and the new employer instead of the old employer, the intention was to preserve the employee/employer rights and liabilities. It certainly was not intended to extend them. When the contract was made the old employer and Hollande had no intention of creating a restraint clause in respect of the new company's clients. The clause was enforceable only in respect of clients of the old company.

The decision also refers to, but does not deal with, two other questions:

1. Hollande was a director and employed as a director. There was no attempt to make him a director of the new company. Could it be that in cases like this *regulation 5(1)* (under the 1981 regulations) did not apply and no transfer takes place?

2. There were allegations that the sale was in breach of a shareholders agreement to which the old company was a party – would this have an effect on the transfer of Hollande's contract?

Case study

A different result was reached in *McCall v Initial Supplies Ltd [1990] Tolley's Employment Service Cases Ct Sess.*

Facts

This case deals with another restraint clause prohibiting the solicitation and dealing with the original employer's clients for a period of one year after the termination of employment. In this case, the employee transferred to Initial and then left to set up his own business. At this stage Initial sought an interdict (injunction).

Findings

The court refused to exercise its discretion to grant an injunction. It refused to substitute the new for the old employer because that would substantially alter the practical scope and effect of the restraint clause.

Is the answer to the above to put in a new restraint clause? The employee cannot agree to any detrimental change to his contract terms (*regulation 12* of the 1981 TUPE regulations and *regulation 4* of the 2006 regulations and *Foreningen AF Arbedjsldere I Danmark v Daddy's Dance Hall A/S ECJ [1988] IRLR 315*). So, if the clause is wider it will be unenforceable, as in *Credit Suisse First Boston (Europe) Ltd v Lister [1998] IRLR 700 CA*. However, if the clause was redrafted along the lines of *Morris Angel*, it is possible the court might take a different view.

Performance-related pay and bonuses   [6.12]

This is another area where the literal transfer of the term to the new employer can change the nature and effect of the term completely. It is the intention of the Directive to ensure the employee's rights are safeguarded and, with the increasing use of pay and profit-related elements as a significant part of the employee's remuneration, they cannot be ignored. As with restraint clauses, the courts are not applying a strict literal interpretation to the clause after the transfer.

The European Court of Justice is firmly of the view that the employee should not suffer financially as a result of the transfer.

In *Merckx and Neuhys v Ford Motors Co Belgium SA [1996] IRLR 467 ECJ*, the European Court was of the opinion that a detrimental change had occurred to Merckx and Neuhys' terms when although the new employer had agreed to continue to apply the turnover-related pay formula in their contracts, he would be doing so on his turnover and would not guarantee that this would result in as high a payment as they had received in the Ford Group. This clearly suggests the right to performance-related pay, profit-related pay (PRP) and bonuses transfer.

Case study

The point was then considered in *Unicorn Consultancy Services Ltd v Westbrook [2000] IRLR 80 EAT*.

Facts

Westbrook belonged to the Atkins PRP scheme. To obtain payment the scheme required the employee to be employed in the Atkins group on the first day of the month preceding the payment month. Before that date Westbrook had been transferred under TUPE to Unicorn.

Findings

The EAT held that Unicorn had to pay the sum Westbrook had earned under the scheme. Under *regulation 5* of the 1981 TUPE regulations and now *regulation 4* of the 2006 regulations, the obligation was deemed made by Unicorn. Unicorn had to make the payment.

It should be noted that the employees who transferred had earned their PRP because they had worked throughout the profit period. The case does not deal with the employee who has only worked for part of the period. The EAT realised there would be difficulties working out the profits in such cases.

The EAT scrutinised the terms of the scheme very carefully and concluded that the requirement to be employed on the first of the month preceding the payment date was an administrative matter and not a substantive qualifying issue.

The EAT did not have to deal with payment in future years in the above case but this point cannot be ignored, especially where the payment is an important part of the pay package.

Case study

This matter was dealt with in *Mitie Managed Services Ltd v French [2002] IRLR 512 EAT*.

Facts

Mrs French had worked for Sainsbury's and participated in a profit-sharing scheme in which the profit could be taken as cash or shares. Mrs French had opted for shares. The section in which she worked was transferred under TUPE first to Pitney Bowes Management Services Ltd and then to Mitie. From the date of the first transfer the transferred staff insisted they were still entitled to their profit share, including the Sainsbury's shares. If they were entitled on the first transfer to Pitney Bowes, this liability would transfer to Mitie.

Findings

The tribunal had applied *regulation 5(2)* of the 1981 TUPE regulations literally to the facts and insisted the staff were entitled to Sainsbury's shares that the new employer would have to purchase in the market. The EAT decided otherwise. It held that a literal application of *regulation 5(2)* of the 1981 regulations had to be avoided. The new employers would be subject to the rules of the Sainsbury's scheme, which Sainsbury's could change but into which it would have no input. Nor would the employees have an input into the profit. Assessing the amount due would be difficult. The new owners, unlike Sainsbury's, could not issue new shares but would have to buy them in the market. The EAT agreed with the *Unicorn* decision that it is not a simple case of construing the contract terms and applying them. It concluded that:

> 'The entitlement of the transferred employees in a case such as this, which has complications absent from, say, *Unicorn*, is to participation in a scheme of substantial equivalence, but one which is free from unjust, impossible or absurd features. In most cases we would expect the transferee to be able to negotiate a scheme of such equivalence with the transferred employees or their unions. If a negotiated conclusion is impossible, then it is appropriate for an application to be made to an employment ➡

> tribunal, probably under section 11 of the Employment Rights Act, for a determination of the relevant particulars of employment.'
>
> The parties were given time to negotiate a replacement scheme.
>
> This decision concurs with the European Court in *Merckx and Neuhys v Ford Motors Co Belgium SA*, although that particular case was not referred to in the case.

Bonuses are frequently expressed as being discretionary or even as being at the board's or a manager's absolute discretion. That does not mean they are not contractual. The discretion has to be exercised in accordance with mutual trust and confidence and can only be exercised where there is expressed to be a discretion, say, in fixing targets or determining the size of the bonus 'pot'. The bonus as expressed for the year of the transfer will be binding. It may be reasonable to presume new targets can be set for the next year.

In conclusion, acquiring employers should not ignore the importance of profit and performance-related schemes and bonuses. To do so, could be a costly mistake.

Stock options [6.13]

Although the latest case, *Mitie*, has put forward the solution of a reasonable replacement scheme, it is still worth reviewing two earlier cases where the applicants tried to enforce the option scheme itself. For this to occur, the scheme must be separate from the employment contract and the outcome will depend entirely on the wording of the scheme.

> ## *Case study*
>
> ### *Facts*
>
> In *Chapman and Elkin v CPS Computer Group plc [1987] IRLR 462 CA*, the transferred employees successfully enforced the share option scheme itself. They were employed by a wholly owned subsidiary of CPS Group and were invited to participate in the CPS share option scheme. They duly paid for their options. The business of the company for which they worked was then sold to Glassmill. The scheme provided that if an employee was dismissed for redundancy as defined in the *Employment Protection (Consolidation) Act 1978 (EP(C)A 1978)* (now the *ERA 1996*), he could exercise his options within six months of the termination of his➡

employment. CPS refused to allow them to exercise their options so they sought damages for breach of contract.

Findings

The Court of Appeal decided that TUPE could not change the definition of redundancy in the *EP(C)A 1978*. Before TUPE, the contracts would have terminated on the transfer and they would have been redundant. TUPE preserved the employment but did not affect the definition of redundancy. The employees were therefore redundant and it was breach of contract to refuse them their option rights. The court was also of the opinion that the case was not directly concerned with the employment contract as the share option contract was a separate one. In this respect the courts have progressed their thinking and now the link with employment would probably be upheld.

Case study

Facts

In *Thompson v ASDA MFI Group plc [1988] IRLR 340 Ch D*, Thompson had been employed by Wades, an ASDA subsidiary. As such he was entitled to join the ASDA savings-related share scheme. The scheme provided that if the employee ceased to work for a company in the group his options would lapse. ASDA then sold its shareholding in Wades causing Thompson's share options to lapse.

Findings

On construction of the scheme he had ceased to be employed by a group company and he lost his options. The result would have been the same if, instead of selling the shares in Wades, ASDA had sold the business. In either instance, Thompson would cease to be a group employee.

A well-drafted scheme outside the employment contract would appear to have benefits for the employers – but not the employee.

Negotiation arrangements [6.14]

Many contracts, particularly in the public sector, include terms relating to the way in which the contract terms can be identified. These may be by reference to collectively agreed terms or perhaps to nationally agreed terms. With these clauses the courts and tribunals have taken the literal approach. This requires a careful analysis of the contract terms.

Case study

Facts

In *William West and Sons (Ilkeston) Lts v Fairgieve [2000] IRLB 632 EAT*, the transferor had entered into an agreement with the Transport and General Workers' Union (TGWU) giving it bargaining rights. It had also written any resulting collective agreements into the contract of employment. After the transfer the transferor agreed new wage rates with the TGWU. Transferred employees claimed they were entitled to these new terms.

Findings

The EAT decided that under *regulation 6* of the 1981 TUPE regulations (now *regulation 5* of the 2006 regulations) the collective agreements transferred to the new employer but with the new employer's name substituted for that of the transferor. Any agreement reached by the new employer with the TGWU would automatically be part of the employment contract. The rewritten contract precluded any possible entitlement to wage rates agreed between the union and its previous employer.

In *Glendale Grounds Management v Bradley [1998] (EAT 484/97)*, the collective agreement was only incorporated after the 'approval of the council'. The EAT substituted the new employer for the council. This meant that the collective agreement could only be incorporated if the new employer gave his approval and the new employer had not approved the agreement.

Case study

BET Catering Services v Ball [1997] IDS 583 EAT.

Facts

There had been a transfer of school meals service from Richmond Borough Council to BET. BET continued to recognise the union. The contract provided that staff would be paid in accordance with the➡

National Joint Council (NJC) for manual workers. BET could not participate in the NJC because it was not a local authority.

Findings

It was held the contract incorporated future changes agreed by the NCJ.

Case study

A similar conclusion was reached in *Whent v T Cartledge Ltd [1997] IRLR 153 EAT.*

Facts

Brent had contracted out services and the terms of the employees transferred provided that Brent was a member of the NJC for administrative, professional, technical and clerical services. The union was de-recognised. The employer had said that he would agree and discuss terms with the employees but had not done so. Meanwhile, a pay rise was agreed at the NJC as well as to Brent staff.

Findings

The agreement transferred and NJC terms applied.

Although these cases concern pay they will apply to all terms covered by the arrangement, including hours and holidays.

Contracts (Rights of Third Parties) Act 1999 [6.15]

The basic common law rule is that a person who is not a party to a contract cannot sue upon it (there is a different rule is Scotland which does grant some rights to third parties). This was changed by the *Contracts (Rights of Third Parties) Act 1999* which allows the contracting parties, expressly or implied, to grant enforcement rights to persons who are not parties to the contract. This will enable an employer who wishes to protect his transferring employees to place duties on the acquiring employer as to the way the employees will be treated. These duties might include undertaking no redundancies for two years or the acquirer shadowing the transferring employer's terms and conditions for two years. The employees would then be able to enforce that contractual promise themselves. However, it is possible to contract out of the Act and it is not uncommon for this to be the case. This means only the transferring employer can enforce such promises. More often than not, there is little incentive for him to do so.

Two-tier workforces [6.16]

The unions are concerned at the development of two-tier workforces, especially in the contracting out of public services. They would like to see a requirement that any new staff taken on to work in the public service unit concerned would be entitled to the same terms and conditions as existing staff and could not be employed on less advantageous terms. The Confederation of British Industry would like to see a voluntary code under which employers agree to take on employees on fair and reasonable terms. It remains to be seen whether two-tier workforces can be avoided, either through legislation or code.

Liability for negligence [6.17]

At first it was assumed by some that tortious rights (the rights of the person wronged) and liabilities, such as claims for misrepresentation and personal injuries, did not transfer under *regulation 5(2)* of the 1981 TUPE regulations and that the regulation was restricted to contract rights. The wording only requires a connection with the contract and is quite wide enough to include tortious liabilities.

Regulation 5(2)(a) (of the 1981 regulations) states:

'All the transferor's rights, powers, duties and liabilities under or in connection with any such contract, shall be transferred by virtue of this regulation to the transferee.'

In *The Secretary of State for Employment v Spence [1986] IRLR 248 CA*, Balcombe LJ confirmed that 'in connection with' covered not only statutory but also tortious liability. A county court then acted on this and held that the wording in the *National Health Service and Community Care Act 1990*, which is a mirror image of the wording in TUPE, effectively transferred liability for injuries caused by negligence whilst employed by the transferring employer to the acquiring employer (*Wilson and ors v West Cumbria Health Care NHS Trust [1994] IRLB 506*).

It is now clear beyond doubt that tortious liability and, in particular, liability for negligence and failure to provide a safe system of work does transfer to the incoming employer.

This means the acquiring employer buys an uninsured risk. In the private sector, employers have to be insured under the *Employers' Liability (Compulsory Insurance) Act 1969 (EL(CI)A 1969)* for the benefit of their employees. The insurer's liability is only secondary liability. The insurer is only liable if the employer is liable. So, if an employee has a back injury while employed by the transferring employer who is properly insured, but he transfers under TUPE to the acquiring employer, the transferring employer and his insurance company escape liability and the claim has to be brought against the acquiring employer.

The acquiring employer will also be insured under the Act but the policy will not cover accidents arising before the acquiring employer assumed responsibility for the employee. The net effect is the transferring employer and his insurance company that should be responsible are not. The acquiring employer obtains an uninsured risk and the employee loses the benefit of the *EL(CI)A 1969*.

A simple solution was available. Under the Directive, member states are authorised, if they so wish, to provide for joint and several liability between the transferring and acquiring employer. This would enable the court to apportion loss in accordance with fault. Therefore, if the transferring employer is solely liable he would bear the full cost. Because he is liable the employee could claim against his insurance company. If it is a continuing unsafe situation loss would be apportioned between the employers.

Under *regulation 17* of the 2006 regulations, the transferor and transferee will be jointly and severally liable for liabilities to employees for injury or disease arising from their pre-transfer employment in those cases where the transferor is a public sector employer not subject to, or exempted from, the requirement to affect Employer's Liability Compulsory Insurance.

As far as the private sector is concerned the new regulations have nothing to add to existing case law (see below). The Government believed the matter should be dealt with as a commercial negotiation. In this respect it is simpler to transfer rights completely to the acquirer. Unfortunately, it is extremely difficult in practice to obtain an indemnity to cover this liability.

Case study

Facts

In *Bernadone v Pall Mall Group and Martin v Lancashire County Council [2000] IRLR 487 CA*, the Court of Appeal took an extremely purposive interpretation of the TUPE regulations to ensure fairness. In both these ➡

cases the employee had been injured and had then been transferred under a TUPE transfer to the new employer. The questions before the court were:

- did the liability to provide a safe system of work transfer?

- if so, was there any way in which the insurance company would have to cover the liability?

Findings

The court first decided that tortious liability did transfer to the acquirer. *Regulation 5(2)* (1981 regulations) refers to liability 'in connection with employment'. There is no requirement that the duty has to be contractual. The employer's liability arises because of employment and is therefore in connection with employment. Also, the employer's liability to ensure a safe workplace arises in contract, where it is an implied contractual term and statute as a tort. It would be strange if the contractual liability transferred but the tortious liability remained with the transferring employer. There can now be no doubt tortious liability transfers.

Turning to the insurance policy, the court pointed out that the transferring employer has a vested or a contingent right to claim an indemnity under the insurance policy. This, the court decided, was also a right of the transferor 'in connection with employment' and therefore it too transferred to the acquirer. Taking a purposive view of *regulation 5(2)* (1981 regulations), the court brushed aside arguments that TUPE could only apply to contracts and liabilities directly arising between the transferring employer and the employee and that it could not have been intended to cover contracts between the transferor and third parties, such as the insurance company. Bernadone and Martin could sue the acquirer who could in turn claim an indemnity from the insurance company.

The case undoubtedly achieves justice, the employee can still take advantage of the *EL(CI)A 1969*, the acquiring employer is covered by insurance and the insurance company who took the premium for the risk must cover the loss. Applying the principles of joint and several liability may have been a simpler route to the same end.

Bernadone is of no help though if the outgoing employer is not insured. In the public sector, employers are exempt from the requirement to have insurance cover and so they do not normally have external insurance. Here the contractor is still taking on an uninsured risk. *Regulation 17* of the new 2006 regulations now effectively addresses this point.

That said, the existence of insurance cover or limited joint and several liability does not relieve the acquiring employer from the need to check the health and safety situation. The transferring employer will probably reveal outstanding claims and these and any contingent claims will be covered by the transfer of the insurance protection or the public sector joint and several liability provision.

What may not be revealed are so-called embryonic claims. These are situations where the danger exists before the transfer but the injury occurs after the transfer. This can be illustrated by 'stress' cases. In personal injury claims for mental illness based on work-related stress, the employer is only liable if he should have been aware of the risk to the employee. This may be because it was obvious, as when an employee is trying to do the work of two or three people, or because the employee has brought his problems to the attention of the manager.

The acquiring employer will find it very difficult to obtain this information but if the outgoing employer was or should have been aware of the risk, then the acquirer will also be deemed to know and will be liable for the injury occurring after the transfer. Where the risk is physical, a safety officer visiting the site should be able to identify areas of risk. As far as mental illness is concerned, risk factors are identified by the Health and Safety Executive in its leaflet *Work-related Stress*.

Statutory rights   [6.18]

The statutory rights given to employees are also 'connected with employment' and also transfer with the employee to the new employer under *regulation 4* of the 2006 TUPE regulations.

One of the most important rights transferring under TUPE is that of continuity of employment. The employee's right to exercise many statutory rights, such as unfair dismissal, redundancy and maternity leave, depends on the employee having sufficient continuity of employment. Under *regulation 4* of the 2006 TUPE regulations, the transferring employee takes his accrued continuity of employment with him and so cannot be treated by the acquirer as a new employee. Given the necessary continuity he may be able to claim unfair dismissal and redundancy even if dismissed the day after the transfer.

There are some situations where the employee may have worked for the employer before and after the transfer, but not be able to use *regulation 4* because he was not employed by the transferor immediately before the transfer, or did not transfer until after the transfer was complete. As these employees do not transfer under TUPE, they cannot rely on *regulation 4*. Any claims they have remain against the transferring employer and they do not transfer on the same terms and conditions. However, their continuity of employment may be preserved under *section 218* of the *ERA 1996* which provides that if a trade, business or an undertaking is transferred from one person to another:

- the period of employment of an employee in the trade, business or undertaking at the time of the transfer counts as a period of employment with the transferee; and

- the transfer does not break the continuity of employment.

The situation to be considered here is where, although there is an actual gap in employment, there is no gap in continuity. This is due to the way in which continuity is calculated.

Under *section 212* of the *ERA 1996*:

- continuity is calculated in weeks running from Sunday to Saturday; and

- any part of a week in which a contract of employment exists is counted as a full week, so if an employment contract is in existence on one day of the week, the whole week is counted for the purpose of continuity.

Example

An employer who has been unable to find a purchaser for his business decides to close it and retire. He dismisses his two employees with wages in lieu of notice on Monday 1 July. On Thursday 5 July, out of the blue, Newco offer to buy the business. The transfer takes place on the following Monday 8 July and Newco immediately offers employment to the dismissed employees who start work on Friday 12 July. The employees will not transfer under the TUPE regulations as they were not employed immediately before the transfer. The dismissal is not connected with the transfer. It was because the employer had decided to close down. The employees have no TUPE protection.

The employees have been transferred to a new employer under *section 218* of the *ERA 1996* so the transfer itself will not break continuity. There is no gap in continuity. In the week 30 June to 6 July there is an employment contract up to and including 1 July so the whole week until the 6 July is included in the continuity calculation. In the following week, there is employment on the 12 July so again the whole week from the 7 July is included for the purposes of continuity. There is no gap in employment.

Even if there is a gap in employment, continuity may be protected under *section 218*. Unlike TUPE, *section 218* does not specify that the employee has to be employed immediately before the transfer, nor does it say he has to be employed immediately afterwards. In early cases, some judges did try to incorporate the need to be employed immediately before the transfer. However, this was finally rejected in *Macer v Aberfast Ltd [1989] IRLR 139 EAT* where the EAT followed the reasoning of the House of Lords in *Litster v Forth Dry Dock and Engineering Co Ltd* and decided to interpret the provision in such a way that the continuity of employment was preserved.

The EAT concluded the transfer could take place over a period of time (no indication is given as to how long this may be) and that employment could be terminated before the transfer and recommence after the transfer. Thereby, continuity could be preserved.

Case study

Facts

The facts in *Macer* are extremely complicated. Macer was managing director of Computer Technology Recruitment Ltd (CTR). CTR became insolvent and it was decided to sell CTR to Recruitment, a subsidiary of Aberfast. On 31 December, all employment with CTR ended. The employees were assured their jobs were safe and they would be deemed to have commenced work with Recruitment on 1 January. Macer was offered employment as managing director of Recruitment from 12 January so creating a gap of twelve days in his employment. The transfer took place 18–19 January. Macer could not rely on *regulation 5(2)* of the 1981 TUPE regulations because he was not employed by CTR immediately before the transfer. Aberfast had deliberately engineered a gap in Macer's employment to break continuity under *section 218* of the *ERA 1996*.

Findings

The plan to break continuity of employment failed. The EAT's purposive interpretation of *section 218* prevented Aberfast from using such a mechanical device.

Case study

A and G Tuck v Bartlett [1994] IRLR 162 EAT. ➡

Facts

Bartlett worked for A and G Tuck (Slough) Ltd and an associated company as production manager. The business of A and G Tuck (Slough) Ltd was transferred to A and G Tuck Ltd whilst Bartlett was on vacation. Bartlett was asked by A and G Tuck (Slough) Ltd (in whose employ he remained) to work for the new owner for the next two weeks. At the end of that time he was invited to become production manager for the new owner but the new owner avoided all requests for a contract of employment. The question was whether the period of two weeks during which he was employed by the old owner but worked for the new one prevented continuity running.

Findings

Bartlett could not take advantage of *regulation 5* of the 1981 TUPE regulations (now *regulation 4*) because it only applied where the contract would otherwise have terminated due to the transfer and his clearly did not. Continuity was preserved by the ordinary continuity rules in *section 218* of the *ERA 1996* that provides that if a trade, business or undertaking is transferred from one person to another then employment will be continuous. The argument that there was a gap of two weeks following the transfer did not succeed.

Case study

Justfern Ltd v D'Ingerthorpe [1994] IRLR 164 EAT.

Facts

D'Ingerthorpe was a lecturer at a training college that closed when the owner left the country. D'Ingerthorpe claimed unemployment benefit for two weeks before commencing employment at the college that had been bought by Justfern. D'Ingerthorpe later claimed he had been unfairly dismissal by Justfern. Justfern argued the two-week gap broke D'Ingerthorpe's continuity of employment and he therefore had insufficient continuity to bring the claim.

Findings

Section 218 of the *ERA 1996* again preserved his continuity and D'Ingerthorpe could go ahead with his claim. ➡

Claims for all the other statutory rights will transfer. This will include working time, holidays, minimum wage protection, protection relating to union membership, family rights, part-time and fixed-term contracts and discrimination. It does not matter that the fault or breach was entirely that of the transferring employer and the acquiring employer had acted impeccably. The liability will transfer in full.

Case study

DMJ International Ltd v Nicholas [1996] IRLR 76 EAT.

Facts

When Mrs Nicholas transferred under TUPE from D J Mouldings to DMJ International she was employed on a part-time basis. She had previously been employed full time but had been forced to retire at 60 and be employed part time. She was later made redundant from DMJ International. She then brought several claims against DMJ, including sex discrimination relating to her retirement.

Findings

The EAT held that the alleged act of sex discrimination was, under *regulation 5* of the 1981 TUPE regulations, deemed to have been done by the acquirer and any claim would have to be brought against the acquirer.

There is one statutory right that may not transfer. Under *regulation 10* of the 1981 regulations and *regulation 13* of the 2006 regulations, the transferring employer has to consult the representatives of a recognised trade union or elected representatives. Failure to do this enables the union or elected representatives to seek an order for a protective award from the tribunal. This can be for as much as 90 days' pay. The individual employee can then enforce the award. Does this right transfer?

In *Kerry Foods Ltd v Creber [2000] IRLR 10 EAT* (see **4.6** for the facts of this case), the EAT said that it did. The EAT decided that the duty to consult arose from the individual contracts and as such transferred to the new employer under *regulation 5(2)* of the 1981 regulations.

This case was distinguished in *Transport and General Workers Union v McKinnon, JR Haulage Ltd and ors [2001] IRLR 597 EAT* where the EAT pointed out that the employees were seeking compensation which arose under TUPE itself, whereas *regulation 5* of the 1981 regulations was concerned with the transfer of rights existing outside TUPE. The EAT decided the liability for failure to consult did not transfer.

Policies, procedures and other matters [6.19]

This chapter has concentrated on the legal rights that transfer under *regulation 4* of the 2006 TUPE regulations. Policies, procedures, collective agreements and other matters outside the contract do not transfer. That does not mean they should be ignored. Although it may be possible to change them without legal difficulties they are nonetheless important. These matters and the culture of the transferring unit all need to be subjected to investigation. Differences between cultures can prevent the transfer being a 'good fit'.

Although policies and non–contractual procedures do not transfer they can have an impact on the transferee.

Example

Miss A works for Oldco. Her manager at Oldco sexually harasses her. She is frightened to bring a formal grievance because of the consequences and the culture of Oldco is not conducive to her grievances being dealt with professionally. The part of the business in which Miss A works is transferred to Newco and that company becomes her new employer under the TUPE regulations. The manager does not transfer. Now free of fear and retribution she brings a discrimination claim. Newco will be liable.

Due diligence [6.20]

The prospective contractor or purchaser of a business needs to know the terms of employment as well as any outstanding or incipient claims in order to make a sensible bid for the business. The new regulations impose legal requirements in this respect. *Regulation 11* of the 2006 regulations requires the transferor to notify the transferee of all the employees' rights and obligations that will be transferred (called 'employee liability information'). In the new regulations, the employee liability information must be provided at least two weeks before the completion of the TUPE transfer, unless this is not reasonably practicable. The employee liability information to be provided includes:

- The identity of the transferring employee.

- Their age.

- The information contained in their written statement of particulars of employment.

- Details of any disciplinary actions or grievances in the last two years.

- Details of actual or potential legal action brought by the employees in the previous two years.

Under *regulation 12* of the new 2006 regulations, the employment tribunal has power to award the transferee compensation for any loss suffered as a result of the transferor's failure to provide the employee liability information, with a minimum award of £500 per employee (unless the employment tribunal considers that it is unjust or inequitable to award the minimum).

It should be noted that some organisations do put terms in their contracts requiring contractors to provide similar information towards the end of the contract so as to enable tenderers to properly bid for the business. These terms cannot be enforced because the bidders are not party to the contract, but compliance is normal.

Aside from the employee liability information statutory requirements, the contractor should undertake his own due diligence. He needs to check the terms and liabilities not only at the time of the due diligence, but also before the transfer. New claims may arise and terms can change either as the result of routine changes, such as annual wage increases, or as a result of individual events. Wherever possible the incoming contractor should seek some form of undertaking or warranty as to the validity of the information. An indemnity should be sought where possible. There is no legal obligation to provide such protection and it can be difficult to persuade an outgoing contractor to give an indemnity. It remains to be seen whether the levels of statutory penalty for non-compliance referred to above have a positive impact on the free passing of information prior to a transfer.

Guidelines   **[6.21]**

Due diligence may include:

- the employees' terms and conditions of employment, including terms in related documents, such as handbooks;

- related agreements, such as stock options and profit share arrangements;

- the non-pension elements of the pension scheme;

- policies and procedures – check whether these are contractual;

- collective agreements – check whether these are incorporated into the contract;

- the length of service, age, absence record and general work record of the employees;

- details of claims made against the transferor;

- details of claims that the transferor believes may be made;

- pre-transfer dismissals, the reason for them and the way they were conducted;

- check whether the consultation process with the trade union or employee representatives has been properly conducted; and

- the culture of the transferring unit to assess whether it accords with the acquiring organisation.

Some of this information will be personal information and protected under the law of confidentiality and under the *Data Protection Act 1998*. The Information Commissioner has issued the section of the Employment Practices Data Protection Code that deals with the disclosure of employee records in transfers and mergers. The Code was finally issued and came into force in its entirety in 2005.

Warranties and indemnities [6.22]

- [The transferor] warrants that the information supplied to [the transferee] relating to the terms and conditions of employment of the transferring employees is, to the best of his knowledge, correct as of [date].

- [The transferor] undertakes to perform and observe all its legal obligations in connection with the contracts of employment of the transferring employees up to and including the transfer date and will indemnify [the transferor] against any liability arising from [the transferor's] failure to perform and observe such obligations, any settlement of such liability and any costs and expenses reasonably incurred in relation to such liability or settlement thereof.

- [The transferor] warrants that all salary payments and other outgoings relating to or accruing in respect of any relevant employee before the relevant transfer date will be the responsibility of [the transferor] and [the transferor] will indemnify [the transferee] in relation to such accruals.

- [The transferor] will indemnify [the transferee] against each and every liability which relates to or arises out of any act or omission by [the transferee] or any other event or occurrence prior to the transfer date, the settlement of such liability and reasonable costs and expenses incurred in relation to such liability, or the settlement thereof, which [the transferee] may incur as a result of the transfer in respect of any contract of employment concerning the transferring employees.

Where there is a change of contractor and the outgoing contractor will not give an indemnity it may be possible to obtain one from the organisation contracting out the service.

- [The organisation] agrees to indemnify [the contractor] in respect of any legal claims, any settlement of such claims and any costs and expenses reasonably incurred by [the contractor] in relation to such claims arising out of the employment or the termination of employment of any person employed by any previous contractor in the provision of [the services] on your premises prior to this agreement and being claims made against [the contractor] as a result of the agreement to provide services under this contract.

Key points and new developments [6.23]

- Where an employee transfers to a new employer under TUPE he does so on his pre-transfer terms and conditions and any other rights, contractual or otherwise, which he may have will transfer with him.

- If the employee is dismissed before the transfer for a reason connected with the transfer then the employment liabilities attaching to the employee will transfer to the new employer, including the liability for his dismissal – see *Litster* and *regulation 4* of the 2006 regulations.

- Criminal liabilities do not transfer.

- Pension schemes do not transfer, although non-pension benefits included in the scheme will transfer (see also the *Pensions Act 2004*).

- Non-contractual policies and procedures do not transfer.

- Some policies and procedures may have become contractual through customary use.

- Restraint clauses may need to be adjusted to prevent their becoming wider in scope after the transfer.

- The latest case law on performance-related pay and stock options decided the new employer had to provide an equivalent scheme to that of the old employer.

- If the contract provides that terms will be such as are agreed between the union and the outgoing employer, then the name of the incoming employer is substituted for that of the outgoing employer and after the transfer only collective agreements with the incoming employer will be incorporated into the contract. Agreements with the outgoing employer are irrelevant.

- If the contract provides that terms will be those agreed by an external body, for example a NJC (including one on which the outgoing employer had representation), then that term transfers and new terms agreed by that external body are incorporated automatically into the contract. It does not matter that the incoming employer has no influence over those terms.

- Personal injury claims transfer. In the private sector, the benefit of the outgoing employer's insurance policy will also transfer. The public sector is now served by the joint and several liability protection afforded by *regulation 16* of the 2006 regulations.

- Statutory rights, including continuity of employment, unfair dismissal, redundancy, unpaid wages and discrimination rights, also transfer to the new employer.

- There is some confusion over the transfer of the right to a protective award but it probably does not transfer.

The New 2006 regulations – April 2006 [6.24]

- The transferor must provide the transferee with details of the rights and liabilities of transferring staff before the transfer takes place.

- There is joint and several liability on the transferor and transferee in respect of claims for personal injury or industrial disease.

Questions and answers [6.25]

Question

The employment terms of staff transferred under TUPE state that hours, pay and holidays will be as agreed between the transferring employer and the union. The transferring employer and the union have just reduced weekly hours from 48 to 40. The transferred employees are insisting that their hours are also reduced to 40. What is the position?

Answer

Under *regulation 4* of the 2006 TUPE regulations, the transferred contract is deemed made by the new employer. That means the name of the new employer replaces that of the old employer in the contract. Therefore, as from the transfer only terms agreed after that date between the new employer and the union are incorporated in the contract. The hours are unchanged at 48.

➡

If the contract had provided that the terms would be those of the NJC and it reduced the hours to 40, then the hours would be reduced. Replacing the old with the new employer would not affect this clause.

Question

An employee transferred under TUPE six weeks ago. He has now produced a letter from his previous manager agreeing that he could take three months' paid leave to complete a computer course. When we asked the outgoing contractor about the terms and conditions of employment we were only told of the standard terms and not about this agreement. Is he entitled to paid leave?

Answer

Assuming the manager had authority to grant the leave, yes he is. It does not matter that the incoming employer does not know about the term. Terms transfer automatically. Knowledge of them is not required.

Question

A government department has just contracted out its IT work to our business. An employee has approached us and informed us that she has severe work-related upper limb disorder, will be off work for six months and will be bringing a claim against us for failing to provide a safe system of work. Are we liable?

Answer

Unfortunately you are. Claims in tort for personal injuries are claims 'in connection with employment' and these transfer under *regulation 4* of the 2006 TUPE regulations. Although it may seem unfair, as you were not at fault, the liability is yours. If you had taken a transfer from the private sector the position would have been different. The liability would still have transferred but the benefit of the compulsory employer's liability insurance would also have transferred so you would have been able to claim an indemnity from the outgoing employer's insurance policy.

However, under *regulation 16* of the 2006 regulations, joint and several liability to cover liability for injuries and diseases in TUPE transfers from the public to the private sector was introduced. This allows the loss to be➡

137

apportioned in accordance with fault. Most would fall to the government
department in this case.

7. Pensions

The problem with pensions [7.1]

An employee's pension rights are an important element of his employment package. Indeed, they are an important employee benefit. However, there are obvious difficulties attached to the transfer of pension rights. To give the same rights the new employer would have to fund the transferring employee's participation in the outgoing employer's pension fund or provide a mirror image scheme. The former raises practical problems, quite apart from Inland Revenue rules. The latter would, especially in the contracting sector, lead to a fragmentation of pension rights and increasing administrative costs.

Perhaps it is not surprising that although the requirement for the transfer of terms and conditions of employment under Article 3(1) of the EU Acquired Rights Directive 1977 (77/187/EEC) ('the Directive') and *regulation 4* of the *Transfer of Undertakings (Protection of Employment) Regulations 2006 (SI 2006/246)* (TUPE) is, on the face of it, wide enough to include pension rights, both the Directive and TUPE exclude pensions from transfer. The reality of the situation is that neither provision is a shining example of clarity.

The statutory provisions [7.2]

Article 3(3) of the Directive provides that:

> 'Paragraphs 1 and 2 [these provide for the transfer of terms and conditions and collective agreements] shall not cover employees' rights to old age, invalidity or survivors' benefits under supplementary company or inter-company pension schemes outside the statutory social security schemes in member states.

> Member states shall adopt measures necessary to protect the interests of employers and of persons no longer employed in the transferor's business at the time of transfer within the meaning of Article 1(1) [this defines a transfer] in respect of rights conferring on them immediate or prospective entitlement to old age benefits, including survivors' benefits, under supplementary schemes referred to in the first sub paragraph.'

This was transposed into *regulation 7* of the 1981 TUPE regulations. *Regulations 5* (transfer of terms and conditions) and *6* (transfer of collective agreements) of the 1981 regulations did not apply:

'(a) to so much of a contract of employment or collective agreement as relates to an occupational pension scheme within the meaning of the Pension Schemes Act 1993, s 1 [previously the Social Security Pensions Act 1975]; or

(b) to rights powers duties or liabilities arising under or in connection with any such right or subsisting by virtue of any such agreement and relating to such a scheme or otherwise arising in connection with that person's employment and relating to such a scheme.'

Now reflected in *regulation 10* of the 2006 regulations.

Pension arrangements that transfer [7.3]

What is clear is that neither statutory provision has the effect of producing a total embargo on the transfer of all rights relating to or connected with pensions. First, there are several pension arrangements which fall short of being an occupational pension scheme and which will, therefore, transfer. For example, a term under which an employer agrees to pay a regular sum into the employee's personal pension plan does not create an occupational pension scheme and so will transfer.

Second, there may be rights wrapped up in the pension scheme that are not connected with old age or survivors' benefits, such as private medical insurance, life insurance and long-term disability benefit. These rights do transfer.

Some scheme rights can be best described as mixed, being based on an event unconnected with old age but granting some pension rights. This came before the UK courts in *Frankling v BPS Public Sector Ltd [1999] IRLR 212 EAT*.

Case study

Facts

In *Frankling*, the Eastbourne NHS Trust payroll service was outsourced to BPS. The transferring staff were employed on Whitley Council terms and conditions, one of which (section 45) provided that redundant employees were entitled to enhanced redundancy benefits, and another (section 46) allowed employees aged over 50 who had at least five years' service to take an enhanced immediate pension. When Mrs Frankling was made redundant, BPS refused to provide her with the enhanced pension benefits. ➡

Findings

The Employment Appeal Tribunal (EAT) decided that although the enhanced pension benefits were triggered by redundancy, they in fact related to benefits payable in old age. The benefits could not transfer under *regulation 5* of the 1981 TUPE regulations but were caught by the 1981 *regulation 7* exclusion.

The *Frankling* case has not received universal approbation and the Government proposed to amend TUPE to provide for the transfer of mixed pension and non-pension benefits. This has been overtaken by the decision of the European Court in *Beckmann v Dynamco Whicheloe McFarlane Ltd [2002] IRLR 578 ECJ*.

Case study

Facts

In *Beckmann*, Mrs Beckmann, like Mrs Franklin, had originally been employed in the NHS under Whitley Council terms. She was transferred under TUPE and later made redundant. She was over 50 and had the necessary five years' service. Dynamco paid her the enhanced redundancy payment but not the enhanced pension terms.

Findings

The European Court, taking a purposive interpretation in order to protect the employee's entitlements, decided 'old age benefits' were restricted to benefits to which the employee was entitled because she had reached the age of retirement. It said that the exclusion from transfer had to be construed narrowly and was exhaustively restricted to the listed benefits. The benefits claimed by Mrs Beckmann were paid because she had been made redundant, not because she had reached retirement age, and so they transferred to the new employer. The effect of this decision is considerable and will have great impact on organisations that have undertaken TUPE transfers from the public sector.

Case study

Facts

In *Martin and ors v South Bank University (C-4/01) [2004] IRLR 74 ECJ*, M, D and W were lecturers at an NHS nursing college and employed under General ➡

Whitley Council (GWC) conditions of service. These GWC conditions provided a system of early retirement rights. In November 1994 the nursing college became part of SBU. In 1997 SBU offered early retirement rights that differed from the GWC rights. The applicants claimed they were entitled to the more favourable GWC terms.

Findings

The ECJ held that the GWC benefits were not excluded from transferring on a TUPE transfer. Furthermore, employees who transfer are not bound by their agreement (as in this case) to accept diminished terms for early retirement in circumstances where these have been offered by the transferee in order to harmonise terms across the workforce.

The Government considered the *Beckmann* and *Martin* cases in the consultation leading up to the new 2006 regulations and concluded no changes were required. It felt case law was clear and should be followed in that judgments such as *Beckmann* and *Martin* merely interpreted the requirements of the *Acquired Rights Directive*, as fully implemented in the existing regulations, and were consistent with the Government's own view of the intended effect in this regard.

Guidelines [7.4]

- Old age benefits are restricted to those payable on retirement and must be given a narrow interpretation.

- Benefits triggered by something other than retirement age are not old age benefits – this will apply to redundancy and early medical retirement.

- The list of excluded benefits – old age and survivors' benefits is exhaustive and to be interpreted narrowly.

Occupational pension schemes [7.5]

Occupational pension schemes do not transfer. There were several valiant attempts to interpret the Directive and TUPE regulations so as to secure the transfer of some occupational pension schemes.

Case study

The first attempt was *Perry v Intec Colleges Ltd [1993] IRLR 56 ET*. In this case, the tribunal looked at the duty to preserve the employee's 'immediate and prospective' pension rights in Article 3(3) of the Directive.

➡

Facts

Perry's employment was transferred under TUPE from the YMCA to Intec. His YMCA contract afforded him better pension rights than his Intec contract.

Findings

The tribunal held that although under *regulation* 7 of the 1981 TUPE regulations contractual pension rights did not transfer, the provision of *regulation* 5 of the 1981 regulations providing for the transfer of contractual terms had to be interpreted in line with Article 3(3) and the need to protect immediate and prospective pension rights. In the opinion of the tribunal, an employee's immediate pension rights were those accrued to the transfer date and the prospective ones were those accruing after that date. To protect these rights it decided to add at the end of *regulation* 7 of the 1981 regulations:

'But any contract of employment transferred by virtue of regulation 5 shall be deemed to include such rights as are necessary to protect the interests of the employee in respect of rights conferring on him immediate or prospective entitlement to old age benefits, including survivors' benefits under supplementary pension schemes.'

This would mean that the new employer would have to provide a similar scheme to that of the outgoing employer.

This view was rejected in *Walden Engineering Co Ltd v Warrener [1993] IRLR 420 EAT*. In this case, the employee unsuccessfully argued that a contracted-out pension scheme was not a supplementary pension scheme but a statutory scheme and so it had to transfer. The EAT decided that a line had to be drawn between state social security schemes and supplementary or contractual schemes. Contractual schemes did not transfer. A contracted-out scheme was a statutory scheme, not a social security scheme.

The Directive's use of the words 'company or inter-company pension schemes' are misleading in that they suggest that public sector schemes are not caught by the exception. The *Frankling v BPS Public Sector Ltd* case confirms that public sector schemes are contracted out within the meaning of the Directive.

The standard view that the retirement element of pension schemes does not transfer is confirmed in *Adams v Lancashire CC and BET Catering Services Ltd [1997] IRLR 436 CA*.

> ### Case study
>
> *Facts*
>
> In this case, employees moved from local government service where they enjoyed pension provision to BET which, because their earnings were too low, did not allow the employees to join the BET scheme. The employees argued they should have been provided with an equivalent pension provision, basing their claim on the duty to protect both accrued and prospective rights as put forward in *Perry v Intec Colleges Ltd*, and the fact that pensions are pay under Article 141 (formerly 119) under the Treaty of Rome for the purposes of equal pay.
>
> *Findings*
>
> The court decided that although pensions were pay under Article 119, they did not transfer under Article 3(3) of the Directive and that *regulation* 7 of the 1981 TUPE regulations correctly incorporates Article 3(3). Two decisions of the EFTA Court have also confirmed the opinion that pension schemes do not transfer – *Eidesund v Stavenger Catering A/S [1996] IRLR 684 EFTA Ct.* and *Langeland v Norsk Fabricom A/S E-2/95 EFTA Ct.*
>
> *Regulation 10(3)* of the 2006 regulations make it clear in statute there will be no risk to the transferor of successful breach of contract or unfair constructive dismissal claims if the transferee fails to afford transferred employees any given level of occupational pension entitlement following a relevant transfer.

Negligent statements – liability [7.6]

> ### Case study
>
> *Hagen and ors v ICI Chemicals and Polymers Ltd and ors [2002] IRLR 31 QBD.*
>
> *Facts*
>
> This was an unusual transfer in that it depended on the agreement of the employees to transfer. After the transfer the employees claimed they had➡

been induced to agree to transfer because of certain promises and undertakings given to them by both their transferring and new employer.

Findings

The High Court rejected all their claims except for one relating to the pension benefits available after transfer. In respect of pensions, the High Court decided that the transferring employer, ICI, owed the employees a duty to take reasonable care in giving them information about the pension scheme. The court held that ICI had breached this duty of care by not informing certain employees that their pension rights might be adversely affected. The information given to the employees on this matter prior to the transfer was inadequate and misleading. Moreover, the employees had relied on the information actually given to persuade them to transfer. ICI was held liable for negligent misstatement. The High Court went on to hold this liability remained with ICI. The liability did not transfer because occupational pension schemes are specifically excluded from transferring by *regulation* 7 of the 1981 TUPE regulations.

Changing attitude [7.7]

As personal pension provision gains greater importance there is increased pressure to provide for some form of pension transfer. For some time the public sector has insisted that incoming employers make pension provision for the transferred employees. The pension provision has to be broadly comparable and approved by the Government Actuary's Department (GAD) in accordance with public criteria. This has the advantage of allowing service contractors in the public sector to operate one rather than several contracts, so avoiding the administrative costs of fragmentation.

When compulsory competitive tendering was replaced by the concept of 'Best Value', local authorities reached an agreement with the unions and contractors which gives employees the option of remaining within the Local Government Pension Scheme (LGPS) or transferring to the contractor's scheme. This will only apply if the contractor's scheme matches the LGPS in every material respect.

Reform [7.8]

In addition to the replacement Directive (the new Acquired Rights Directive 1998 (98/50/EC) ('1998 Directive')), which permits member states to provide for the transfer of pension rights, the Government intended to take advantage of the changes to the Acquired Rights Directive 1977 and provide for the transfer of pension rights, or at least for there to be some pension provision by the transferee. The Government reformed the public and private sectors by adopting two very different approaches.

The public sector [7.9]

A statement of practice issued by the Cabinet Office in January 2000 declared that the Government is committed to ensuring the public sector is a good employer and a model contractor and client. It wants a pragmatic approach to modernising public services in the pursuit of quality services and value for money for the taxpayer. It seeks such organisational change through clarity and certainty about the treatment of staff involved. The policy has no statutory basis or force but represents the policy which government departments are required to follow and provides guidance for the rest of the public service. It may impact on private sector employers currently tendering for business or those businesses which were previously performed by government employees.

The Code of Practice, *Staff Transfers From Central Government: A Fair Deal For Staff Pensions*, issued in June 1999, provides guidance on the practical application of the Government's policy statement.

The Code is mainly concerned with transfers between the Government and the private sector when contracts are awarded under public private partnership (PPP) deals. The Code recognises that pensions are an important element in overall remuneration of staff, particularly within the public services where there are occupational pension schemes offering a high quality of benefits.

The Code sets out the standard practices that the Government will follow when its employees are transferred to other employers. The principles the Government will apply are as follows:

- to treat staff fairly;

- to do so openly and transparently;

- to involve staff and their representatives fully in consultation about the process and its results; and

- to have clear accountability within government for the results.

There are two separate but related aspects to treatment of pensions in a business transfer:

1. Staff should continue to have access after the transfer to a good quality occupational pension scheme under which they can continue to earn pension benefits through their future service.

2.   Staff should be given options for the handling of the accrued benefits that they have already earned.

Central to the process is the requirement for an assessment of whether pension arrangements being offered to employees by their new employer are 'broadly comparable' to those provided by their existing employers. This requirement relates only to the period of employment after the change of employer. Exceptionally, if comparability is not available, there is a requirement for the valuation of any detriment on pensions to be offset by elements of the remuneration package outside the pension scheme.

This statement of practice sets out the principles on which GAD undertakes its assessments of broad comparability. Assessments may be commissioned by a public service employer or by a contracting authority on a one-off basis in relation to a specific group of staff. They may also be commissioned by a private sector employer with a view to obtaining a 'passport' that his pension scheme is broadly comparable to a specific public service scheme for any group of employees who may transfer from that scheme to his employment over a given period.

For a passport, where a specific group of employees cannot be identified, the tests are conducted using a very large range of employee profiles containing different characteristics affecting the value of pension rights, including, but not limited to:

* age;
* gender;
* salary level; and
* length of service.

In the public sector the Government intends to follow the Code detailed above which it clearly regards as a generous policy.

The private sector   [7.10]

In the private sector the *Pensions Act 2004* introduced, for the first time, a minimum standard of occupational pension entitlement to be afforded to all transferred employees who had such entitlement prior to the transfer. This minimum 'safety net' requires the transferee to match employee contributions, up to 6 per cent of salary, into a stakeholder pension, or offer an equivalent alternative. The new regulations that came into force in April 2006 make no changes to pensions upon the transfer of a relevant undertaking.

Due diligence: avoiding problems with pensions [7.11]

The acquiring employer should check:

- the existence of a pension scheme;
- whether the scheme contains non-pension benefits, such as medical insurance and life insurance;
- the pension retirement age; and
- whether retirement benefits can be triggered by an event occurring before retirement age.

Key points and new developments [7.12]

- Pension provision in occupational pension schemes does not transfer.
- Other pension arrangements do transfer.
- Non-pension benefits included in the pension scheme transfer.
- Pension benefits triggered by an event other than retirement, such as redundancy, do transfer.

Questions and answers [7.13]

Question

Does the employee's right to long-term disability insurance transfer under TUPE if the benefit is included within the pension scheme?

Answer

Yes it does. Only benefits due upon retirement are excluded from transfer.

Question

The transferring employer paid the equivalent of five per cent of the employee's salary into a personal pension plan of the employee's choice. Does the acquiring employer have to match this level of contribution or is this a pension right and, therefore, does not transfer? ➡

Answer

This is a pension right. But *regulation 10* of the 2006 TUPE regulations only excludes occupational pension schemes from transfer. This is not an occupational pension scheme under *section 1* of the *Pensions Schemes Act 1993* – the right to this level of contribution will transfer.

8. Automatic Unfair Dismissal

Security of employment   [8.1]

Article 3 of the EU Acquired Rights Directive 1977 (77/187/EEC) ('the Directive') and *regulation 4* of the *Transfer of Undertakings (Protection of Employment) Regulations 2006 (SI 2006/246)* (TUPE) may protect the employee's terms and conditions of employment, but they do nothing to give the employee security of employment and prevent his dismissal. Article 4 and *regulation 7* address the issue of security of employment. They provide that if the dismissal is connected with the transfer then the transfer is not a valid ground for dismissal. There is only one exception and that is where the transfer-related dismissal is shown to be for an economic, technical or organisational (ETO) reason that entails changes in the workforce. Where the reason or principal reason for the dismissal is the transfer of the undertaking, *regulation 7* of the 2006 regulations makes dismissals automatically unfair unless the employer can demonstrate that he had an ETO reason for the dismissal.

Is a transfer-related dismissal valid?   [8.2]

Some commentators held the view that the dismissal was not just unfair, it was actually invalid, and that, in the absence of an ETO reason, the employment continued despite the apparent dismissal. This view was based on a combination of Article 3(1) of the Directive which provides that the transferor's rights and obligations will transfer to the new employer, and Article 4 which provides that the transfer 'shall not in itself constitute grounds for dismissal' unless there was an ETO reason which entails changes in the workforce.

This formed the basis of the decision of the Court of Appeal in *Wilson v St Helens Borough Council and Meade and Baxendale v British Fuels Ltd [1997] IRLR 505 CA*. Relying on those two Articles, the court insisted on reinterpreting *regulations 5* and *8* of the 1981 TUPE regulations (now *regulations 4* and *7* of the 2006 regulations) to ensure that dismissals connected with the transfer were prohibited unless they were connected with an ETO reason which entails changes in the workforce. This meant that, in the absence of an ETO reason, any employee dismissed for a transfer-related reason before the transfer would still transfer to the new employer and the dismissal of an employee post transfer would be ineffectual, unless there was an ETO reason.

On appeal, the House of Lords corrected this misapprehension (*Wilson v St Helens Borough Council and Meade and Baxendale v British Fuels Ltd [1998]*

IRLR 706 HL). It thoroughly reviewed the Directive, the TUPE regulations and the decisions of the European and the UK courts concluding that the Court of Appeal's interpretation could not be supported. If the Court of Appeal was right then the Directive and the regulations need not have concerned themselves with compensation for dismissal. If there was an ETO reason, the dismissal was not unfair so no compensation would be due. If the dismissal was not for an ETO reason, the dismissal was prohibited and void and the employee would transfer to the employment of the new employer.

The Lords pointed out that the European Court had consistently treated dismissals connected with the transfer as valid dismissals, even where there was no ETO reason. It unanimously decided that transfer-related dismissals were effective and governed by *regulation 8* of the 1981 regulations. This view was subsequently confirmed in *Jules Dethier Equipment SA v Dassy [1998] IRLR 266 ECJ*. The European Court held that, under Article 4, when an employee had been unlawfully dismissed it was the liability for that dismissal which transferred to the new employer.

Dismissal of an employee because of a relevant transfer [8.3]

Set out below are *paragraphs 1* to *5(b)* of *regulation 8* of the 1981 TUPE regulations.

'(1) Where either before or after a relevant transfer, any employee of the transferor or transferee is dismissed, that employee shall be treated for the purposes of Part X of the Employment Rights Act 1996 [the part dealing with unfair dismissal] as unfairly dismissed if the transfer or a reason connected with it is the reason or principal reason for his dismissal.

(2) Where an economic, technical or organisational [ETO] reason entailing changes in the workforce of either the transferor or the transferee before or after a relevant transfer is the reason or principal reason for dismissing an employee:

(a) paragraph (1) above shall not apply to his dismissal; but

(b) without prejudice to the application of section 98(4) of the 1996 Act (test of fair dismissal), the dismissal shall for the purposes of section 98(1)(b) of that Act (substantial reason for dismissal) be regarded as having been for a substantial reason of a kind such as to justify the dismissal of an employee holding the position which that employee held.

(3) The provisions of this regulation apply whether or not the

employee in question is employed in the undertaking or part of the undertaking transferred or to be transferred.

(4) Paragraph (1) above shall not apply in relation to the dismissal of any employee which was required by reason of the application of section 5 of the Aliens Restriction (Amendment) Act 1919 to his employment.

(5) Paragraph (1) above shall not apply in relation to a dismissal of an employee if:

    (a) the application of section 94 of the 1996 Act to the dismissal of the employee is excluded by or under any provision of Part X of the 1996 Act or of sections 196–197, 199–200, 202, 208–209, 236(3) and (4), or sections 237 or 238 of the Trade Union and Labour Relations (Consolidation) Act 1992; or

    (b) the application of Article 20 of the 1976 Order to the dismissal of the employee is excluded by or under any provision of Part III or Article 76 of that Order.'

The above demonstrates that is very wide ranging in its coverage. It is concerned with:

- dismissals occurring before and after the transfer;
- dismissals effected by the transferring employer or by the acquiring employer; and
- dismissals of employees in the unit transferred and also those retained by the transferring employer in the employment of the acquiring employee whose employment will be affected by the transfer.

It is surprising that there are no reported cases on this latter point. However, it is clear that, under *regulation 8(3)* of the 1981 regulations, an employee who did not transfer but whose work as a result of the transfer was unilaterally changed by the employer would be an affected employee and could claim constructive dismissal as a result of the transfer. This concern for affected employees who are not part of the transfer group runs through the Directive and the 1981 TUPE regulations. It can also be seen in the duty imposed on both employers to consult employees who might be 'affected' by the transfer under *regulations 10* and *11* of the 1981 regulations and under *regulations 13 to 15* of the new 2006 regulations.

The new 2006 regulations (*regulation 7*) clarify the meaning of *regulation 8* of the 1981 regulations. The new *regulation 7* sets out three different categories of dismissal:

- First, dismissals for which the sole or principal reason is the transfer itself or a reason connected with the transfer that is not an ETO reason;

- Secondly, dismissals for which the sole or principal reason is not the transfer itself, but is a reason connected with the transfer that is an ETO reason;

- Thirdly, dismissals for which the sole or principal reason is unconnected with the transfer.

Dismissals in the first category are automatically unfair under the unfair dismissal legislation. Dismissals in the second category are potentially fair under the unfair dismissal legislation – i.e. fair, subject to the normal test of reasonableness in that legislation. The regulations have no bearing on dismissals in the third category, as such dismissals are unrelated to the transfer, even though they may be made around the time of such a transfer.

Regulation 7 and the rules for unfair dismissal [8.4]

Regulation 7 of the 2006 regulations and *regulation 8* of the 1981 regulations do not create a new TUPE right, they simply apply the existing unfair dismissal provisions in *Part X* of the *Employment Rights Act 1996* (*ERA 1996*) to dismissals connected with TUPE. The following is a brief summary of the requirements for bringing an unfair dismissal claim.

Continuity of employment [8.5]

The right to claim unfair dismissal is restricted to those who have the required minimum continuity of employment – currently one year. Employees with less than one year's service dismissed because of the transfer cannot bring an unfair dismissal claim. This was not settled law for some time.

In *Milligan v Securicor Cleaning Ltd [1995] IRLR 288 EAT*, it was decided that minimum continuity was unnecessary as *regulation 8* of the 1981 regulations made all dismissals automatically unfair. This led to an amendment to *regulation 8* – a new *regulation 8(5)* – restoring the minimum continuity of service requirement. As it turned out this was unnecessary since *Milligan* itself was overruled in *R v Secretary of State for Trade and Industry, ex parte UNISON [1996] IRLR 438 Div Ct*.

In this case, the court said the purpose of the Directive is to preserve rights, not to provide employees with rights they did not previously have. An employee with less than one year's continuity of employment would not normally be able to bring an unfair dismissal claim. There are some exceptions to this rule, for example dismissals relating to discrimination, maternity and family rights and union membership do not have a minimum employment requirement. Also,

153

when Belgium questioned the European Court as to whether it was lawful for it to exclude certain categories of workers, such as students, from its version of TUPE, the court held that if workers did not otherwise have these rights they did not gain them under the Directive.

The claimant must have been dismissed [8.6]

The unfair dismissal claimant must meet all the unfair dismissal law requirements, including showing that he has been dismissed.

There has been some confusion over constructive dismissal. *Section 95(1)* of the *ERA 1996* sets out three ways in which a contract may end that will be treated as dismissal. These are:

'(a) the contract under which he is employed is terminated by the employer (with or without notice);

(b) the employee is employed under a contract for a fixed term and that term expires without being renewed under the same contract; or

(c) the employee terminates the contract under which he is employed (with or without notice) in circumstances in which he is entitled to terminate it without notice by reason of the employer's conduct.'

The third category of dismissal, constructive dismissal, requires the employer's breach to be a fundamental breach of an actual contract term. The term may be express or implied. Confusion arises because the employee's right to refuse to transfer to the new employer under *regulation 4(9)* of the 2006 TUPE regulations does not refer to a 'fundamental breach of contract' but to a substantial change to 'his working conditions', a term that could encompass more than the strict breach of a contract term.

Case study

This was the basis of the decision of the Employment Appeal Tribunal (EAT) in *Rossiter v Pendragon plc [2002] IRLR 483 CA.*

Facts

Rossiter had transferred to Pendragon from Lex Ford. His employment terms were maintained but they included a commission arrangement that the employer had the right to amend. Rossiter resigned after Pendragon➡

---

sought to exercise its power to amend the commission scheme. Rossiter alleged that the amendment was a detrimental change to his working conditions under which he would stand to lose some £3,000 a year. The EAT upheld his claim. The EAT decided that constructive dismissal for a claim made under *regulation 8* of the 1981 regulations was not the same as constructive dismissal under the *ERA 1996*. The EAT decided that breach of contract was not necessary in a claim under *regulation 8*, a change to the working arrangements which fell short of breach of contract would suffice. It insisted that the right to claim unfair dismissal under TUPE was exactly the same as under the *ERA 1996*.

Findings

The Court of Appeal disagreed. Rossiter had to show Pendragon had breached his contract and it had not. Rossiter had not been constructively dismissed.

The new regulations (*regulation 4*) provide some clarity to this 'confused' position. Where a transferred employee finds that there has been or will be a 'substantial change' for the worse in their working conditions as a result of the transfer, they have the right to terminate their contract and claim unfair dismissal before an employment tribunal on the grounds that the actions or proposed actions of the employer had constituted or would constitute a de facto termination of their employment contract. An employee who resigns in reliance on this right cannot make a claim for pay in lieu of a notice period to which they were entitled under the contract.

This right exists independently of an employee's common law right to claim constructive dismissal for an employer's repudiatory (fundamental) breach of contract.

Example

An employer divides the country into sales regions. A salesman is contractually assigned to the Yorkshire region and there is no power in the contract to change his assigned region. After a TUPE transfer, and acting unilaterally, the new employer decides the employee will, in addition, cover Humberside. That would be breach of a contract term and the salesman could reasonably resign and claim constructive dismissal.

Care must also be taken with fixed-term contracts. When a fixed-term contract expires, it is treated as a dismissal for unfair dismissal purposes unless it is renewed. At one time it was possible to exclude unfair dismissal rights arising on expiry of the contract and, as the contract terms transfer in their entirety to the acquiring employer, the acquiring employer would obtain the advantage of any exclusion. The power to waive unfair dismissal rights was removed by *section 18* of the *Employment Relations Act 1999*. So a transferred employee with at least one year's continuity of employment will be able to claim an automatic unfair dismissal if his contract is not renewed.

Reason for dismissal [8.7]

In order to show the dismissal is fair the employer must first produce a valid reason for dismissal. The valid reasons are set out in *section 98(1)* and *(2)* of the *ERA 1996*. They must relate to:

- the employee's capability or qualifications;
- conduct;
- redundancy;
- continued employment being in contravention of the law; or
- some other substantial reason.

The defence provided in *regulation* 7 of the 2006 regulations that the dismissal is due to an ETO reason entailing a change in the nature of the workforce now falls into the category of redundancy.

Reasonable to dismiss [8.8]

If the employer can show an ETO reason for the dismissal, that merely proves a ground for dismissal. Unfair dismissal law also requires the employer to show that it was fair to dismiss for that reason. This should not be too heavy a burden. It involves showing the decision was one that a reasonable employer could have made and followed a proper procedure. There are well-established rules for dismissal and disciplinary procedures and guidance in the *ACAS Code of Practice on Disciplinary and Grievance Procedures* issued October 2004. Since October 2004, minimum statutory procedures apply to all dismissal, disciplinary action and grievance procedures. These procedures must be written into the contract and breach by the employer could result in an increase of compensation of between 10% and 50%.

Case study

Gibson v Ciro Cittero (Menswear) plc [1998] IDS 620 EAT. ➡

Facts

The case concerns the transfer of retail clothing shops. Ms Gibson had been entitled to hold a key to the shop and to open and close it. The new employer decided to improve the security arrangements by giving keys to senior staff and to make a payment to the key holder. Ms Gibson was no longer a key holder so her terms had been changed.

Findings

The EAT decided the employer had a valid organisational reason for the change and was therefore able to rely on the ETO defence to prove the existence of a good reason for dismissal. But that was not enough. It had to be shown that it was fair to dismiss for that reason and this meant that all the factors were taken into consideration. The case was remitted to a tribunal for reconsideration on this point.

Remedies [8.9]

The remedies are those available for unfair dismissal under the *ERA 1996*. Unfair dismissal claims must be brought in the employment tribunal within three months of the termination of the contract. Extensions of time are only given where it can be shown that it was not reasonably practicable for the applicant to bring the claim in the allotted time.

The most common remedy is compensation. This is divided into two parts.

Basic award [8.10]

This is calculated on a similar basis to redundancy pay. It is based on length of service, age and pay. Pay is capped at £290 per week and is reviewed every February in line with the current RPI.

- Aged up to and including 20, the employee receives half a week's pay for each year of continuous employment.

- Between 21 and 40, one week's pay per year of continuous employment.

- Forty-one and over, 1½ times a weeks' pay for each year of continuous employment.

Only 20 years can be taken into account and the years with the highest pay out are used first.

Compensatory award [8.11]

This is capped at £58,400 and again reviewed annually each February. It covers expenses incurred as a result of dismissal (excluding legal costs), losses incurred and benefits that the employee would have had but for dismissal. The employee has to mitigate his loss and compensation is reduced if he has contributed to his dismissal. The new rules on dispute resolution in the *Employment Act 2002* (that came into force in October 2004) increase the employee's compensation by 10%–50% if the employer does not follow the minimum dismissal, disciplinary or grievance procedures. The employee who does not comply with the procedures will suffer a similar reduction.

It is possible for the tribunal to recommend the re-engagement or reinstatement of the employee, but these orders are not common. The employer cannot be forced to take the employee back, but compensation is increased if the employer unreasonably refuses to do so.

It must also be remembered that the employee may be able to bring a breach of contract claim. An employee dismissed for an ETO reason has not broken his contract. He must be given his full contractual notice. The employer may wish to make a payment in lieu of notice. In Scotland, the employer has the implied contractual right to make a payment in lieu of notice monies, elsewhere the employer only has a contractual right to do so if there is an express contract term. If a payment in lieu is made without contractual authority that is a technical breach of contract. Of course, if wages in lieu of notice are properly calculated the employee suffers no loss and a claim is most unlikely. However, because the employer is terminating the contract by breach, any restraint of trade clauses (restrictive covenants) in the contract become unenforceable. It follows that where there are vital restraint clauses the employer should take due care.

Settlement of claims [8.12]

The various pieces of legislation granting employees employment protection rights also provide that any attempt to limit or exclude those rights will be void. There are two ways in which statutory employment claims can be settled:

1. By reaching an agreement using the services of an ACAS Conciliation Officer (usually once proceedings have been issued).

2. The execution of a statutory compromise agreement after the employee has obtained independent legal advice (possible before proceedings have been issued).

Each piece of legislation specifies whether the rights can be settled or compromised in this way. There is no such provision in TUPE. In fact, the opposite applies. *Regulation 18* of the 2006 regulations renders any attempt to limit or exclude the rights given to the employee under *regulation 4* (transfer of terms and liabilities), *regulation 7* (unfair dismissal), *regulation 13* (consultation of representatives) or *regulation 15* (protective awards) void. These TUPE rights cannot be settled or compromised. On the other hand, unfair dismissal and redundancy claims brought under the *ERA 1996* can be settled and compromised. Claims for unfair dismissal or redundancy relating to TUPE dismissals are brought under the auspices of the *ERA 1996* as amended by TUPE. So it may be possible to settle and compromise those particular claims.

Regulation 18 is aimed at excluding claims and preventing the employee having access to a tribunal to stop him initiating a claim. Where the employer has actually exercised his right and brought a claim there is no reason why the settlement and compromise provisions should not apply.

Defending dismissals [8.13]

TUPE is only concerned with dismissals connected with the transfer or, to be more precise, dismissals where the 'reason or principal reason' is the transfer. These are automatically unfair under *regulation 8* of the 1981 TUPE regulations and now further clarified by *regulation 7* of the 2006 regulations (see above at **8.3**). Where the reason is unconnected with the transfer the employee cannot claim automatic unfair dismissal even if the dismissal is close to the transfer date. For example, if an employee is dismissed the day before the transfer for harassment of a co-worker the dismissal will not be transfer related. This does not mean the employee is unable to bring an unfair dismissal claim. It means that TUPE does not apply. Any claim would have to be brought against the transferring employer. Liability for the claim does not transfer to the acquirer.

Unfortunately not all examples are so clear. The most problematic situations are those where the employer makes changes to the workforce to prepare the business for sale or where the receiver or administrator reorganises the business to sell the viable part. If the sale is due to the financial circumstances of the business and not due to the transfer, the dismissal costs will stay with the transferring employer. But if the reason is related to the transfer then the liability for the dismissed employee will transfer subject to the ETO defence. This is not an easy line to draw.

Case study

Longden and Paisley v Ferrari Ltd and Kennedy International [1994] IRLR 157 EAT. ➡

159

Facts

Ferrari was in the hands of administrative receivers and planning to dismiss all the staff. Kennedy was considering purchasing Ferrari and, in order to preserve the business during negotiations, provided money to keep the business going. It also indicated the staff it thought essential to keep the business alive asking that they be retained and not dismissed as had been planned with the others. The next day Mrs Longden, who was not on the essential list, was dismissed. Eight days later Kennedy purchased an option on Ferrari and five days after that it purchased the business by an asset sale from the receivers.

Findings

The EAT held this was not a series of transactions effecting the transfer to Kennedy. It was 'effected' by the one simple transaction of an asset sale. Mrs Longden was dismissed before that sale and the reason was not the prospective sale but Ferrari's financial difficulties. The prospective sale caused the retention of staff that would otherwise have been dismissed, not the dismissal of those whom Kennedy did not consider essential. Mrs Longden had no claim under *regulation 8* of the 1981 regulations. Ferrari was only liable for redundancy.

The situation is complicated by the use of the definite article. *Regulation 8* of the 1981 regulations referred to the dismissal being unfair if '*the* transfer or a reason connected with it is the reason or principal reason for his dismissal'. It is 'the' transfer, not 'a' transfer. Does this require an actual transfer to be in the offing? Or is the intention to transfer with the transferee, not yet identified, enough? There is no definitive answer.

Case study

Some cases have taken the narrow view, as in *Ibex Trading Co Ltd (in administration) v Walton [1994] IRLR 564 EAT.*

Facts

The Alpine Double Glazing Co had gone into liquidation. The administrator informed the staff their wages would be reduced. Those who refused to accept the reduction were dismissed as redundant on 16 October, effective 4 November. On 11 November the business was sold. By the date of the hearing the acquiring employer was also in liquidation. ➡

Findings

The EAT decided that, under *regulation 8* of the 1981 TUPE regulations, dismissals were automatically unfair only if connected with 'the' transaction. This meant that a particular transaction had to be in mind. It would not matter that the transaction ultimately fell through and the transferee was replaced. Where, as here, the administrator intends to sell but no particular purchaser is in view, the dismissals are only connected with 'a' transaction and fall outside *regulation 8*. Other cases have taken a more generous interpretation.

Case study

In *Harrison Bowden Ltd v Bowden [1994] ICR 186 EAT*, the EAT decided it was not necessary for there to be an identified transferee for *regulation 8* to operate.

Facts

The company that had employed Bowden since 1988 was in financial difficulties and administrative receivers were appointed. They advertised for purchasers and Harrison showed an interest. Most of the employees, including Bowden, were dismissed on grounds of redundancy on 31 January 1991. On 4 February Bowden was asked to return to help out. The sale took place on 8 February and on 12 February Bowden accepted employment with the purchaser. He was dismissed on 12 March and claimed unfair dismissal. The question was whether he had sufficient continuity of employment, bearing in mind the break in his employment.

Findings

The EAT accepted his dismissal on 31 January was unfair because it was connected with a transfer to a possible buyer and was to facilitate that sale. Therefore, the contract transferred under TUPE and Bowden had sufficient continuity to bring his claim. The EAT treated 'the' transfer as 'a' transfer.

Case study

Bowden was followed in *Morris v John Grose Group Ltd [1998] IRLR 499 EAT*. ➡

Facts

A motor company was in the hands of the receivers and being prepared for sale. Morris and several other employees were dismissed to make the business more saleable. At the time of the dismissal no prospective purchaser had been identified. Three days later John Grose Group Ltd were introduced to the receivers and 36 days later they agreed to buy. The lack of an identified purchaser persuaded the tribunal that the dismissal was not connected with the transfer.

Findings

The EAT disagreed with the tribunal and overruled it. The EAT held it was sufficient that there was a possible transfer. They held 'the' transfer means 'transfer' or 'a' transfer. In conclusion, there does not have to be a contract or an identified purchaser for *regulation 8* of the 1981 regulations to apply.

If the dismissal is connected with the transfer then it is necessary to see if there is a valid ETO defence under *regulation 8(2)*. The way in which the ETO defence applies to pre-transfer dismissals was set out in *Litster v Forth Dry Dock and Engineering Co Ltd [1989] IRLR 161 HL:*

- It must first be decided whether the dismissal would have been for a reason connected with the transfer. If it is not, then *regulation 8* does not apply and the outgoing employer has sole responsibility for the dismissal. If it is, then the dismissal is automatically unfair under *regulation 8(1)*.

- Then there must be a check to see if there is an ETO reason requiring a change in the workforce. If there is then there is a valid and fair ground for the dismissal under *regulation 8(2)*.

- If there is an ETO reason then any existing liability will remain with the outgoing employer. The outgoing employer could be liable for any redundancy payment, or for unfair dismissal if he has failed to follow a proper procedure or has unfairly selected for redundancy, or for damages for breach of contract if due notice has not been given.

- In the absence of an ETO reason the employee will have been employed immediately before the transfer and liability for the dismissal will transfer to the incoming employer.

Dismissal and the ETO defence – the relationship in practice   [8.14]

The interrelationship between *regulations 8(1)* and *8(2)* of the 1981 TUPE regulations was a source of confusion. The more generally accepted view was that *regulation 8(1)* makes the dismissals automatically unfair unless the defence in *regulation 8(2)* comes into play. In *Warner v Adnet [1998] IRLR 384 CA*, the Court of Appeal insisted the two subparagraphs should be read together in this way, rejecting the argument they were mutually exclusive. The effect of the mutually exclusive interpretation is once it had been found that the reason or principal reason for the dismissal was the transfer, the dismissal was automatically unfair and the ETO defence in *regulation 8(2)* could not be used.

In *Warner*, the court, approving the tribunal's decision, held that:

> 'It was right for (the tribunal) first to consider the position under regulation 8(1) and to conclude that the principal reason for the dismissal was the transfer. That was, by its nature, a provisional or prima facie finding, even though not expressed as such. The tribunal had then considered the escape provisions of 8(2), and they found that the economic reason was established. Regulation 8(1) was then disapplied.'

The court held the dismissal was fair.

In the later case of *Kerry Foods Ltd v Creber [2000] IRLR 10 EAT*, without referring to *Warner*, the EAT adopted the mutually exclusive interpretation.

Case study

Facts

In *Kerry Foods*, WH Luke & Sons manufactured sausages. The company was in financial difficulties and receivers were appointed. Nineteen employees were dismissed on 27 January, ten more on 31 January and, a sale of the brand name and goodwill having been made to Kerry, the remaining employees were dismissed on 2 February 50 minutes before the Kerry deal was complete.

Findings

This was held to be a transfer of an undertaking. Kerry ensured that Luke's factory could not be used for sausage manufacture and continued to manufacture for the St Luke's clients at their own factory under the same St Luke's brand name. The EAT first decided there was a transfer of ➡

---

an undertaking and then that all employees had been dismissed for a reason wholly or mainly connected with the transfer. So, under *regulation 8(1)* of the 1981 regulations, the dismissals were connected with the transfer and were automatically unfair. The EAT accepted that, if the dismissals were for an ETO reason, then they would not be unfair. But it decided that if the dismissal was for an ETO reason, then it would not be for a reason connected with the transfer but for a reason connected with the ETO reason. *Regulations 8(1)* (dismissal connected with the transfer) and *8(2)* (ETO dismissals) were mutually exclusive; a dismissal could not be connected with the transfer and also be for an ETO reason. Once it had been decided the dismissals were connected with the transfer they could not proceed to consider whether it was an ETO reason. *Kerry* did not consider the *Warner* decision.

A full review of all the cases in *Thompson v SCS Consulting Ltd [2001] IRLR 801 EAT* resulted in the EAT deciding that the mutually exclusive interpretation was wrong. The EAT held there were two clear steps in determining the interrelationship between *regulations 8(1)* and *8(2)* of the 1981 regulations. The first step was to see if the reason or principal reason for the dismissal was the transfer. The second step was to see if there was an ETO defence.

If there was an ETO defence then any liability remains with the transferring employer; it does not transfer to the incoming employer. Because of *Kerry* uncertainty was created. The 2006 regulations clarify the position and now (under *regulation 7*) ensure a finding that the dismissal is connected with the transfer will not prevent the application of the ETO defence.

Considering the ETO reasons   [8.15]

In post transfer dismissals it will be the ETO reasons of the new employer that will be taken into account. In pre-transfer dismissals, whose reasons need to be considered? Suppose the incoming employer insists that the outgoing employer reduces the number of staff? Or the company contracting out services insists that the new contractor makes some staff redundant?

Case study

In *BSG Property Services v Tuck [1996] IRLR 134 EAT*, it was decided that it was the needs of the dismissing employer which had to be taken into account.   ➡

Facts

In this case, Mid Bedfordshire District Council, in the mistaken belief that TUPE did not apply, made its maintenance staff redundant and engaged BSG to do the work. The notice terminating Mid Bedfordshire employees' contracts, although given before the transfer, did not expire until after the transfer to BSG had taken place. BSG did not take on any of the redundant staff because it wanted the work to be done by self-employed tradesmen.

Findings

The EAT assessment of the situation was as follows:

- there was a TUPE transfer;

- the employees were still employed at the time of transfer (notice had not run out);

- the employees transferred to BSG under TUPE;

- the employees were not redundant from the council because they transferred to BSG;

- the council was the dismissing employer so the council's needs determined whether there was an ETO reason;

- as the employees were not redundant there was no ETO reason for the council;

- BSG may well have had an ETO reason – but that was irrelevant as it was the council's needs alone which had to be considered;

- the dismissals were therefore unfair under *regulation 8(1)* of the 1981 TUPE regulations; and

- the liability for the unfair dismissals and any other outstanding liabilities transferred to BSG which was deemed to have acted as the council had done.

This case highlights the importance of identifying the reasons behind any dismissals occurring before the transfer.

An ETO reason entailing changes in the workforce [8.16]

Whether, in a particular instance, there is or is not an ETO reason is largely a question of fact for the tribunal.

Harmonisation of terms [8.17]

The first thing to notice about the ETO defence is it is not sufficient to show there is an ETO reason for the dismissal. In addition, that reason has to necessitate a change in the workforce. This is a considerable barrier to the harmonisation of the employment terms of the existing and the newly acquired staff. Harmonisation of terms may well be a valid organisational reason for the dismissal, but it does not involve a change in the workforce. The employer needs the same workforce but on different terms.

Case study

Delabole Slate Ltd v Berriman [1985] IRLR 305 EAT.

Facts

Delabole had acquired the quarry in which Berriman worked. After the transfer it decided to pay him in accordance with its existing collective agreement. This entailed a reduction in his guaranteed weekly wage so Berriman resigned and claimed constructive dismissal.

Findings

The EAT was quite clear that the change to the terms did not require a change in the workforce and therefore the ETO defence did not apply. Berriman had been unfairly dismissed under *regulation 8(1)* of the 1981 TUPE regulations.

Change in job content [8.18]

The need for a 'change in the workforce' gives the impression that the identity of at least one employee must change. This is not so. A change in the work requirements can be an ETO reason. It will be a question of degree whether this is an organisational or, perhaps, a technical change.

Case study

This is illustrated by *Crawford v Swinton Insurance Brokers Ltd [1990] IRLR 42 EAT.* ➡

Facts

Mrs Crawford had worked for CJD Law as a typist and clerk. She was permitted to work at home when she wanted to and was supplied with a car for company and personal use. She was also company secretary. When the business was transferred to Swinton she was told that:

- there would be less secretarial work as it used standard letters;

- she would have to work as an insurance broker;

- she would have to work office hours;

- she could not work at home;

- she would not have a car; and

- she would no longer be company secretary.

Findings

The EAT said the workforce connotes the whole body of employees as an entity and corresponds to the 'strength' or the 'establishment', so a change in occupation can be a change in the workforce. However, before the tribunal could decide whether the job changes amounted to an ETO reason it had to investigate the employer's motives for the change. For example, the move from secretarial to insurance work could be an operational reason but the removal of the car and permission to work at home might not be. Of limited importance was the loss of the position of company secretary as it did not involve her in many duties. The case was sent back to the tribunal for reconsideration.

In order for *regulation 8* of the 1981 regulations to come into operation the employee had to be dismissed. Where there is an imposed change in terms and conditions, the imposed change must take the form of a fundamental breach of the contract of employment.

Enforced changes to contract terms are one of the most frequent examples of TUPE-related dismissals. Often the dismissal will be a constructive dismissal where the employee resigned as a result of the employer's breach of contract (see *Rossiter v Pendragon plc* (**8.6**) and the application of the 2006 regulations to situations of substantial change in working conditions post transfer).

167

Changes not involving a contract breach [8.19]

Changes to non-contractual policies or procedures or, as in *Rossiter*, the exercise of a contractual power to adjust commission rates will not amount to constructive dismissal so the question of an ETO reason will not arise.

Workforce reduction by the transferring employer [8.20]

The reason for the reduction is absolutely critical. There are many reasons put forward to reduce the workforce on or around the time a business is transferred. The most common situations are detailed below.

Change is required – even without a sale [8.21]

Case study

Thompson v SCS Consulting Ltd.

Facts

The business was in the hands of a receiver but Open Text UK was considering a purchase. The receiver then informed Open Text UK and SCS that he intended to dismiss all the employees immediately. The receiver agreed to delay the dismissals to enable Open Text UK, which wanted to keep key employees, to identify those to be retained. Thompson was not on that list and was dismissed.

Findings

It was agreed there was a TUPE transfer and it was decided the transfer was the reason for Thompson's dismissal. But the EAT went on to decide that the receiver could use the ETO defence. The business was overstaffed, inefficient and insolvent. The receiver would need to reduce staff to make the business viable even if there was no sale.

Dismissal to improve the chances of a sale [8.22]

On the face of it, dismissal to improve the chances of a sale could be an economic reason, but it is not.

Case study

Wheeler v Patel and J Golding Group of Companies [1987] IRLR 211 EAT.

Facts

Golding owned a shop. He employed Mrs Wheeler in the shop. The shop was sold to Patel. After the sale Mrs Wheeler was told by Golding her employment would end on 26 January, just three days before the completion of the sale. Patel did not employ Mrs Wheeler. Golding said that he dismissed Mrs Wheeler at the request of Patel, although it is not entirely clear that Patel insisted on the dismissal. The key issue before the EAT was whether a desire to obtain a better price could be an economic reason justifying the dismissal.

Findings

The EAT, bearing in mind the need for a purposive interpretation, decided that 'economic' must be given a more restricted than literal meaning. If a wide definition was taken it would be impossible to find a situation where the employer would be unable to rely on an economic reason. The economic reason had to be related to the business itself. Mrs Wheeler's dismissal was not related to the business but for the desire for a sale.

Case study

Gateway Hotels v Stewart [1988] IRLR 287 EAT.

Facts

A loss making hotel was sold by Gateway to Lytpark. Lytpark insisted all the hotel employees should be dismissed. Eventually, in order not to lose the sale, this was done.

Findings

The EAT, following *Wheeler*, decided this was not an economic reason entailing a change in the workforce. It was concerned with the sale, not➡

> with the business. Also, there were other possible purchasers interested in the business that might not have required the dismissal of the workforce.

Grant of the contract is conditional upon a reduction in the workforce [8.23]

The Court of Appeal has distinguished this from a desire for a sale and held that it is a valid economic reason connected with the business. The difference here is the acquiring employer has no choice. This dismissal is a contract condition.

Case study

Whitehouse v Chas A Blatchford and Sons Ltd [1999] IRLR 493 CA.

Facts

Whitehouse worked for James Stubbs and Co before it lost its contract to supply prosthetic appliances to the Northern General Hospital and Blatchfords. One of the terms of the contract between the hospital and Blatchfords was that Blatchfords would reduce the staff costs. Without this undertaking Blatchfords would not have got the contract. Whitehouse was made redundant to reduce costs.

Findings

The Court of Appeal held this was an economic reason. It was not to get a quicker or better sale. It was an essential part of the business. Whoever was successful in obtaining the contract, including Stubbs, would have been subject to the same condition.

Change of service methods [8.24]

Many service contractors will want to change the way they deliver the service. Where the service change results in a major reorganisation this can be an organisational reason entailing a change in the workforce.

Case study

Porter and Nanayakkara v Queen's Medical Centre (Nottingham University Hospital) [1993] IRLR 486 QBD. ➡

Facts

Following a series of murders by a nurse, the Trent Regional Health Authority decided to change its provider of paediatric and neonatal services. It awarded the contract to Queen's Medical Centre which decided to provide the service in a completely different way. The reorganisation meant the posts previously held by Porter and Nanayakkara no longer existed. However, there were other posts that they could have filled. They had to compete for the new posts and were not successful.

Findings

The court held that the reorganisation did not prevent TUPE applying. The court pointed out that most new providers will make changes and that scientific development will make changes very likely in the provision of medical services. So Porter and Nanayakkara's dismissals were for a reason connected with a transfer. But the court found that the reorganisation amounted to an ETO reason and so the dismissals were not automatically unfair. Once there was an ETO reason, the new employer was free to choose whom it wished for the new posts. It did not have to appoint Porter and Nanayakkara simply because they were capable of doing the work.

The reorganisation will have to be considerable, not minor, to amount to an ETO reason. A major change affecting only a few or even one employee could be an ETO reason if related to an organisational need.

Redundancies [8.25]

In non-TUPE situations redundancies can occur for many reasons. For example:

- the employees are excess to requirements;

- the employees lack the necessary skills to operate new methods or procedures;

- the need to cut costs; and

- the need to relocate.

If the dismissals are for a reason wholly or principally related to the transfer then they will be for an economic or organisational reason and will entail a change to the workforce. This is a complex area of the law related to managing business transfers and for this reason redundancy dismissals are dealt with separately in **CHAPTER 12 – REDUNDANCIES**.

Costs [8.26]

In *Wilson v St Helens Borough Council* (see **8.28**), the House of Lords accepted that the cost of operating an undertaking could be an ETO reason.

In this case neither the transferring nor the acquiring employer could afford to run a care home at its current level of costs. The financial costs were not sustainable. St Helens only accepted the transfer of the management of the home on the condition it added no financial burden to it. Changes were inevitable no matter who ran the home and these changes would have to include less staff and a reduction in labour costs.

This will not apply to the contractor who puts in a low bid and then needs to reduce labour costs to make a profit.

Timescale [8.27]

Time will eventually allow the link (the nexus) between the transfer and a dismissal to be broken. But exactly when it can be said that the dismissal is, through the passage of time, no longer related to the dismissal remains unclear. Inevitably, it will depend on the facts and circumstances of each particular case.

Example

Suppose an organisation, in order to protect its transferring employees, agreed to include in the contract fee sufficient funds to allow the contractor to provide the transferring staff with benefits equivalent to those they would have enjoyed had they stayed in the employment of the organisation, including pay increases and non-contractual redundancy payments, for a period of two years. In theory, any contract changes causing dismissals immediately after the two years could be related to the transfer.

Case study

The unreported case of *Taylor v Connex South Eastern [2000] EAT.* ➡

Facts

Taylor was a chartered accountant employed by British Rail. He moved to Connex upon the privatisation of British Rail in 1996. His position was deputy company secretary. Detrimental changes to his contract were introduced in 1998. Taylor refused to accept the changes and was dismissed.

Findings

The EAT held a change of terms some two years after the transfer was connected with the transfer. In this case the EAT did not think it was time alone which broke the link, but the longer the time the greater the opportunity for some event to break the link. His claim that his dismissal was connected with the transfer was upheld.

Wilson v St Helens Borough Council [8.28]

The cases of *Wilson v St Helens Borough Council and Meade and Baxendale v British Fuels Ltd* illustrates many of the points discussed in this chapter.

The facts of the two cases are similar in that in both the employees were dismissed before the transfer and then employed on less beneficial terms by the acquiring employer.

Case study

Facts

In *Wilson*, Lancashire County Council had the contract to manage a controlled care home owned by a trust. When Lancashire could no longer afford to run the home the management contract was offered by the trust to St Helens. St Helens accepted the contract but only on the condition that it did not become an additional financial burden. It would be able to avoid this burden only by a reorganisation and a scaling down of some of the home's activities. The number of employees would be reduced and the payments to those retained would be cut. There were 162 employees at the home. Lancashire made them all redundant but agreed to find jobs for those who did not want to transfer. In all, 72 employees transferred to St Helens on new employment terms. Of these some moved to new posts in the home that carried additional responsibilities and pay. Others ended up with fewer responsibilities and less pay. ➡

In *Meade*, British Fuels Ltd was formed following the merger of two coal carrying companies. Before the merger the employees were made redundant and paid their redundancy pay. They were then employed by the new merged company on new harmonised but less advantageous terms.

Findings

The House of Lords made the following points:

- Dismissals connected with the transfer of an undertaking are automatically unfair under *regulation 8* of the 1981 TUPE regulations (now *regulation 7* of the 2006 regulations). This applies to dismissals before and after the transfer. So the dismissals in both cases are covered by *regulation 8(1)* and are automatically unfair, unless there is an ETO reason under *regulation 8(2)*.

- Such dismissals are not void but are effective dismissals. Employment is terminated and the terms of the contract will no longer apply. The employees' remedies lie in breach of contract and unfair dismissal.

- The actual employment of a dismissed employee does not transfer to the new employer.

- Unless the employees were dismissed for an ETO reason, any employment liabilities relating to the dismissed employees will transfer to the new employer under *regulation 5* of the 1981 regulations now *regulation 4* of the 2006 regulations (as in *Litster v Forth Dry Dock and Engineering Co Ltd*).

- As the old contract has ended, the dismissed employee can be engaged on new detrimental terms but may be able to claim unfair dismissal compensation and, although this is unlikely, re-engagement or reinstatement.

- The only defence available to the employer against an unfair dismissal claim is that of an ETO reason requiring a change in the nature of the workforce. If this defence exists the dismissal will not be unfair.

- The employee cannot agree to a detrimental change to any term where the change is due to the transfer because *regulation 12* of the 1981 regulations makes agreements reducing the rights afforded to the employee under the TUPE regulations void. This is further supported by *regulations 4* and *18* of the 2006 regulations (this is discussed fully in **CHAPTER 9 – CHANGING TERMS AND CONDITIONS**). ➡

- There is no identified period of time after which it can be said that the change is unconnected with the transfer. In each case it will depend upon the facts.

- Changes prior to the transfer may similarly be connected to the transfer.

Meade was quite straightforward. The dismissal terminated the contract but was automatically unfair. The employees could, legally, be taken on under new detrimental contract terms. They were not entitled to a continuation of their previous terms. There was no ETO reason and so no defence to a claim for unfair dismissal. The terms were effectively changed but the employees could claim unfair dismissal.

In *Wilson*, the dismissal effectively removed the old terms. This time the Lords found there was an ETO reason. No organisation could afford to run the home without changes. Even if Lancashire County Council had continued to manage the home it would have had to reduce costs. There was an economic reason for the change to the terms and this was a good defence to an unfair dismissal claim. In this case, the terms changed but there was no unfair dismissal liability to transfer.

Employees can be taken on under new terms but they will have to be dismissed first and the price for that dismissal will be compensation for unfair dismissal. The maximum compensatory award for unfair dismissal is currently £58,400. Such dismissals could prove costly.

Key points and new developments [8.29]

- Dismissals where the reason or principal reason for the dismissal is the transfer of an undertaking are automatically unfair.

- Dismissals for reasons connected with the transfer are valid dismissals (they are not overturned by the TUPE regulations) even though the employee may be able to bring an unfair dismissal claim.

- Unfair dismissal claims under TUPE are subject to the same requirements as unfair dismissal claims under the *ERA 1996*.

- Dismissals for reasons unconnected with TUPE are not automatically unfair.

- The longer the gap between the transfer and the dismissal the less likely the dismissal will be for a reason connected with the transfer.

- If there is an ETO reason which entails a change in the workforce the dismissal will be for a good reason, but the dismissing employer will still have to show it was fair to dismiss for that reason and a proper procedure was followed.

- The following have been held to be ETO reasons:

  — too many staff;

  — relocation;

  — cost; and

  — new method of production or delivery of service.

- The following have been held *not* to be ETO reasons:

  — harmonisation of terms;

  — to speed the sale of a business; and

  — to get a better price for the business.

- Because there can be confusion as to whether a dismissal can be both connected to the transfer and for an ETO reason or whether the two reasons for dismissal are mutually exclusive, the 2006 regulations provide that dismissals for an ETO reason are a subset of reasons connected with the dismissal.

Questions and answers [8.30]

Question

Can an employer harmonise policies and procedures or must he continue to apply those of the outgoing employer to the transferring employees?

Answer

Only contract terms transfer to the new employer. It will depend on whether the policies and procedures are contractual. If they are then they have to be observed however inconvenient that may be. If they are not contractual they may be harmonised. Where harmonisation is taking place employees and appropriate trade union representatives should always be consulted. Ascertaining the status of policies and procedures is an important part of the due diligence process. ➡

Question

Will an employee who is dismissed before the transfer become an employee of the acquiring employer?

Answer

No. The dismissal is effective and employment ends. If the dismissal is connected with the transfer it is automatically unfair unless the employer can show that he has an ETO reason requiring a change in the workforce. If the employer can show that he has an ETO reason, the dismissal will be for a valid reason. This on its own will not make the dismissal fair, it only supplies a good reason for the dismissal. The employer will have to show that it was fair to dismiss for that reason and that he followed a proper procedure.

If the dismissed employee is taken into the employment of the acquiring employer, the acquiring employer can engage him on new detrimental terms and these will be the legal terms of his employment. Unless there is an ETO defence the acquiring employer will also be liable for any claims relating to the unfair dismissal.

Question

Can an employee with less than one year's service bring a claim for unfair dismissal where the dismissal is TUPE related?

Answer

No. The normal rules for bringing unfair dismissal claims apply so the employee will need one year's continuity of employment.

Question

What is an ETO?

Answer

An ETO is an economic, technical or organisational reason requiring a change in the workforce. It is important to note the need for a change in the workforce. This excludes wage reductions or the harmonisation of terms and conditions of employment as they do not require a workforce ➡

change, just the same workforce on different terms. However, in the *Wilson v St Helens Borough Council* case, where the transferring home was so over staffed and expensive to run that no-one would have been able to continue to operate it without changes, that did amount to an ETO reason. Redundancies and reorganisations have been accepted as ETO reasons, although with reorganisation it is a question of degree.

9. Changing the Terms and Conditions

The need for change   [9.1]

We live in a world in which the pace of change is growing ever faster and employment is no exception to this. Not only do employees have increased expectations of control over their employment conditions, but employers are also demanding increasing flexibility to meet changing market demands and to improve profitability. The ability of human resource management to meet changes in demand will, to a considerable extent, depend on its ability to change contract terms. Changing terms is not easy at the best of times but when the change is a transfer under the *Transfer of Undertakings (Protection of Employment) Regulations 2006 (SI 2006/246)* (TUPE) it is extremely difficult. Most employees are resistant to change. This is particularly so when moving from one employer to another and to an unknown entity.

General rules for changing terms   [9.2]

Putting the restrictions imposed by TUPE to one side, there is no inherent power to change contract terms no matter how old, inconvenient or unreasonable they may be. Once a contract has been made, the terms remain unchanged unless the parties agree to a variation or the employment is terminated and the employee re-engaged on new terms. A well-drafted better contract may contain some provision for changing the terms but such contracts are by no means universal. Below is a simple checklist for reviewing the power to vary the contract:

- Is the provision you wish to change a contract term?

- Where it is a term, is there any flexibility to change it within the contract wording?

- Is there any mechanism elsewhere within the contract for changing terms?

- Will the employee accept and agree to the proposed change?

- As a last resort, is dismissal of the employee and re-engagement on new terms a viable option in the circumstances?

The component parts of this checklist need to be looked at in detail.

A contract term [9.3]

Checking the provision to be changed is actually a contract term is always the logical starting point. Often policies and procedures issued in conjunction with a contract of employment are not contractual. Occasionally, the policy or procedure itself may expressly state that it does not form part of the contract terms and is issued as guidance only with no intention of being contractually binding. Where this occurs, changes can be effected easily. It is still advisable to consult with the employees concerned and get their agreement to the change prior to implementation.

Discretionary elements of a contract are often contractual through implication, custom and practice. Care must be taken not to assume that the use of the word 'discretionary' means the term falls outside of the contract terms and that changes can be safely implemented without the risk of breaching the contract.

Flexibility within the contract terms [9.4]

Some terms and conditions contain express flexibility. For example: 'You are employed as an Administrator and will be required to perform any tasks or undertake any duties as may reasonably be requested by your line manager that fall within your capabilities and as the needs of the business dictate.'

Other clauses often containing flexibility include:

- hours;
- location;
- overtime; and
- shifts and rosters.

Where such flexibility is present there exists the ability to change terms to reflect the new hours, role or workplace environment. Effecting reasonable change will not breach the contract of employment. Changes will need to comply with the implied contractual duty of mutual trust and confidence. This involves:

- having a good reason for the change;
- ensuring the change is reasonable;
- informing and consulting the employee before the change is implemented;
- giving any available help to enable the employee to meet the change; and
- giving time to meet the change.

Other mechanisms for change [9.5]

If there is no flexibility in the contract term itself all may not be lost. There may be machinery in the contract for changing the term, such as negotiating a new collective agreement or issuing a new handbook. Much will depend on the specific contract wording and the facts and circumstances of any particular case.

The employee accepts change [9.6]

If there is no machinery for change within the contract then it may still be possible to effect change by consultation and agreement. Offer the new term to the individual employees. If they accept the term then there is a valid variation to the existing contract terms. Mutually agreed variation means the contract changes do not amount to a breach of contract. Acceptance can be express (oral or in writing) or implied from conduct. Acceptance through conduct is fraught with difficulties. If the variation involves an immediate change in activity, such as working different hours, then working the new hours is implicit acceptance. The employee can negate this implicit acceptance by indicating he does not accept the term and is working under protest. If the variation does not have an immediate impact, for example giving the employer the power to change the hours but involving no immediate change to the hours worked, then it is almost impossible to imply acceptance. Most employers tie changes to an offer the employee is unlikely to refuse, such as a wage increase.

Dismissal and re-engagement [9.7]

If all else fails the employer has the option of dismissing and re-engaging the employee on the new terms. This is the least attractive way to change terms. Three problems have to be avoided:

1. Breach of contract.
2. Unfair dismissal.
3. Collective redundancy consultation.

Breach of contract [9.8]

Most contracts contain a clause that details the notice due upon termination. Where no such clause exists, the statutory minimum periods of notice will apply (one week's notice for each complete year of service up to a maximum of twelve weeks). The statutory period of notice may be implied into the contract of employment. Quite simply, breach of contract is avoidable by serving the appropriate period of notice under the contract.

Unfair dismissal [9.9]

The employee has done nothing to deserve dismissal. However, if the employer can show there is a genuine business reason for the change that will be 'some other substantial reason' for dismissal under *section 98* of the *Employment Rights Act 1996*. This will provide a valid ground for the dismissal. The tribunal may question the existence of the need for the change and whether the change selected actually met the need.

Case study

The Employment Appeal Tribunal (EAT) raised both these questions in *Evans v Elemeta Holdings [1982] IRLR 143 EAT.*

Facts

Although the employer had operated a voluntary redundancy scheme for several years, Evans had never volunteered for redundancy. A new manager decided to consolidate part of the redundancy payment into the basic wage and introduce mandatory unpaid overtime on weekdays and for up to four hours on a Saturday.

Findings

The EAT maintained that the voluntary system had worked satisfactorily and so the manager could not show any need for the change. Even if he had shown a good reason for some mandatory overtime, the EAT thought the system chosen was extreme and unnecessary. Elemeta failed to show a valid reason for the change.

In addition to having a valid reason for the change the employer must also follow a proper procedure. Since the case of *Polkey v AE Dayton Services Ltd [1987] IRLR 503 HL*, employers have been required to consult employees individually before dismissing them, unless consultation would be pointless. Failure to consult will make the dismissal unfair.

Furthermore, since the Disputes Resolution section of the *Employment Act 2002* came into force in October 2004, the employer has to follow the mandatory contractual procedure set out in *Schedule 2*. Failure to follow this procedure will make the dismissal automatically unfair and could result in an increase of up to 50% in the employee's compensatory award.

Collective redundancy consultation requirements [9.10]

Depending on the number of employees the employer proposes to dismiss, he will have to follow the collective redundancy consultation procedures in *section 188* of the *Trade Union and Labour Relations (Consolidation) Act 1992* and the *Collective Redundancies and Transfer of Undertakings (Protection of Employment) (Amendment) Regulations 1999 (SI 1999/1925)*. This is because the definition of redundancy for collective consultation (but not for redundancy pay) was widened to include any dismissal for a reason or reasons unconnected with the employee. In *GMB v Man Truck and Bus Ltd [2000] IRLR 636*, the EAT confirmed that dismissals undertaken in order to change the terms were dismissals for a reason unconnected with the employee and so were redundancies. The process of collective consultation and the penalties for breach are discussed in detail later in **CHAPTER 12 – REDUNDANCIES**.

The Directive and TUPE restrictions on changing terms [9.11]

The EU Acquired Rights Directive 1977 (77/187/EEC) ('the Directive') itself does not specifically prevent the employee agreeing to a change in his employment terms on or after his transfer. The Directive is designed to protect the employee's original rights and, in particular, his terms and conditions of employment by ensuring that he will still enjoy those terms after the transfer. This would be completely defeated if the employer was to be able to persuade a reluctant employee to change those protected terms.

Case study

It is, therefore, not surprising that the European Court came to the conclusions it did in *Foreningen AF Arbedjsldere I Danmark v Daddy's Dance Hall A/S [1988] IRLR 315.*

Facts

The case concerned the transfer of the lease on some restaurants and bars from Irma Catering to Daddy's Dance Hall.

Findings

The European Court of Justice (ECJ) decided that the Directive covered the transfer. Tellerup had previously worked for Irma and was then engaged by Daddy's Dance Hall. The terms of his new contract, taken as a whole, were no less advantageous than those of his previous contract, but➡

> they were not identical. Some were better and some were worse. In so far as the individual terms were better they were valid and enforceable, but the detrimental terms could not be enforced. So far as it was concerned his previous terms applied.
>
> The court agreed that the acquiring employer had exactly the same powers to change the contract terms under contract and national law as the previous employer had. These passed to him under Article 3 (1981 TUPE regulations, *regulation 5* now *regulation 4* of the 2006 regulations). It went on to add 'that in no case (can) the transfer of the undertaking itself . . .constitute the reason for this alteration.'
>
> The key principle in this case was clear. The European Court decided an employee was legally incapable of agreeing to a change in any individual term that was a change to his detriment.

Some time later, *Daddy's Dance Hall* was followed in *Rask v ISS Kantineservice A/S [1993] IRLR 133 ECJ*. In *Rask*, the court stated:

> 'Consequently, in so far as national law allows the employment relationship to be altered in a manner unfavourable to employees in situations other than the transfer of an undertaking, in particular as regards their conditions of pay, such an alternative is not precluded merely because the undertaking has been transferred in the meantime and the agreement has been made with the new employer. Since, by virtue of Article 3(1) of the Directive the transferee has subrogated to the transferor's rights and obligations under the employment relationship, that relationship may be altered with regard to the transferee to the same extent that it could have been to the transferor, providing that the transfer of the undertaking itself may never constitute the reason for that amendment.'

So, the new employer has the same power to change the terms as the old one, but with one major exception. There can be no detrimental change if the reason for the change is the transfer of the undertaking. The changes in *Rask* were relatively minor. The pay date was changed form the last Thursday in the month to the last day of the month and the shoe and laundry allowance was removed, although the overall pay remained the same.

Transfer – the sole reason for change [9.12]

Several cases since *Daddy's Dance Hall* have questioned whether its key principle – that an employee is incapable of agreeing to a detrimental change to a term of his contract – only applies when the transfer is the sole reason for the change.

Does it extend to situations where, although the change is not solely because of the transfer, the transfer is the principal reason for the change, or is simply connected with the change?

Case study

Ralton v Havering College of Further and Higher Education [2001] IRLR 743 EAT.

Facts

In this case, three college lecturers employed on the terms of the 'silver book' (a collective agreement between local authorities and the unions) transferred on those terms to the college. Two were on fixed-term contracts and when these contracts expired they were offered employment on the college's terms, not on those of the silver book. The third was on an indefinite contract but accepted an offer of promotion on the college's terms. All three claimed that they should be employed on silver book terms whilst their employment relationship with the college continued.

Findings

The EAT indicated that the transfer had to be the sole reason for the change, basing its conclusion on the reference to 'solely' and 'sole justification' in several European Court decisions, including *Daddy's Dance Hall*.

There are two main strands to the EAT's decision (which are discussed below):

1. The terms on which the employees transfer under the Directive.

2. The change was connected with the transfer and therefore impermissible.

The terms of transfer [9.13]

In *Ralton*, the EAT held that the employees transfer on the terms they enjoyed before the transfer. The objective of the Directive is to maintain their rights but not to increase them. Had they remained in the employment of the local authority, the local authority would probably have renewed the fixed-term contracts on silver book terms and included the silver book in the promotion contract, but they were not legally bound to do so. The EAT emphasised that the college could not be more restricted in its actions than the local authority and could not be subjected to a requirement to apply the silver book throughout any employment the lecturers might have with them when such a condition did not apply to the local authority. The employees transferred with their existing terms and conditions but with no more. The college was free to offer its own terms on contract renewal and on promotion.

Change connected with the transfer [9.14]

The EAT found that other factors had affected the college's decision to change the terms. The demand for courses, the renewal of the fixed-term contracts and the promotion had all played a part. The transfer was not the sole reason for the change so the change was valid.

TUPE does not specifically refer to changes to the terms either and, like the Directive, restricts itself to dismissals. However, in relation to dismissals, TUPE does not require the transfer to be the sole reason for the dismissal but to be the 'reason or principal reason' for the dismissal. To insist, as *Ralton* does, that there can be no other influence on the decision, far from protecting the employee this would allow the Directive to be sidelined by a relatively unimportant factor. It would be better practice to apply *Foreningen AF Arbedjsldere I Danmark v Daddy's Dance Hall A/S* to cases where the transfer was the reason or principal reason for the change.

Case study

This very point was reviewed by the European Court in the case of *Martin and ors v South Bank University (Case C-4/01)*.

Facts

The applicants were employed at the Redwood College of Health Studies as nursing lecturers. Their employment was governed by the terms and conditions of the General and Nurses and Midwives Whitley Council (GWC) and they were members of the NHS pension scheme. This scheme provided payment of enhanced retirement pension and compensation on employees ceasing work in the following situations:

- redundancy;

- in the interests of the efficiency of the service; and

- on organisational change.

➡

186

Redwood College became part of South Bank University (SBU). SBU notified staff they would not be able to remain in the NHS pension scheme and offered three options:

1. Leave the NHS pension scheme and start a new arrangement.

2. Transfer from the NHS scheme to one of SBU's schemes.

3. Leave the NHS pension scheme alone and not take out a new pension scheme.

The applicants did not accept the terms and conditions of employment of SBU. The applicants joined the Teacher's Superannuation Scheme and applied to transfer their existing NHS pension benefit into that scheme. Martin was not able to do this because she was over 60 at the time of the transfer of the undertaking. Because of changes to be imposed by the Government, SBU wrote to all academic staff aged over 50 advising them that early retirement may not be available after 31 March 1997. The staff were given the opportunity to take early retirement before that date. Martin took early retirement. She complained that they should have received the more favourable early retirement package available under GWC terms and conditions.

Findings

The ECJ held that:

- rights which are contingent upon either dismissal or premature retirement by agreement with the employer fall within the definition of 'rights and obligations' to be safeguarded in the event of a transfer;

- early retirement benefits are not old age, invalidity or survivor's benefits within the meaning of the Directive;

- obligations arising from a contract of employment are transferred, regardless of the fact that those obligations derive from statutory instruments and regardless of the practical arrangements adopted for such implementation;

- an employee may not agree to forgo his rights arising from a contract of employment;

- the transferee cannot, under the Directive, offer retirement benefits that are less beneficial if the transferor could not have made such detrimental changes to the terms of employment;

- the fact the transferee states he cannot offer early retirement benefits➡

187

> in future must be taken into account in order to determine whether the transfer was a reason for change;
>
> - whether the transfer of an undertaking is the reason for change must be assessed in the light of all the circumstances of the case; and
>
> - provided the change in terms and conditions is permissible under national law and the transfer of the undertaking is not the main reason for the change, the agreement between the employee and employer to vary conditions of employment is valid.

In *Wilson v St Helens Borough Council and Meade and Baxendale v British Fuels Ltd [1998] IRLR 706 HL* (see **CHAPTER 8 – AUTOMATIC UNFAIR DISMISSAL** for full facts of these cases), Lord Slynn raises the question of the relationship between a dismissal for a reason relating to the transfer and a variation that the employee has accepted.

> 'The question as to whether and in what situations, where there has been a transfer and employees have accepted the dismissal, claimed compensation based on it and worked for a long period after the transfer, there can be a valid variation by conduct is not an easy one.'

Because the House of Lords decided that *Wilson* was a straight case of dismissal followed by new terms rather than an agreed variation, it did not deal with the issue raised by Lord Slynn. It was decided that a consensual variation of employment terms was ineffective in the event of a TUPE transfer.

Changes which are not due to the transfer [9.15]

Whether the change is due or largely due to the transfer or not will always depend on the facts. *Ralton v Havering College of Further and Higher Education* provides two examples where the change may not be due to the transfer:

1. The renewal of a fixed-term contract.

2. The acceptance of promotion.

Another possibility could be a major reorganisation. For example, if an organisation grows rapidly for various reasons – additional work from clients, the share acquisition of companies and TUPE transfers – it may be necessary to undertake a dramatic restructure. This would include the staff acquired by TUPE transfers as well as the other staff. Would this be solely connected with the transfer? Would the transfer be the principal reason for the change? Arguably, the reason would be growth and the need to reorganise to meet new customer demand. If the change was connected with the transfer then the economic, technical or organisational (ETO) defence should apply (see **9.18**).

Some events occurring after the transfer may be unconnected to it, for example changes to professional standards, introduction of work rosters because customers are demanding access to services in the evenings and at weekends and new technology.

The new regulations [9.16]

The 2006 regulations ensure that employees are not penalised when they are transferred by being placed on inferior terms and conditions. So, not only are their pre-existing terms and conditions transferred across on the first day of employment with the transferee, but the regulations also impose limitations on the ability of the transferee and employee to agree a variation to terms and conditions thereafter. The conflicting case law and confusion highlighted in the above sections of this chapter may now be balanced with the aims of the new regulations (*regulations 4 and 5*) which set out three clear categories of contractual variations:

- First, variations for which the sole or principal reason is the transfer itself or a reason connected with the transfer that is not an ETO reason – i.e. *is not* an 'economic, technical or organisational reason entailing changes in the workforce';

- Secondly, variations for which the sole or principal reason is not the transfer itself, but *is* a reason connected with the transfer that is an ETO reason;

- Thirdly, variations for which the sole or principal reason is unconnected with the transfer.

Purported variations in the first category are to be void – i.e. ineffective. Variations in the second category are to be potentially effective – i.e. effective, subject to being agreed between the parties (or their representatives). The regulations are to have no bearing on variations in the third category as such variations are unrelated to a relevant transfer.

The new regulations reflect the Government's view of the correct case law interpretation of the *Acquired Rights Directive* in this regard.

Cutting the link between transfer and change [9.17]

One key question is whether time alone can cut the link between the transfer and the change. In *Wilson v St Helens Borough Council*, Lord Slynn declared:

'I do not accept the argument that the variation is only invalid if it is agreed on or as a part of the transfer itself. The variation may still be due to the transfer and for no other reason even if it comes later. However,

189

it seems that there must, or at least may, come a time when the link with the transfer is broken or can be treated as no longer effective.'

But this is not a fixed period of time and in *Taylor v Connex South Eastern Ltd [2000] IDS Brief 670*, the EAT explained that the causal link weakened over time because the longer the period of time the greater the opportunity for some event to intervene and break the link:

'The mere passage of time does not, in itself, constitute a weakening to the point of dissolution of the chain of causation.'

Using the ETO defence [9.18]

Where the employer wishes to change the contract terms and that change is connected with the transfer it may still be possible to vary the contract without running into legal problems. The process is based on *Wilson* and it is akin to taking a sledgehammer to crack a nut. The process is based on dismissal, to remove the old terms, and re-engagement, to bring in the new ones. The difficulties are that the dismissals will not be connected with the employee and so, depending on the number the employer is proposing to dismiss it, may be necessary to follow the collective redundancies consultation procedure. The dismissal will be connected with the transfer so it is essential that there should be an ETO defence available.

Dismissal, re-engagement on new terms and the ETO defence [9.19]

Guidelines on using dismissal, re-engagement on new terms and reliance upon the ETO defence are as follows:

- the employer must have a situation that would be a valid ETO defence;

- the employer should produce a draft proposal for changing the terms;

- the draft proposal should be capable of change during the passage of the consultation process;

- depending on the number of employees the employer is proposing to dismiss, the employer will have to complete the collective redundancy consultation process (discussed fully in **CHAPTER 12**);

- during consultation, the employer and union or elected representatives may agree the new terms;

- the consultation has to be with a view to reaching agreement;

- the individual employees must also be consulted;

- the employer can then give notice to terminate the employment; and

- the employees may then be employed on the new terms.

Until the 2006 regulations the ETO defence only applied to dismissals. It did not apply to variations. The new regulations attempt to clarify the uncertainty relating to variation of the contract and to avoid the convoluted process detailed above.

The new power to vary contained in the 2006 regulations is a limited one. There must be an ETO reason entailing a change in the workforce. It will not, for example, allow straightforward harmonisation of terms.

A choice of existing or new terms   [9.20]

Some employers offer transferred employees the choice of remaining on their existing terms or taking up the ones offered by the new employer. Often this is a choice between generous redundancy terms and additional benefits in kind, such as a car and medical insurance. However free from pressure this choice may be, legally it does not work. Although, in practice, it seems to operate quite well because if the employee has made his choice he probably likes the terms and does not sue.

The legal problem is *Foreningen AF Arbedjsldere I Danmark v Daddy's Dance Hall A/S*. In this case, the European Court insisted on an item-to-item comparison and made it clear it did not matter that overall the two packages were equally favourable. This means the employee choosing the new package still retains all those terms in the old contract which are better than the equivalents in the new one or which are absent from the new one. In effect, cherry-picking of the best terms.

Pre-transfer changes   [9.21]

Ralton v Havering College of Further and Higher Education makes it clear that employees only transfer on their existing terms and conditions. Apocryphal stories abound of vengeful, unsuccessful contractors increasing their employees' wages or making generous redundancy schemes contractual just to spite the successful bidder. Could it work the other way round? What if the outgoing employer was willing to change the terms to bring them more into line with those of the incoming employer? This occurred in the highly unusual tax case of *Mairs (HM Inspector of Taxes) v Haughey [1993] IRLR 551HL*.

Case study

Facts

The *Mairs* case concerned the privatisation of Harland and Wolff. The employees would transfer via a transfer of an undertaking to a new company, Harland and Wolff 1989 Ltd, on new terms and conditions. The main change was that, after two years, the employees would forgo their contingent right to enhanced redundancy payments. For this they would receive a payment of 30% of the payment that would have been made had they been made redundant and £100 for each completed year of service. The case related to the tax to be paid on the sum and no TUPE issue was raised.

Findings

The employees won their case. There was no tax due on the payment because being for loss of a contingent liability it was not classified as an emolument. The case does raise the possibility of an agreed variation before the transfer albeit this must now be viewed in light of the 2006 regulations (see **9.16** above).

In many ways the case is similar to *Wilson v St Helens Borough Council* as even the union recognised that no one would take on the enormous redundancy liability. But the difference is that in *Wilson* the employees were dismissed. If the employees are dismissed (and an imposed change is a constructive dismissal), the dismissal is automatically unfair unless the employer can rely on the ETO defence.

In *Mairs*, their terms were varied by agreement. There was no dismissal. The outgoing employer issued new terms. The employees signed a statement that read: 'I hereby confirm that I accept the new terms and conditions on the basis set out in that letter and the termination of the existing H&W redundancy scheme.' But the new agreed terms did not come into effect until the transfer was complete and work started for the new employer.

This case is an example of a variation agreement connected with the transfer and made with the transferring employer before the transfer, but containing detrimental terms. One view is that it may be nothing more than yet another example of employees who find the deal satisfactory and do not bother to enforce their legal rights.

Compromise agreements [9.22]

If the situation did not involve the transfer of an undertaking it would be possible to agree the change and to protect against any claim by using a compromise agreement (see **CHAPTER 8**). Compromise agreements are used in two different situations:

1. Where the employee has started to exercise a right.

2. Where the employee is agreeing to forgo a right he has not attempted to exercise.

An example of the first situation would be where the employee brings a claim for unfair dismissal. The compromise agreement, or COT3, can be used to reach an effective settlement. TUPE does not inhibit this type of use. In the second situation, it is not clear whether compromise agreements or COT3s are valid in these circumstances. The employee is agreeing to exclude or limit his rights under *regulation 4* of the TUPE regulations (transfer of terms and liabilities) and/or *regulation 7* (unfair dismissal). This is clearly forbidden and rendered void by *regulation 18*. But it does seem strange that an agreement entered into voluntarily under the auspices of an independent third party should not be valid. Indeed, compromise agreements are used but employers should realise that in these particular circumstances they do not amount to a 100% guarantee.

Key points and new developments [9.23]

• There is no inherent right allowing the employer to vary contract terms. If the contract does not contain flexible terms or some mechanism for changing terms the employer will have to persuade the employee to agree to the change or, as a last resort, dismiss and re-engage on the new terms.

• Dismissal and re-engagement are treated as redundancy for the purposes of collective redundancy consultation and the employer will have to go through the redundancy consultation process.

• The acquiring employer acquires all the rights the transferring employer has to change the contract terms both under the contract and at common law. But he may not use those rights if the reason or principal reason for the change was the transfer.

• If there is an ETO situation the employer can dismiss the employee and re-engage on new terms. The ETO defence will be a valid defence to unfair dismissal.

• Time itself will not break the link between the change and the transfer, but the longer the gap the greater the opportunity for some event to intervene and break the link.

- The employee cannot contract out of his rights under TUPE so he cannot agree to any detrimental change to his contract terms, although he can agree to beneficial ones. Detriment is assessed on a term-by-term basis, not by comparing the contractual packages.

- Because the employee cannot contract out of his TUPE rights, compromise agreements are probably ineffective.

- The 2006 TUPE regulations allow employers to change employment terms where they have an ETO defence without having to dismiss and re-engage the employee.

Questions and answers   [9.24]

Question

Following a transfer of a smaller business into ours, I have inherited an employee who was previously employed (according to her contract terms) as general office manager and administrator. I would like to amend slightly her duties and responsibilities now she has transferred over to our organisation. Am I in any position to impose change without breaking her contract terms?

Answer

If you look carefully at her existing contract terms you may find there is some built-in flexibility for change. For example, her job title might say that she is required to perform any duties and tasks within her capability upon reasonable request from the line manager and as the needs of the business dictate. In this case, you will have the flexibility to impose modest changes to the employee's duties and responsibilities. Where the contract is silent, you should always seek to agree changes with the employee. Once agreement has been reached and recorded there can be no argument that you have breached her contract terms.

Question

Two van drivers recently transferred into our organisation. In their first week it was necessary to make alterations to their working hours to fit in with our operational requirements. The drivers are currently working the changed hours but they have never said they are happy with them. They➡

have said nothing. I am worried they may refuse to work the new hours at some point in the future. Can I accept their lack of complaint as acceptance of the new terms?

Answer

The current position is unsafe in law. You are right to be concerned. To assume by the employees conduct (the performance of the new hours) that they have accepted them is fraught with difficulty, particularly here where the new hours have been recently imposed. The employees could lodge a protest to the new hours and that would negate any implied acceptance. Over a period of time, usually several weeks, it is possible to imply acceptance through conduct where the new terms have an immediate impact, such as a change to hours. To avoid confusion, the best practice is to actively seek written agreement to the new hours. Such variations are likely to be deemed void under the 2006 regulations unless you can show the sole or principal reason for the variation is not the transfer itself, but is a reason connected with the transfer that is an ETO reason.

Question

Employees who have transferred under TUPE are quite happy to transfer onto the new employer's terms and conditions, giving up their contractual redundancy package in return for a company car and a share option scheme. Is this new agreement enforceable?

Answer

Yes and no. Employees are quite free to agree to any improved term but both *Foreningen AF Arbedjsldere I Danmark v Daddy's Dance Hall A/S* and *regulation 18* of the 2006 TUPE regulations make it impossible for them to contract out of any beneficial term where the reason, or principal reason, is the transfer. So, they can agree to the car and the profit share but would retain the redundancy rights.

Question

If an employee transfers across to the new employer on the same terms and conditions as he enjoyed with the old employer and those terms included a provision entitling the old employer to change the terms, can the new employer use that provision and change the term? ➡

Answer

He can if the change is not for a reason or mainly for a reason connected with the transfer. This, once again, is the combined effect of case law such as *Daddy's Dance Hall* and the 2006 regulations.

10. Indemnities and Warranties

Information [10.1]

Whenever there is a transfer of an economic entity under the *Transfer of Undertakings (Protection of Employment) Regulations 2006 (SI 2006/246)* (TUPE), the new employer acquires the staff on the same terms and conditions as those they previously enjoyed with the transferring employer. All the rights and liabilities connected with that employment transfer and the transferee is deemed to have done or failed to do everything that the transferring employer has done or failed to do in respect of that employment. It is not surprising that organisations considering taking on board activities under TUPE want details of the staff and their liabilities before they reach their final decisions. What is perhaps surprising is that it was not until the 2006 regulations came into force in April 2006 that this matter was dealt with. It was not addressed by either the EU Acquired Rights Directive 1977 (77/187/EEC) ('the Directive') or the 1981 TUPE regulations.

The new 2006 regulations [10.2]

The new 2006 regulations recognise the prospective contractor or purchaser of a business needs to know the terms of employment as well as any outstanding or incipient claims in order to make a sensible bid for the business. The new regulations impose legal requirements in this respect. *Regulation 11* of the 2006 regulations requires the transferor to notify the transferee of all the employees' rights and obligations that will be transferred (called 'employee liability information'). In the new regulations, the employee liability information must be provided at least two weeks before the completion of the TUPE transfer, unless this is not reasonably practicable. The employee liability information to be provided includes:

- The identity of the transferring employee.

- Their age.

- The information contained in their written statement of particulars of employment.

- Details of any disciplinary actions or grievances in the last two years.

- Details or actual or potential legal action brought by the employees in the previous two years.

Under *regulation 12* of the new regulations the employment tribunal has power to award the transferee compensation for any loss suffered as a result of the transferor's failure to provide the employee liability information, with a minimum award of £500 per employee (unless the employment tribunal considers that it is unjust or inequitable to award the minimum).

Focus on consultation [10.3]

Until the 2006 TUPE regulations both the Directive and the 1981 TUPE regulations concentrated on the position of the employee and paid only scant attention to the position and needs of the respective employers. It was the failure to address the full practical implications of business transfers that caused problems. It remains to be seen whether the new 2006 regulations have gone far enough to fully relieve the problems of the past. Both the Directive and the 2006 regulations deal with the need to let the employees know what is happening by imposing a duty on both the transferring and acquiring employers to consult employee representatives in respect of employees who may be affected by the transfer. Moreover, there is a duty to explain the reasons for the transfer and any measures the company envisage taking which will affect the employees (Article 6 of the Directive and *regulation 13* of the 2006 regulations).

To enable the transferring employer to consult his transferring employees on their likely position after the transfer, the acquiring employer has to give the relevant information to the transferring employer (*regulation 13* of the 2006 regulations) (dealt with in **CHAPTER 11 – COLLECTIVE CONSULTATION**).

Contractual requirement for information [10.4]

In addition to the new statutory information requirements detailed in **10.2** above, there is a discernible tendency for organisations contracting out services to put a clause in the contract requiring the contractor to provide information on employment terms, labour costs and perhaps even prospective employment liabilities. This information is usually required a set time before the re-tendering process takes place.

There will normally be a requirement to notify of any changes to the information and sometimes no change can be made without the consent of the organisation. If the contractor was to make a change without consent, for example a five per cent wage increase, this would be a valid and enforceable change to the employee's terms and the term would transfer with the employee to the acquiring employer. If the organisation had warranted that the employment details supplied by the contractor were correct and then notified this to the prospective contractor, the contractor could sue the organisation and the organisation could sue the outgoing contractor. The warranties included on these contracts are often extremely onerous and should only be signed after careful consideration.

Sample clauses [10.5]

- The organisation [name] will provide an indemnity to any new contractor in relation to the employees transferring to the new contractor. The existing contractor [name] undertakes to provide a list of all employees who are specifically assigned to the contract or working wholly or mainly on the contract on [date] and of their terms and conditions of employment. The contractor [name] will notify the organisation [name] immediately if there is any change to this information.

  The contractor [name] warrants that the information supplied is correct.

- The contractor [name] will notify the organisation [name] of any claims which have been made or which the contractor [name] has reason to believe may be made by a transferring employee against the contractor [name].

- The contractor [name] warrants that he has fulfilled all his contractual, statutory and common law obligations in respect of the transferring employees.

Once the transfer is complete then full details can be transferred to the acquiring employer as he steps into the shoes of the outgoing employer.

Restrictions on the disclosure of personal information [10.6]

Statutory obligations apart, it should not be assumed that the employer is free to disclose personal information. He is not. He is restrained by the common law of confidentiality under the *Data Protection Act 1998* (*DPA 1998*). No matter how explicit the terms between the organisation and the contractor may be, they cannot alter the confidentiality and data protection rules.

The critical issues are:

- what information can be disclosed before the transfer? and
- when can this information be disclosed?

Confidentiality and the common law [10.7]

The first restriction is the law of confidentiality. This prevents a person who receives information that he knows, or ought to know, is confidential from disclosing that information to a third party or using it for his own benefit. Although most frequently used to prevent employees disclosing their employer's confidential information, it also applies to employers.

Case study

Dalgleish v Lothian and Boarders Police Board [1991] IRLR 422.

Facts

In this case, the local authority sought the names and addresses of the board's employees to check whether they had paid their poll tax.

Findings

The court held that the information had been provided by the employees in confidence and there was no express or implied consent to disclosure.

The rule of confidentiality is not absolute. The employer may be under a legal duty to disclose the information (as under the new regulations detailed in **10.2** above) or disclosure may be in the public interest. An example of the latter is where employees can make disclosure under the *Public Interest Disclosure Act 1998*. In *Dalgleish*, there was no public interest and, at least as yet, there is no legal duty to disclose.

Confidentiality is an effective bar to the disclosure of confidential personal information. But confidentiality will not prevent the disclosure where the individual is not identifiable. Where the employee holds a unique position it may be difficult to grant him anonymity. It may, however, be possible to include him in a group of staff and give the information for the group. Anonymised information should be sufficient to meet the bidder or prospective contractor's needs. Full details are only transferable after the transfer.

Statutory restriction [10.8]

The second restriction is contained within the *DPA 1998*. Personal information can only be disclosed in accordance with Data Protection Principle 1. The Act applies to 'processing' which is widely defined. It covers everything from collection through access, use and disclosure to destruction. For the purposes of this section of the book the relevant provisions of the Act can be restricted to disclosure. Any disclosure will have to be both lawful and fair and, in addition, one of the following conditions must be met:

1. The data subject (in this instance the employee) has given their unambiguous consent; or

2. The disclosure is necessary for the performance of a contract to which the data subject is a party or in order to take steps at the request of the data subject before entering into a contract; or

3. The disclosure is required by law; or

4. The disclosure is needed to protect vital interests of the subject; or

5. Disclosure is necessary for a task in the public interest or the exercise of official authority vested in the controllers (the employer) or a third party to whom data are disclosed; or

6. For the legitimate interest of the controller or third party, except where these interests are overridden by the interests of the data subject.

Consent under the Act [10.9]

As the disclosure is not required by law only disclosure with consent (1) and the legitimate interests of the employer or third party (6) are of possible help. Consent is a very difficult concept. The employee will have to be aware of the disclosure before he can consent. Simply telling him will not amount to consent. Consent cannot be implied because the employee has not objected. Contractors who are aware that they may have to disclose personal details on transfer of undertakings could put a suitable clause in the employment contract. Even this possible solution has been questioned. If the employee has to sign the contract to get the work is that consent? And can he withdraw consent once it has been given? Despite these doubts, a contract term appears to be the best way to deal with the problem under current law.

Important data protection principles [10.10]

There are other data protection principles that have to be noted. In particular, no more information should be disclosed than is necessary (Principle 3) and there must be adequate security. On the latter point, the employer should insist that the persons to whom the information is disclosed should use it only for the purpose for which it was disclosed, not disclose it to any unauthorised person and return or destroy the information after use. It may be appropriate to disclose the information via a secure data room. It is questionable whether the organisation needs to have the information. It may be that the role of the organisation is to warrant to the contractor that the new contractor or bidder is the person to whom access should be given.

It is not clear when the legitimate interests of the controller (the employer) or a third party (the organisation or bidder or new contractor) will outweigh those of the employee. Given the strong emphasis in the Directive on the need to protect personal information the evidence would have to be very persuasive. It is unlikely to be of use.

Sensitive information [10.11]

Certain rules exist with regard to sensitive information. Sensitive information includes information on:

- racial or ethnic origin;

- political opinions;

- religious or other beliefs;

- trade union membership;

- data concerning health or sexual life; and

- the commission or alleged commission of any offence, including any sentence.

In these circumstances, in addition to the general conditions above, the following rules apply:

- the data subject must have given his *explicit* consent; or

- disclosure is necessary for the purpose of exercising or performing an obligation or right confirmed or imposed on the data controller by employment law; or

- it is necessary to protect the vital interests of the data subject; or

- it is carried out in the course of activities of a non-profit making body which exists for political, philosophical, religious or trade union purposes; or

- the information has deliberately been made public by the data subject; or

- it is necessary in connection with legal proceedings or obtaining legal advice; or

- it is necessary for the administration of justice; or

- it is necessary for medical purposes.

This is a very restrictive list. It makes disclosure of health information difficult although information on absences may probably be disclosed.

Sending information abroad [10.12]

Another difficulty concerns sending information abroad. This is particularly important if the prospective acquiring employer has a foreign domicile or is controlled outside the EU. As the Data Protection Directive 1995 (95/46/EC) applies throughout the European Economic Area (EEA), information can be sent to any country within the EEA. The EU Commission has also decided that Switzerland and Hungary provide adequate protection for personal information (more countries are likely to be added to this list). In addition, the Commission has reached a Safe Harbor Agreement with the USA that will allow the transfer of information to US organisations that have voluntarily signed up to the Safe Harbor Principles. The agreement is subject to American law. The Principles ensure that individuals know:

* the use to which the information is put;

* to whom the information may be revealed or transferred;

* that the information is held securely;

* it is accurate and current; and

* that they have access.

Enforcement will be by the Federal Trade Commission and, for airlines, the Department of Transportation. If the information is to be sent elsewhere the employer will need to ensure the adequate protection of the information or obtain the individual's consent.

The Data Protection Code – employment records [10.13]

For consideration in conjunction with *regulation 11* of the 2006 TUPE regulations on employee liability information, in August 2002, the Information Commissioner produced a Data Protection Code on Employment Practices. Part 2 of the Code deals with employment records and includes a section that covers the management of business transfers called *Mergers and Acquisitions*. It gives useful guidance on the application of the *DPA 1998*.

The Code recognises that business merges and acquisitions will generally involve the disclosure of worker data. This may take place during evaluation of assets and liabilities prior to the final merger or acquisition decision. Once a decision has been made it is also likely to take place either in the run-up to or at the time of the actual merger or acquisition. The Code reminds businesses that a new employer's use of workers' information acquired as a result of a merger or acquisition is constrained by the expectations the workers will have from their former employer's use of the information.

The Code sets out six practice 'benchmarks':

1. Ensure, wherever practicable, that information handed over to another organisation in connection with a prospective acquisition or merger is anonymised.

2. Only hand over personal information prior to the final merger or acquisition decision after securing assurances that it will be used solely for the evaluation of assets and liabilities, it will be treated in confidence and will not be disclosed to other parties, and it will be destroyed or returned after use.

3. Advise workers, wherever practicable, if their employment records are to be disclosed to another organisation before an acquisition or merger takes place. If the acquisition or merger proceeds make sure workers are aware of the extent to which their records are to be transferred to the new employer.

4. Ensure that if you intend to disclose sensitive personal data a sensitive personal data condition is satisfied.

5. Where a merger or acquisition involves a transfer of information about a worker to a country outside the EEA ensure that there is a proper basis for making the transfer.

6. New employers should ensure that the records they hold as a result of a merger or acquisition do not include excessive information and are accurate and relevant.

The Code offers further specific guidance:

- Wherever practicable, information from which individual workers cannot be identified should be used. Details such as names and individual job titles should be omitted. This might be possible where, for example, a company merely want to know how many workers of a particular type are employed and their average rates of pay. In other cases, a company might require detailed information about particular workers in order to appraise a company's human resources assets properly. Each situation will turn on its own facts and circumstances.

- Consider the removal of names to protect privacy, even if identification is still possible.

- It is important to gain formal assurances about how the information will be used. Should the merger or acquisition not take place information should be returned or destroyed by the shredding of paper or the expunging of electronic files.

- Businesses may not always expect to be involved in mergers or acquisitions and may not, therefore, have told their workers at the time they were recruited what would happen to their personal information in such an event. In some circumstances, the corporate finance exemption from the

DPA 1998 may be relevant and may relieve companies of the obligation to inform workers of the disclosure of their information. This could occur, for example, where providing an explanation to workers could affect the price of a company's shares or other financial instruments.

- Finally, it is the new employer who has the responsibility for the type and extent of personal data retained and who will have liability for it under the Act. The new employer must not assume that the personal data he receives from the original employer is accurate or relevant and not excessive in relation to its purposes. Within a few months of the merger or acquisition he should review the records he has acquired, for example by checking the accuracy of a sample of the records with the workers concerned, and should make any necessary amendments.

Key points and new developments [10.14]

- Except in respect of its statutory obligations under the 2006 TUPE regulations in respect of employee liability information, an employer has no general right to disclose confidential personal information without the employee's consent. Disclosure may be made if required by law or in the public interest.

- The *DPA 1998* prevents the disclosure of personal information without consent although information can be disclosed where there is a legal duty to do so or where the interests of the employer or third party override those of the employee.

- The service contract itself may require the employer to disclose employment information prior to re-tendering, but this will not override common law principles of confidentiality or the *DPA 1998* and must, at its least, mirror the transferring employer's statutory obligations.

- Anonymous information can always be disclosed.

- Information may be disclosed if the employee consents.

- The 2006 regulations place a duty on the transferring employer to disclose all rights and liabilities to the new employer in good time before the transfer.

- The Information Commissioner has provided guidance on the application of the *DPA 1998* to mergers and transfers in the Data Protection Code on Employment Practices, Part 2 – Employment Records.

Questions and answers [10.15]

Question

If a bidder seeks the personal details of staff that might transfer after the re-tendering for a service contract does that information have to be provided?

Answer

Information can always be provided in a form under which an individual cannot be identified. If the process is not completed this information should suffice. Other than where the transferring employer is legally obliged to do so (under the new 2006 regulations, *regulations 11* and *12*), the provision of identifiable information should be avoided as this may breach the *DPA 1998* and be in breach of the common law rule of confidentiality.

Question

Our organisation recently contracted out its catering services to an external contractor. In the contract was a clause requiring the contractor to provide information on employment terms and particularly on wages and labour costs. There is also a requirement to notify us of any changes to these terms and labour costs. Our consent is required before any changes are made to labour costs. We did this to protect our position and that of any other contractor when the time comes to re-tender the contract for the catering services. It has been brought to our attention that the current contractor has significantly increased pay and conditions to staff working within the catering services that were contracted out. No consent was sought. What is our position?

Answer

It would appear the contractor has breached the terms of the contract. Should you suffer financial loss as a result of this breach, for example additional cost at re-tendering, your organisation could sue for damages attributable to the contractor's breach of contract. ➡

Question

We currently hold a security contract. The process of re-tendering has commenced. Under the contract we are obliged to provide information on the staff working on the security contract in advance of the re-tendering process. We have been asked to provide details of the employees' sick records over the period of the contract. Are we able to do this under the provisions of the *DPA 1998*?

Answer

Special provisions apply to the disclosure of sensitive information. The law in this area is not clear. It is probable that to disclose anonymised general details of the amount of absence in respect of a particular workforce is not in breach of the *DPA 1998* provisions. However, disclosure of specific details on each individual with regard to the reasons for their sickness absence will breach the provisions of the Act without explicit agreement from the employee to make such disclosure. In short, general information on the staff collectively will be permissible. Individual personal information will require consent.

Question

An American company has agreed to buy part of our business. It has asked us to transfer all personal files to its American office once the transfer is complete. Is it entitled to the files and do we have to send them to the USA?

Answer

Once the transfer is complete the transferor can transfer information to the transferee, the American company, without breaching any law. At this stage, it is deemed to have acted as your company has done. Nowhere is it provided that you have to transfer the actual files, though some organisations do so. However, before sending information to the USA you should ensure that the company has signed up to the Safe Harbour Agreement. If it has not you will need the consent of the individuals to send the information. You could instead offer to send the information to the UK base in charge of the transferred business.

11. Collective Consultation

The legal requirement [11.1]

Whenever a transfer of an undertaking takes place, the transferring and acquiring employer must consult representatives in respect of all the employees in their respective workforces who may be affected by the transfer (the definition of 'affected employee' is discussed in **11.10**). This consultation is required by both the EU Acquired Rights Directive 1977 (77/187/EEC) ('the Directive') and by the *Transfer of Undertakings (Protection of Employment) Regulations 2006 (SI 2006/246)* (TUPE). It may not be the only consultation required in law. If there are to be redundancies then there will have to be collective redundancy consultation under *section 188* of the *Trade Union And Labour Relations (Consolidation) Act 1992 (TULR(C)A 1992)*. The purpose of this requirement is that because redundancies involve dismissals the individual employee must be consulted to avoid liability for unfair dismissal. This chapter is only concerned with consultation in respect of the transfer. Redundancy consultation is dealt with in **CHAPTER 12 – REDUNDANCIES**.

The Directive and TUPE [11.2]

The Directive in Article 6 requires both the transferring and the acquiring employer to inform and consult representatives of employees affected by the transfer but does not specify how this will be done. Lacking any guidance, the Government assumed the normal national pattern should be followed and so limited consultation under TUPE (and for redundancy) to representatives of recognised independent trade unions.

In *The Commission of the European Communities v United Kingdom [1994] IRLR 392 ECJ*, the European Court decided the UK had not fully implemented the Directive because employers could avoid their consultation duty by the simple device of not recognising a union. As a result of this finding, TUPE was amended by the *Collective Redundancies and Transfer of Undertakings (Protection of Employment) (Amendment) Regulations 1995 (SI 1995/2587)*. Further amendment followed in the form of the *Collective Redundancies and Transfer of Undertakings (Protection of Employment) (Amendment) Regulations 1999 (SI 1999/1925)*. The 1995 amendments gave the employer the choice of consulting a recognised union or elected representatives. The 1999 version insists that the employer will consult recognised union representatives and only consult elected representatives when there is no recognised union.

The meaning of 'appropriate representatives' [11.3]

Regulation 13(3)(a) and (*b*) of the 2006 TUPE regulations provides that the appropriate representatives will be as follows:

'(a) if the employees are of a description in respect of which an independent trade union is recognised by their employer, representatives of the trade union; or

(b) in any other case, whichever of the following employee representatives the employer chooses;

(i) employee representatives appointed or elected by the affected employees otherwise than for the purposes of this regulation, who (having regard to the purposes for and the method by which they were appointed or elected) have authority from those employees to receive information and to be consulted about [the transfer] on their behalf,

(ii) employee representatives elected by them, for the purposes of this regulation.'

The employer's choice [11.4]

It follows that where there is no recognised union the employer can choose between a standing body (2006 TUPE regulations, *regulation 13(3)(b)(i)*) or ad hoc elected representatives (*regulation 13(3)(b)(ii)*). The problem with the standing body is that it must have authority to be informed and consulted on TUPE matters and it is not clear whether implicit authority will be enough. As there is increasing consultation with workplace representatives, standing bodies of representatives should ensure that their constitution gives them the power to be consulted and to receive information on any matter relating to employment or statutory rights.

Electing representatives [11.5]

If representatives have to be elected the employer has the duty of arranging the election. The basic requirements of the duty are set out in *regulation 14* of the 2006 TUPE regulations.

The requirements for the election of employee representatives under *regulation 14(1)* of the 2006 regulations are that:

- the employer will make such arrangements as are reasonably practical to ensure that the election is fair;

- the employer will determine the number of representatives to be elected so that there are sufficient representatives to represent the interests of all the affected employees, having regard to the number and classes of those employees;

- the employer will determine whether the affected employees should be represented either by representatives of all the affected employees or by representatives of particular classes of those employees;

- before the election the employer will determine the term of office as employee representatives so that it is of sufficient length to enable information to be given and consultations under *regulation 13* to be completed;

- the candidates for election as employee representatives are affected employees on the date of the election;

- no affected employee is unreasonably excluded from standing for election;

- all affected employees on the date of the election are entitled to vote for employee representatives;

- the employees entitled to vote may vote for as many candidates as there are representatives to be elected to represent them or, if there are to be representatives for particular classes of employees, may vote for as many candidates as there are representatives to be elected to represent their particular class of employee;

- the election is conducted so as to secure that:

  — so far as is reasonably practicable, those voting do so in secret; and

  — the votes given at the election are accurately counted.

Should a representative cease to act as a representative (he might resign as a representative or his employment may end) and as a result some employees are no longer represented, a by-election has to be held.

Considerations for the employer [11.6]

The employer is given considerable scope in establishing the election rules but has to make the following decisions:

- Who will manage the election? Will a person be appointed to be a scrutineer (it need not be an outsider)?

- How many representatives will there be?

- How will the representative's constituencies be decided?

- How will requests for nominations be made?

- Can there be self-nominations?

- How will voting take place? The fairest and most secure way is by a written ballot. But will this be a workplace or a postal ballot?

- Who will count the votes?

- Who will deal with complaints?

The election does not have to be contested. If there are only sufficient nominations for the representative places the nominees are declared elected.

If there are no nominations at all then there is no collective consultation, but the information that should have been given to the representatives must then be given to the individual employees. The employer must have given sufficient time for the election before he can move to informing the affected employees instead of informing and consulting the representatives.

So individual consultation is not an alternative option to collective consultation, it is only a fall back when there are no elected representatives. However, there is nothing to prevent the employer keeping the individual employees informed and asking for their views alongside the collective information and consultation procedure.

Rights of the representatives [11.7]

Under the terms of *section 61* of the *Employment Rights Act 1996 (ERA 1996)*, the appropriate representatives are entitled to reasonable time off with pay to fulfil their duties and for training to prepare them for their duties. There is a similar provision for reasonable paid time off to enable the officials of recognised trade unions to fulfil their duties under *section 169* of the *TULR(C)A 1992*. Cases under this section can be used as guidance as to what is deemed 'reasonable'.

According to the decision of *Hairsine v Hull City Council [1992] IRLR 211 EAT*, pay will be calculated on the basis of the sum they would have earned had they been working their scheduled hours. Reasonable time off will include preparation time. Again, in accordance with case law, the timing and extent of the period of time off must be reasonable and take into account the needs of the employer's business.

The representative must be given access to the affected employees and, in addition, the employer must provide the representatives with the appropriate accommodation and facilities.

Protection from dismissal [11.8]

Representatives are given special protection in the performance of their duties. Union officials are protected against unfair dismissal (without the need for one year's continuity of employment) and action short of dismissal (victimisation and other unfavourable treatment) under *sections 146* and *152* of the *TULR(C)A 1992*. These rights have been extended to representatives and to candidates standing for election as representatives (*ERA 1996, ss 47* and *103*).

The information and consultation 'trigger point' [11.9]

A literal reading of Article 6(1) of the Directive would lead to the conclusion that consultation need not begin until the agreement to transfer has been finalised:

'the transferor and transferee shall be required to inform the representatives of their respective employees affected by a transfer . . .'.

The same would apply to *regulation 13* of the 2006 TUPE regulations that requires consultation with representatives where there are employees '... who may be affected by the transfer'.

This is not the position in practice. To commence consultation at the point when the deal was finally agreed would defeat the objective of consultation.

Case study

This is highlighted by the case of the *Banking, Insurance and Finance Union v Barclays Bank plc [1987] ICR EAT.*

Facts

Barclays set up a new investment bank, Barclays de Zoete Wedd (BZW), by merging Barclays Merchant Bank (BMW) with various firms of jobbers and stockbrokers that it had acquired. The business of BMW would transfer to BZW but the employees would not. Instead, the employees would transfer to another new subsidiary, Barclays de Zoete Wedd Services Ltd (BZW Services) which would then supply its labour under a service contract to BZW. Before any transfer was completed, BIFU complained to the tribunal because no information had been supplied nor was consultation taking place. ➡

Findings

Consultation has to take place when a transfer is proposed, even though it may eventually fall through. In this particular case, the Employment Appeal Tribunal (EAT) decided the transfer of employees to a service company was not the transfer of an undertaking.

When is a transfer 'proposed'? [11.10]

It may be clear that the employer cannot wait until the final deal but inevitably it is unclear how certain the possibility must be before the transfer is 'proposed'.

Case study

Institution of Professional Civil Servants v Secretary of State for Defence [1987] IRLR 373 Ch D.

Facts

This case is based on the *Dockyards Services Act 1986*. This Act contains similar provisions to those in TUPE. Under this Act, the management of the Rossyth and Devonport Dockyards was transferred to the private sector.

Findings

Millet J decided the employer had to have formulated some definite plan or proposal that it intended to implement, if necessary, after consultation with the appropriate representatives. Mere contemplation is not enough to trigger consultation.

The last point on consultation with representatives is of considerable importance. The employer will have to consult the representatives 'with a view to reaching agreement' on the measures that will be taken in relation to any affected employees. He must be open to persuasion on this point or the consultation cannot be said to be with a view to reaching agreement.

Information and consultation is required whenever there are or may be employees affected by measures taken in connection with the transfer. This is wider than the employees who may transfer. Employees retained by the transferring employer may find their duties or terms of employment changed and the acquisition of a new business could have repercussions for employees of the acquiring employer as well. These are affected employees. Any union recognised in respect of these affected employees must be consulted and in a representative election they are part of the electorate. Acquiring employers sometimes ignore this last point. As a result, they fail to comply with their information and consultation responsibilities.

There is no minimum number of employees who must be expected transfer to trigger information and consultation. So long as one employee is affected, even though that employee is not expected to transfer, information and consultation must take place.

Period for consultation [11.11]

There is no set period for TUPE consultation, unlike redundancy consultation where the legislation specifies minimum time periods during which consultation must take place. If there is a redundancy situation running alongside the TUPE transfer then the redundancy consultation periods will be a useful guide. But all the Directive and TUPE specify is that the information will be supplied and that consultation will commence. *Regulation 13(2)* of the 2006 TUPE regulations states that:

> 'long enough before a relevant transfer to enable the employer of any affected employees to consult all the persons who are appropriate representatives of any of those affected employees.'

If the employer has to consult ad hoc elected representatives then the elections must be held before the 'long enough' period begins. The time it takes to complete the election exercise is not part of consultation.

How long is long enough? This is rather like asking how long is a piece of string? It is unhelpful to say that it all depends on the circumstances or that it will be decided by a tribunal, but there is little helpful material from which to draw guidance. Perhaps the best guide is *Hough v Leyland DAF Ltd [1991] IRLR 194 EAT*. At the time of this decision, redundancy consultation had to start at the earliest opportunity (it now has to begin in good time) and the EAT decided this was when a specific proposal had been formulated rather than the diagnosis of a problem and a consideration of possible ways to deal with it. Clearly, there can be no duty to consult prior to that date and this is the point at which employers will have to decide when consultation will begin.

The information requirement [11.12]

Both the Directive (Article 6(1)) and *regulation 13(2)* of the 2006 TUPE regulations require certain basic information to be provided to the representatives. Where the employees have failed to elect representatives this information must be supplied directly to the individual employees.

Regulation 13(2) requires the following information to be supplied:

- the fact that the relevant transfer is to take place, when, approximately, it is to take place and the reasons for it;

- the legal, economic and social implications of the transfer for the affected employees;

- the measures which the employer envisages he will, in connection with the transfer, take in relation to those employees or, if he envisages that no measures will be so taken, that fact; and

- if the employer is the transferor, the measures which the transferee envisages he will, in connection with the transfer, take in relation to such of those employees as, by virtue of *regulation 4*, become employees of the transferee after the transfer or, if he envisages that no measures will be so taken, that fact.

Compliance in practice   [11.13]

The information must be given to each representative in writing either by being given to the representative or sent to an address he has notified to his employer or, in the case of a trade union representative, sent by post to the union at the address of its head or main office. It has to be supplied by the consulting employer. This can cause difficulties for the transferring employer as he will not know what steps the acquiring employer may intend to take in relation to transferred employees.

Although the main duty is imposed on the transferring employer where the acquiring employer has failed to provide him with the necessary information, *regulation 15* of the 2006 TUPE regulations allows him to be joined in any action brought against the transferring employer. This is a roundabout way of ensuring that he provides the necessary details.

The reasons and details of the transfer are self-evident. The legal effect of the transfer presumably concerns the effect on the employee's contract, continuity of employment and legal rights. But the social and economic implications are far from clear. They have been lifted straight from the Directive and there is no guidance as to their meaning.

The information given on the measures that are envisaged in respect of the employees must not be treated lightly, particularly when the transferring employer is giving the transferring employees information about the prospective actions of the acquiring employer. If he gets it wrong he could find himself on the wrong end of a claim for misrepresentation. 'Envisages' is wider than 'proposes'; a change is normally envisaged before it is proposed.

Case study

Hagen and ors v ICI Chemicals and Polymers Ltd and ors [2001] IDS Brief 699, HC.

Facts

This transfer was most unusual in that it would not take place unless the transferring staff agreed. They did agree. After the transfer they alleged that promises given to them by both ICI, the transferring employer, and Redpath Engineering Services, the acquiring employer, and which had induced them to agree to the transfer had not been met.

Findings

The High Court rejected all their claims except for one relating to the pension benefits available after transfer. In respect of pensions, the court decided that the transferring employer, ICI, owed the employees a duty to take reasonable care in giving them information about the pension scheme. The court held that ICI had breached this duty of care by not informing certain employees that their pension rights might be more adversely affected by the transfer than the information given to them suggested, and the employees had relied on the information actually given to persuade them to transfer. ICI was liable for negligent misstatement. The court went on to hold that this liability remained with ICI, it did not transfer because occupational pension schemes are specifically excluded from transferring by *regulation 10* of the 2006 regulations.

When it comes to the actual information that has to be supplied the tribunals have taken a fairly strict interpretation. The following rules have been formed:

- the representatives are entitled to information but not to see the original documents, such as the bids or the contracts;

- they are not entitled to the information on which the employer's decisions have been based. The representatives are only entitled to the measures themselves, not to the underlying information. The representatives will no doubt have great interest in this information but they are not entitled to it; and

- the representatives are not entitled to information because they would like to have it.

Under *regulation 13(9)*, information need not be disclosed:

'If in any case there are special circumstances which render it not reasonably practicable for an employer to perform.'

Where the duty of disclosure is imposed upon the employer:

'he shall take all such steps towards performing that duty as are reasonably practicable in the circumstances.'

This is similar to the provision in *section 188* of the *TULR(C)A 1992* in respect of redundancy consultation where it has been decided that to amount to 'special circumstances' the circumstances would have to be 'exceptional', 'out of the ordinary' or so uncommon that it made consultation impractical to consult properly. Insolvency would not, automatically, be a special circumstance. It will all depend on the circumstances. This means the employer has to make a judgement but the tribunal must not use hindsight to review the employer's decision.

Commercially sensitive and confidential information [11.14]

A difficult question relates to commercially sensitive or confidential information. Dealing with personal information first, wherever possible this should be supplied in an anonymised fashion. The advent of the *Data Protection Act 1998* has made tribunals and courts more sensitive to the unnecessary disclosure of personal information. Market sensitive information may also be withheld according to the unreported case of *Nalgo v British Waterways Board [1988] ET*. Questions have arisen concerning information that would affect the market price of shares. The Financial Services Authority (FSA) has recently indicated that disclosing information in confidence might not breach its disclosure rules. Employers would be prudent to check first with the FSA.

Finally, there is nothing to stop employers disclosing additional information on a voluntary basis.

The consultation requirement [11.15]

Consultation with the appropriate representatives must take place whenever the transferring or acquiring employer envisages that he will take 'measures' in relation to any of his employees who are affected by the transfer. If no measures are envisaged the representatives must be so informed. Note the fact that where there is no duty to consult it does not affect the duty to provide information as above.

Both the Directive and the 2006 TUPE regulations provide that the employer only has to consult in respect of the measures he envisages taking in relation to his own employees. So, although the transferor has to inform the transferring employees about the measures the acquiring employer proposes to take in respect of their employment, he does not have to consult on those measures. Indeed, it is difficult to see how he could. Similarly, the acquiring employer only has to consult in respect of his own affected employees. No one has to consult the transferring employees. In practice, arrangements are usually made for the new employer to meet the transferring staff and their representatives.

There need be no consultation if no measures connected with the transfer are envisaged. In *Institution of Professional Civil Servants v Secretary of State for Defence*, Millet J decided that to be connected to the transfer the measures had to be both temporally and causally connected to the transfer. If the measures were measures that would have been taken anyway, they were not connected to the transfer and need not be subject to consultation.

Consultation involves more than the transfer of information. Consultation is specifically required to be with a view to seeking the agreement of the representatives to the measures envisaged. The appropriate representatives must have an opportunity to put their views. Those views must be considered and a reasoned response given. It does not mean that agreement must be reached, but there has to be a serious attempt to reach it.

Breach of the consultation requirement [11.16]

Before the new 2006 TUPE regulations came into force in April 2006, case law deliberated on whether liability for the transferor's failure to comply with his duty to inform and consult passed to the transferee.

> ### *Case study*
>
> *Alamo Group (Europe) Ltd v Tucker and anor [2003] All ER (D) 367*
>
> #### *Facts*
>
> TT Ltd went into administration on 22 June 2000. On 8 September 2000, AG(E) Ltd concluded a contract to purchase TT Ltd. The employees of TT Ltd presented a complaint to an employment tribunal that TT Ltd had failed to comply with its obligation, under *regulation 10* of the 1981 TUPE regulations, to consult with the representatives of its employees who were affected by the sale of the business. ➡

Findings

The EAT found that the sale of TT Ltd to AG(E) Ltd amounted to a relevant transfer for the purposes of TUPE and that TT Ltd had failed to comply with its *regulation 10* (1981 TUPE regulations) obligation. Accordingly, the tribunal awarded the employees compensation of one week's gross wages each. It went on to find the liability to make the compensatory payment under *regulation 10* had transferred to AG(E) Ltd under *regulation 5* of the 1981 regulations.

This decision of the EAT reverses the earlier EAT decision in *Transport and General Workers' Union v James McKinnon, JR (Haulage) Ltd and ors [2001] IRLR 597 EAT* where it was held the transferor retained the liability to pay.

The EAT in *Alamo* swung back in favour of the approach that it is artificial to draw a distinction between the rights which arose out of the contract of employment and those that arose out of statute when considering whether a right was subject to *regulation 5* of the 1981 regulations. The EAT held that the only question that mattered in determining whether liability transferred under *regulation 5* was whether the right arose in connection with the contract of employment or the employment relationship.

Under *regulation 15* of the 2006 regulations no such distinction is required. It provides that the transferor and transferee be jointly and severally liable for any award of compensation made by an employment tribunal for failure by the transferor to comply with these information and consultation requirements. This regulation makes practical sense. It provides an incentive to the transferor to comply with the requirements and allows the employee to choose which employer he brings his claim against, thereby maximising the prospect of recovering compensation.

Enforcement [11.17]

Enforcement claims must be taken to the employment tribunal, usually within three months of the breach.

The statutory claims [11.18]

1. *Failure to arrange for the proper election of representatives, provide the information to the appropriate representatives or conduct proper consultation.*

   The employees or appropriate representatives should complain to the tribunal within three months of the transfer. This period can only be extended if it was not reasonably practicable to bring the claim within that time (2006 TUPE regulations, *regulation 15*). The claim can be brought as soon as breach has occurred, there is no need to wait until the transfer has taken place (*South Durham Health Authority v UNISON [1995] IRLR 407 EAT*).

The following rules apply as to who may claim:

- if the complaint relates to a failure in the election of representatives, any affected employee may bring the claim;

- if it relates to any other breach relating to an employee representative (for example failure to provide information or failure to consult) then the representative or representatives themselves can bring the claim;

- if the breach is in relation to trade union representatives then the union will bring the claim; and

- in any other case an affected employee can bring a claim.

2. *Failure of the transferring employer to provide information on the measures the acquiring employer proposes to take in respect of the transferring employees.*

The liability lies initially with the transferring employer even when the acquiring employer has failed to provide him with the necessary information. Any complaint of failure to provide information on the measures the acquiring employer proposes to take has to be made against the transferring employer. If he wishes to avoid this liability he has to show that it was not reasonably practical for him to comply with his duty because the acquiring employer had not provided him with the information. To do this he must give the acquiring employer notice of this fact. This has the effect of making the acquiring employee a party to the proceedings against the transferring employer (2006 TUPE regulations, *regulation 15(5)*). The tribunal can then decide who is liable and make the award against the appropriate employer.

The protective award [11.19]

The tribunal must first decide if a breach has occurred. If it has, the tribunal may then order the employer (this could be the acquiring employer if he has failed to provide information about the measures he proposes to take in respect of transferring employees) to pay an appropriate sum to the affected employees specified in the award. The amount of the award is at the tribunal's discretion but it may not exceed 13 weeks' pay. Unlike the redundancy protective award where pay above £290 a week (this sum is reviewed annually in February in line with the RPI) has to be disregarded, the pay is not subject to an upper limit.

At one time the award could be set against any wages, or payment or compensation for wages, such as wages in lieu of notice that the employer might have made. As the employee was usually paid during the period prior to the dismissal the chances of the employees obtaining any additional payment were small. This has changed. It is no longer possible to set the award against any other payment, thus providing an additional incentive to bring a claim for failure to inform or consult. On the other hand, the protective award is an incentive to consult properly.

If the employer does not pay the award the employee may complain to the tribunal and the tribunal will order the employer to make the payment.

EU Directive on information and consultation [11.20]

The *Information and Consultation of Employees Regulations 2004* came into force on 6 April 2005 for undertakings employing 150 or more employees. The regulations implement the *EC Information and Consultation Directive* and they apply to undertakings with 100 or more employees from 6 April 2007 and to those with 50 or more employees from 6 April 2008. The European Commission estimates that, once fully implemented by EU member states, the Directive will cover 50% of EU employers.

The 2004 regulations:

• facilitate voluntary agreements where possible rather than lay down detailed rules that apply universally; and

• allow pre-existing arrangements that have both employer and workforce approval to continue where possible.

The obligation will only arise if the workforce requests to be informed and consulted. Under the regulations, employees will be able to request information and consultation arrangements with a written petition from ten per cent of the workforce (subject to a minimum of 15 and a maximum of 2,500 employees). There is then a period of six months for negotiating a voluntary agreement. Where arrangements are already in place that have been agreed with employees, the employer may ballot the workforce to endorse or reject the request and only if a minimum of 40% of the employees endorse the request do the existing arrangements have to be changed.

Businesses are able to agree with their workforce the information and consultation arrangements that best suit their circumstances. However, where no agreement is reached, standard provisions apply and the employer has a further period of six months in which to set up the necessary structures.

A broad range of issues are subject to the obligations contained in the regulations, including issues relating to the economic situation of the company, anything which could cause a threat to employment and decisions likely to lead to substantial changes in work organisation or contractual arrangements (including redundancies and transfers).

Key points and new developments [11.21]

- Both the transferring and acquiring employer must consult in respect of all their employees who will be affected by the transfer.

- If the employer recognises an independent trade union, information and consultation must be with representatives of that union.

- If there is no recognised independent union then the employer may either inform and consult an existing elected body or arrange for the election of representatives.

- If the employees fail to elect representatives the employer must provide the information to the individual affected employees.

- The employer must inform and consult long enough before the transfer for the information requirement to be fulfilled and for consultation to be effective.

- The employer must inform the representatives of the reasons for the transfer, the legal, economic and social implications of the transfers and the measures he envisaged taking in respect of the affected employees.

- The acquiring employer must inform the transferring employer of the measures he envisages taking in respect of any transferring employees.

- Both employers must consult representatives in respect of the measures they will be taking in relation to their own staff.

- Breaches in the election of representatives, the provision of information or consultation can result in an award of up to 13 weeks' pay to affected employees.

- A failure to inform or consult will not make the transfer void.

Questions and answers [11.22]

Question

Does the acquiring employer have to consult his own staff?

Answer

If he has employees who will be affected by the transfer, for example employees whose responsibilities will change or who might be in a pool➡

---

for redundancy, they must be informed about the transfer and consulted on any measures which the employer envisages he may take in respect of them.

Question

If there is no recognised trade union can the employer leave it to the employees to choose their own representatives?

Answer

This used to be possible but the law was changed in 1999. Now the employer must conduct fair elections with, wherever possible, secret voting.

Question

I am head of HR within my organisation and we are embarking on collective consultation. We are at the stage of arranging employee representative elections. There seems to be some flexibility here as to what the employer is required to consider. What are the most important factors that I should take into account?

Answer

There is considerable flexibility in the employer's approach to facilitating the election of representatives. It may be prudent to appoint someone to manage and oversee the election process. You should decide in advance how many representatives would be appropriate and whom they will represent. Nominations should be invited in a set format and this should not neglect employees away from the office for whatever reason. Try to ensure a secret ballot and make arrangements for postal voting. The vote count should be scrupulously fair and a nominated person should handle any complaints with regard to the process on behalf of the employer.

Question

We have now held elections and appointed representatives. One of the representatives is now asking for time off to prepare before each stage of the collective consultation. We think the requested time off is unnecessary. What are the rules? ➡

Answer

The employees' representative is entitled to reasonable time off to perform the required duties. This entitlement is paid. Pay will be calculated on the basis of the sum the representative would have earned had they been working their scheduled hours. Reasonable time off will include preparation time. Again, in accordance with case law, the timing and extent of the period of time off must be reasonable and take into account the needs of the employer's business. In short, the law is designed to give the representative (for a short period of time) similar rights to a trade union official.

Question

One of the employee representatives is proving to be particularly difficult to deal with. I would like to pass information directly to the employees as the consultation progresses. Can I do this without risking a personal claim from the employee representative in question?

Answer

No. Failure to provide the information to an appropriate representative could provoke a statutory claim. If, as here, the claim would be in connection with a breach relating to an employee representative then the representative or representatives themselves can bring the claim. They may do so within three months from the transfer.

Question

Can information be withheld from the representatives?

Answer

Only if the employer can show there are special circumstances. Obviously the burden of proof is heavy, for example insolvency is not a special circumstance. Personal details can probably be withheld along with commercially sensitive information depending on the particular circumstances of the case.

Question

How long must consultation last? ➡

Answer

It is impossible to say. The Acquired Rights Directive 1977 states 'in good time' and the TUPE regulations state 'long enough before the transfer'. It may be easier to pinpoint the date when consultation should first be considered. Relying on earlier redundancy consultation cases this should be when there is a proposal to transfer. A proposal is viewed by the courts as being beyond mere contemplation and therefore capable of 'triggering' the consultation requirement.

Question

Does it matter if an employer does not consult?

Answer

It will not affect the validity of the transfer but it could prove expensive. The tribunal can make an award of compensation of up to 13 weeks' pay to each or specified affected employees.

12. Redundancies

Current regulations [12.1]

Despite the fact that redundancy is one of the most common reasons for dismissals when there is a business transfer, neither the EU Acquired Rights Directive 1977 (77/187/EEC) ('the Directive') nor the *Transfer of Undertakings (Protection of Employment) Regulations 2006 (SI 2006/246)* (TUPE) deal expressly with the question of redundancy. Because the TUPE regulations change the normal rules for the termination of contracts they do affect the employee's entitlement to redundancy rights.

TUPE regulations [12.2]

Before TUPE, an employee's contract of employment ended when the business in which the employee was working transferred to a new employer. If the old employer had not given proper notice to terminate the employment contract at or before the transfer date, the employee could bring a breach of contract claim. He would also be redundant because, having transferred the business, the reason his employer dismissed him would be because he was no longer needed – an obvious case of redundancy.

This situation was completely changed by Article 3 of the Directive and *regulation 4* of the 2006 TUPE regulations. These provisions ensure that those employees engaged in the transferring business will transfer with that business to the acquiring employer. There is now no contract termination and so no breach of contract and no dismissal for redundancy where an employee transfers under TUPE.

ETO dismissals and redundancy [12.3]

The probable cause of confusion in this area of business transfers is that when drafting the 1981 TUPE regulations the draftsmen took into account unfair dismissal but neglected to deal with redundancy.

Section 98(2) of the *Employment Rights Act 1996 (ERA 1996)* sets out the grounds that may make a dismissal fair:

- the capability or qualifications of the employee for performing work of the kind that he was employed by the employer to do;
- the conduct of the employee;

- the employee was redundant; and

- the employee could not continue to work in the position which he held without contravention (either on his part or on that of his employer) of a duty or restriction imposed by or under an enactment.

Section 98(1)(b) adds:

- some other substantial reason of a kind such as to justify the dismissal of an employee holding the position which the employee held.

So, for unfair dismissal purposes, redundancy and some other substantial reason for dismissal are two separate categories.

In *regulation 8(2)* of the 1981 TUPE regulations it was unequivocally stated that, for unfair dismissal purposes, an economic, technical or organisational (ETO) reason entailing a change in the workforce will:

> 'be regarded as having been for a substantial reason of a kind such as to justify the dismissal of an employee holding a position which that employee held.'

That is, it is to be some other substantial reason for dismissal. The 1981 TUPE regulations did not separate redundancy dismissals from other ETO dismissals. They were all ETO dismissals as far as unfair dismissal is concerned.

The rationale was to prevent the employee who transfers to the new employer on the same terms and conditions claiming unfair dismissal compensation. It was felt that purpose could be achieved by making all ETO dismissals fall into the some other substantial dismissal category. There was no need to separate out the redundancy cases.

Loss of redundancy entitlement [12.4]

Prior to the 2006 regulations (*regulation 7*) coming into force in April 2006, the important question was if an employee is dismissed because he was excess to requirements and, under *regulation 8(2)* of the 1981 TUPE regulations, he had been dismissed for an ETO reason and therefore for some other substantial reason, that meant that he could not be redundant and so was not entitled to redundancy pay? Initially, case law supported this view. This meant that TUPE had so altered the grounds for dismissal that an employee who, before TUPE, would have been regarded as redundant, was now no longer redundant and was therefore deprived of a benefit to which he had previously been entitled.

Case study

This was indeed the decision reached in *Canning v (1) Niaz and (2) McLoughlin [1983] IRLR 431 EAT.*

Facts

McLoughlin had sold the business in which Mrs Canning worked to Niaz. Niaz did not need Mrs Canning. Mrs Canning's job was to be filled by a member of his family. McLoughlin dismissed Mrs Canning prior to the transfer. Mrs Canning then claimed redundancy pay from either Niaz or McLoughlin.

Findings

The Employment Appeal Tribunal (EAT) decided that Niaz was not liable in redundancy because he had not dismissed her. McLoughlin had dismissed Mrs Canning and that dismissal was due to the transfer. But the dismissal was not an unfair dismissal because McLoughlin no longer needed Mrs Canning and he could therefore rely upon the ETO defence. Under *regulation 8(2)* of the 1981 regulations she had been dismissed for some other substantial reason and not for redundancy. She had therefore not been made redundant and was not entitled to redundancy benefit.

So regulations designed to protect employees in fact ended up depriving them of their rights.

Clarification of the law [12.5]

In *Canning*, the EAT had confused rules under TUPE that were clearly intended to apply only to unfair dismissal with those for redundancy. There is absolutely no legal reason why a dismissal should not be categorised as for some other substantial reason for TUPE and unfair dismissal purposes, or as redundancy for the purpose of obtaining redundancy benefit.

This was the rationale behind the decisions in *Gorictree Ltd v Jenkinson [1984] IRLR 391 EAT* and *Anderson and McAlonie v Dalkeith Engineering Ltd [1984] IRLR 429 EAT*, which completely rejected *Canning*.

In *Gorictree*, the EAT pointed out that redundancy was one of the most common of the ETO reasons for dismissal. Very clear words would have been needed before *regulation 8(2)* of the 1981 TUPE regulations could be construed as excluding redundancy benefit and the wording did not meet that requirement. Indeed, the wording only says that for the purpose of unfair dismissal an ETO dismissal is to be regarded as for some other substantial reason. It does not say it has to be so regarded for redundancy benefit.

Although never overruled, *Canning* was generally regarded as incorrect and *Gorictree* and *Anderson* were relied on because they held TUPE and redundancy provisions should not be confused and employees dismissed for a valid ETO reason may also be redundant and entitled to redundancy pay.

Regulation 7 of the 2006 TUPE regulations was enacted precisely to overcome the misinterpretation in *Canning*. *Regulation 7* provides that an ETO reason for dismissal, which under the new regulations is potentially fair, is to be regarded as having been by reason of redundancy, where the appropriate test in *section 98(2)* of the *Employment Rights Act 1996* is met.

Normal redundancy rules apply [12.6]

The normal redundancy rules apply to redundancy dismissals caused by business transfers. The reason why redundancy is one of the most common reasons for dismissals is evident from the definition of redundancy itself. In *section 139(1)* of the *ERA 1996*, a person is dismissed by redundancy if the dismissal is wholly or mainly attributable to:

- the fact that the employer has ceased or intends to cease;

  — to carry on the business for the purpose of which the employee was employed by him, or

  — to carry on that business in the place where the employee was so employed, or

- the fact that the requirements of that business;

  — for employees to carry out work of a particular kind, or

  — for employees to carry out work of a particular kind in the place where the employee was employed by the employer,

  have ceased or diminished or are expected to cease or diminish.

This covers not only a reduction in employees in the unit transferred, but also where the transferring employer needs to reduce the number of his retained staff following the transfer and where the acquiring employer finds he has excess staff as a result of the transfer. They all fit within the statutory definition of redundancy.

The qualifying employee [12.7]

The right to a redundancy payment under the *ERA 1996* is restricted to employees who have at least two years' continuity of employment. The employee must also have been dismissed. This is where TUPE begins to bite. Under *regulation 4* of the 2006 TUPE regulations, if the employee transfers to the new employer there is no dismissal and so no redundancy entitlement. In fact, this was the position in law prior to TUPE.

Nor does it matter if there is an actual dismissal. If the employee is dismissed immediately before and because of the transfer, is paid his redundancy pay and then taken into the employment of the new employer he is still not redundant because he will transfer to the new employer under TUPE and the apparent dismissal is disregarded.

Some transferring employers make redundancy payments to the employees transferring with the business. Sometimes because they are not aware that it is a TUPE transfer. Sometimes because they are giving employees a choice of options, for example:

* to transfer to the new employer;

* to accept another job with the transferring employer; or

* to take the redundancy pay and go.

Occasionally, there exists simply a wish to make the payment. The interesting issue is that of the employee who, having taken his redundancy pay, then immediately starts to work for the new employer.

Where a statutory redundancy payment is made to an employee, *section 214(2)* of the *ERA 1996* provides that continuity of employment terminates. To bring a further claim for redundancy the employee will have to accrue another two years' continuity of employment. In addition, *section 122(4)* allows any payment made in respect of statutory redundancy to be set against any basic award to be paid by the employer in an unfair dismissal claim. But this only applies where there is a statutory redundancy. It does not apply to voluntary redundancies. The above examples would be regarded, for the purposes of the legislation, as voluntary redundancies.

In these cases the employee is not redundant. He transfers under TUPE. He is not entitled to any statutory redundancy payment. Continuity of service is not broken. Should his new employer make him redundant, he can receive his redundancy payment all over again.

Case study

Gardner v Hayden Davies Catering Equipment Ltd [1992] IDS 469 EAT.

Facts

Ms Gardener was employed by CT Ltd when the business transferred to Hayden Davies. At this stage she was not entitled to a statutory redundancy payment as she was transferring to Hayden Davies but CT Ltd paid her £930 for redundancy. Shortly after the transfer Hayden Davies made her redundant.

Findings

The EAT decided that she was not redundant and had received redundancy payment to which she was not entitled. The EAT appeared so alarmed at the thought that she would receive her redundancy payment again, in full, that it decided that it would be inequitable not to take the redundancy money already received into account when assessing her statutory redundancy pay. The outcome of this case may be justice, but hardly good law.

Case study

A better view was expressed in *Senior Heat Treatment v Bell [1997] IRLR 614 EAT.*

Facts

Lucas Bryce had sold his business to Senior Heat Treatment. Lucas Bryce gave his staff the option of staying with him, moving to Senior Heat Treatment or taking redundancy. Bell chose redundancy but started work immediately after the transfer with Senior Heat Treatment on the basis of a contract entered into before his employment with Lucas Bryce had ended. But within the year they were made redundant.

Findings

Had this been a genuine statutory redundancy his continuity of employment would have terminated with his redundancy payment and➡

> since that date he would not have accrued the vital two years' continuity to bring a claim. But it was not a genuine statutory redundancy. He had transferred under TUPE. He was entitled to his full redundancy payment based on his continuity of employment with both Lucas Bryce and Senior Heat Treatment.

As the employer seems to receive so little, in fact nothing for his money, can he get it back? The answer is no. The UK does not have a law of unjust enrichment. If the payment was made in full knowledge of the situation it is not returnable. If the employer misunderstood the law he might be able to plead his mistake, but he would have to convince a court that his ignorance was understandable and that he generally assumed that the money was lost.

The opposite side of the coin is that the acquiring employer could well find himself paying the redundancy payment for employees dismissed by the transferring employer under *Litster v Forth Dry Dock and Engineering Co Ltd* (see **5.3**).

Unfair dismissal [12.8]

If the employer has more staff than he needs then he will have an economic or organisational reason for making them redundant and dismissing them. In addition to producing a valid reason for the dismissal he will also have to show that it was fair to dismiss for that reason. In redundancy situations this usually concerns selection and consultation.

Redundancy selection [12.9]

When a business transfer results in staff excess to requirements it may be tempting to select those employees who will be made redundant from the pool of the transferred staff. Restricting the pool in this way could make the redundancy dismissals unfair. The employer has to take into consideration all the employees doing similar work. This may mean looking at employees working on other sites or in other departments.

> ### Case study
>
> *Highland Fish Farmers v Thorburn and anor [1995] IRLB 529 EAT.*
>
> ### Facts
>
> The employer operated several fish farms. Thorburn and his brother had worked at one in Aird but were transferred to another at Torridon. Both➡

sites were in travelling distance of their home. One of the brothers still occasionally worked at Aird. The Torridon site closed and two employees from Aird and one from another site were made redundant. These selections were made on a last in first out (LIFO) basis. The brothers said they should have returned to the Aird site where their length of service would have ensured that they were not selected on the LIFO basis. The employer refused because he would then have to make other staff redundant.

Findings

The EAT decided that the pool from which the selection should have been made included employees at both sites.

'Any reasonable employer faced with two sited in geographical proximity and providing mutual support would not have focussed on one single site as the pool for selection'.

The brothers had been unfairly selected for redundancy.

The actual method and criteria for selection is a matter for the employer, but it must be objective. Typical objective selection criteria might include:

- length of service;

- disciplinary record;

- skills;

- qualifications;

- relevant experience; and

- geographical domicile.

The fact that a particular selection method or set of criteria has been used in the past does not compel the employer to follow that method or justify departing from it. However, if the redundancy selection process has been written into the contract, then a failure to follow that procedure will be a breach of contract entitling the employee chosen for redundancy to damages. Also, the dismissal will almost inevitably be unfair despite there being a valid ground for dismissal.

Consulting the employee [12.10]

TUPE consultation is concerned with consulting representatives. The courts and tribunals have developed a requirement that individual employees should also be consulted in small groups or individually. There is no need to consult if it would be pointless to do so but this is difficult to prove. Consultation is not warning or informing the employee. In *R v British Coal Corporation and ors [1994] IRLR 72 Div Ct*, the court said that it involves the provision of a fair opportunity for the employee to understand fully the matters about which he is being consulted, and to express his views on those subjects with the person consulting and considering those views properly and genuinely.

This consultation can take place simultaneously with the collective TUPE consultation and any collective redundancy consultation (see **12.13**).

Contractual redundancy agreements [12.11]

Contractual redundancy agreements may:

- set out a particular procedure to be followed;

- include provision for retraining;

- determine the method of selection; and

- provide for a more generous payment.

The redundancy terms may be directly incorporated into the contract, frequently via a collective agreement. Further to the *Employment Act 2002* (EA 2002) that came into force in October 2004, there is now a minimum contractual procedure required in all contracts as part of the dispute resolution provisions of that Act.

Case study

Anderson v Pringle of Scotland [1998] IRLR Ct Sess OH.

Facts

This case deals with two separate but important points. The first concerns the incorporation of a collective agreement into a contract. The employer had entered into a collective agreement with the GMB in 1986 that included a redundancy procedure in which selection was on the basis of LIFO. The statement of terms and conditions provided that they should be 'in accordance with and subject to' the provisions of that agreement. But the statement did not refer to redundancy so the employer argued the collective agreement was incorporated only to the extent that one of its provisions was referred to in the statement. ➡

> ### Findings
>
> The court rejected this. The whole agreement was incorporated and so to select other than on a LIFO basis was breach of contract.

On other occasions there is no express incorporation and the question is whether incorporation can be implied from custom. This is possible if the procedure has been published as the organisation's redundancy procedure and has been automatically followed on several occasions. But the argument seems to have been rejected more frequently than it has been followed.

> ### Case study
>
> *Quinn v Calder Industrial Materials Ltd [1996] IRLR 126 EAT.*
>
> #### Facts
>
> A redundancy policy had been applied at the place of work on four separate occasions over a seven-year period. The employees argued this application had, through custom and practice, created a contractual term and condition of the contract of employment.
>
> #### Findings
>
> The EAT refused to hold that a redundancy policy that had been applied on four redundancy occasions between 1987 and 1994 had become a contractual term. Policies will only stand a chance of becoming terms if they have been drawn to the attention of employees by management, or have been followed for a substantial period and all the other circumstances of the case are taken into account. In this case, the payment of the enhanced redundancy payment followed a decision to make the payment on each occasion.

> ### Case study
>
> *Pellow v Pendragon [2000] IDS 634 EAT.*
>
> #### Facts
>
> There had been a consistent custom and practice over 20 years concerning the payment of redundancy pay. The published policy➡

reserved to management the right to determine on each occasion the amount that would be paid. When Lex transferred the garage to Pendragon there was no contractual term relating to redundancy.

Findings

The EAT held that it was no more than a management policy and management was free to determine on each occasion whether additional pay would be made and if so how much.

Collective consultation [12.12]

If there are to be redundancy dismissals, then as well as consulting workplace representatives under TUPE and the individuals to be dismissed in order to avoid unfair dismissals, the employer must also undertake redundancy consultation with representatives of the workforce. This consultation is, in many ways, similar to the TUPE consultation, but it is not identical. The details are found in *section 188* of the *ERA 1996* and are summarised below. However, in practice, the two collective consultations can easily be combined.

Comparison between TUPE and redundancy consultation [12.13]

TUPE consultation	*Redundancy consultation*
Consult representatives of recognised independent trade unions otherwise elected representatives.	As for TUPE.
Consult long enough before the transfer.	Consult in good time and at least for a minimum number of days depending on the number of employees it is proposed to dismiss at any one establishment within a 90-day period.
Consult if only one employee affected.	• No need to consult if under 20 employees are to be dismissed. • Consult for at least 30 days if proposing to dismiss 20–99. • Consult for 90 days if proposing to dismiss 100 or more.

Consultation to be with a view to reaching agreement.	As for TUPE. Consultation is not with a view to reaching agreement if the employer has already made up his mind.
Must be told of: • fact, time and reason for the transfer; • legal economic and social implications of the transfer; • measures he envisages taking n relation to his employees; and • if the consulting employer is the transferor measures which the transferee envisages taking in relation to the transferring staff.	Must be given: • details of the reasons for the redundancy; • number and description of those to be dismissed plus the actual number employed in those categories; • method of selection and the procedure and timing of dismissals; • calculation of benefit; • avoidance of dismissals; • reduction of dismissals; and • mitigating the effect of dismissals.
Sanction is a protective award of up to 13 weeks' pay. A week's pay is not capped.	Sanction is a protective award of up to 90 days' pay. Pay is capped at £290 per week. The cap is reviewed annually in February in accordance with the RPI.

Checklist for the acquiring employer   **[12.14]**

The acquiring employer will need to make careful enquiries if he is to avoid the unexpected costs of redundancy. It is suggested he should check the following and try to obtain a warranty or indemnity to support his findings as required.

• Are there any express terms relating to redundancy?

• Do any implied terms based on publication and automatic application exist?

• Do any collective agreements dealing with redundancy exist?

• Have any employees been recently dismissed and could any of those dismissals be for redundancy?

- Has the employer consulted the dismissed individuals?
- Have the full redundancy (and TUPE) procedures been followed?
- Has full notice been given or have wages been paid in lieu?
- Has a full redundancy payment been made?

The indemnity should cover all payments to the individual, including any protective award.

The individual right to statutory redundancy pay [12.15]

To qualify for statutory redundancy pay the employee must satisfy the following conditions and statutory definitions:

- The employee must have been dismissed. This includes the expiry and non-renewal of a fixed-term contract and constructive dismissal as well as direct dismissal by the employer.
- The employee must have at least two years' continuity of employment.
- The reason for the dismissal must be redundancy. Redundancy is defined in *section 139* of the *ERA 1996* as follows:

'For the purposes of this Act an employee who is dismissed shall be taken to be dismissed by reason of redundancy if the dismissal is wholly or mainly attributable to:

(a) the fact that his employer has ceased or intends to cease;

> (i) to carry on the business for the purposes of which the employee was employed by him, or

> (ii) to carry on that business in the place where the employee was so employed, or

(b) the fact that the requirements of that business;

> (i) for employees to carry out work of a particular kind, or

> (ii) for employees to carry out work of a particular kind in the place where the employee was employed by the employer,

have ceased or diminished or are expected to cease or diminish.'

In short, the employer must need to reduce the number of a particular kind of employee. This could be due to a downturn in trading or a desire to increase profits by reorganising the business or part of it.

No entitlement to redundancy pay [12.16]

The employee is not entitled to redundancy benefit in certain circumstances, as defined by statute, where:

- the employer or an associated employer has offered the employee employment on the same terms and conditions (*ERA 1996, s 138*); and
- the employee has been offered suitable alternative employment but has refused it (*section 141*).

If the employee accepts any offer of employment on different terms, whether that employment is suitable or not, the employee is entitled to a trial period of four calendar weeks in the new job. If during or at the end of that period either the employer or the employee decides that the employment is not satisfactory the employment ends, but the rights the employee had before the trial period began have been preserved and he can still bring his claim for redundancy.

Whether an alternative role is suitable or not is often hotly contested.

Suitable alternative employment [12.17]

Where the employee is no longer required he is not entitled to redundancy pay if the employer offers him suitable alternative employment (*ERA 1996, s 141(3)*). In deciding whether the employment is suitable the tribunal will have regard to the contract terms (pay, hours, benefits etc), place of employment, status and security of employment. If the employment is suitable the employee may, nonetheless, have a good reason for rejecting it.

Sometimes there is alternative work but it may not be suitable. The work should be offered even so because a tribunal may find the employer is unfairly dismissing the employee on the ground that the employee may well have accepted the apparently unsuitable work.

The law no longer requires employers to put offers of alternative employment in writing but it is sensible to do so not only as a matter of proof, but also to give the employee sufficient information for him to reach a decision.

Where an alternative position is available and it is suitable, it will be unreasonable for the employee to refuse it. Two problem areas emerge.

1. When is an alternative job suitable?
2. What will be considered an unreasonable refusal?

When presenting the alternative position to the employee, the employer is under an obligation to clearly identify the new position and to set out the differences between it and the original job that is redundant. Only when this has been done is the employee in a position to make a reasoned decision. There may be many reasons for unsuitability, for example:

- it involves an inconvenient geographical relocation;

- it involves greater travelling time to and from work;

- terms and conditions (hours) interfere with unavoidable or important family commitments;

- it requires the employee to accept terms and conditions (hours, pay, holiday entitlement etc) that are less advantageous than the redundant position;

- it does not carry the level of status and responsibility that the employee enjoyed in his previous position; and

- it requires considerable retraining.

Where the employee puts forward reasons why the job is not suitable and they appear reasonable in the circumstances, a tribunal will be inclined to side with the employee in his refusal of the job offered. Conversely, merely stating the offer is unsuitable without further supporting reasons from the employee is unlikely to be acceptable and the tribunal will be inclined to accept the employer's argument of suitability.

The statutory redundancy payment [12.18]

The amount of statutory redundancy benefit payable to the employee is precisely calculated according to a statutory formula:

1. One and a half weeks' pay for a year of employment in which the employee was not below the age of forty-one.

2. One week's pay for a year of employment (not within paragraph 1) in which he was not below the age of twenty-two; and

3. Half a week's pay for each year of employment not within paragraph 1 or 2.

(See the redundancy pay ready reckoner at **12.28**.)

Only 20 years' employment can be taken into account. Where there is more than 20 years' employment the highest paying years are taken into account first. Once the employee reaches the age of 64 payment is reduced each month by one-twelfth so that at 65 the entitlement is nil (*ERA 1996, s 162*).

The week's wage is subject to a cap, currently £290 per week. This cap is reviewed annually each February in accordance with the RPI.

The individual right to contractual redundancy entitlements [12.19]

The employer may have established a contractual scheme giving greater rights to the employee. A typical example would be where the statutory pay entitlement has been enhanced to provide, for example, one month's pay for each complete year of service. Such rights and entitlements are simple contractual arrangements and where the employer breaches the contract the employee can sue for damages.

More complex are implied contractual entitlements. Such entitlements, although not express, may become contractual through custom and practice. For example, where an employer habitually makes an enhanced redundancy payment of the same magnitude over several years and then in a particular case seeks only to adopt the statutory formula. In this case, the employee may claim the right to the enhanced sum because it has become a contractual right through past application.

The right to claim unfair dismissal [12.20]

There are two key requirements:

1. The individual must have been dismissed.

2. He must have at least one year's continuity of employment.

Redundancy is one of the potentially fair reasons for dismissal (*ERA 1996, s 98*) and the dismissal will be fair if proper selection criteria has been applied and a proper consultation procedure has been followed. The redundancy must be substantively and procedurally fair if a claim for unfair dismissal is to be avoided or successfully resisted.

Where other employees hold similar positions to that of the redundant employee the employer will have to justify his selection. The selection process should be objectively justifiable (see **12.10** above). There are situations where the dismissal will be automatically unfair, for example where an employee has been selected for redundancy:

*   on the grounds of maternity;

*   for asserting of a statutory right;

*   for refusing to work in a shop or betting office on a Sunday; and

- for raising health and safety concerns.

Selection on the grounds of race or sex will be a breach of the *Race Relations Act 1976* and the *Sex Discrimination Act 1975*, respectively.

The employer must consult the employee and consider his views before reaching the decision to make him redundant. Failure to consult will make the dismissal unfair unless consultation would be pointless. Consultation is critical to a fair process and must be meaningful.

Failure to allow or facilitate an appeal against a redundancy selection can lead to an unfair dismissal claim. Such a failure may be regarded as an unfair and unreasonable breach of procedure. It is advisable to allow for an appeal against selection.

Unfair dismissal rights and the Employment Act 200[12.21]

In October 2004, the section of the *EA 2002* dealing with dispute resolution came into effect. It requires employers to inform employees in their written statement of particulars of employment of all dismissal procedures. This will include any redundancy procedures.

In addition, a very basic procedure is set out in *Schedule 2* of the Act. The statutory procedure does require an appeal to be available. This procedure is contractual and failure to follow it will render the dismissal automatically unfair. Because it is contractual an employee will be able to bring a breach of contract claim (though not a redundancy or unfair dismissal claim) from day one if the procedure is not followed. Failure to follow the procedure will result in an increase of between 10%–50% in the compensation awarded to the employee.

Collective consultation – the redundancy rules　　[12.22]

The collective consultation requirements for redundancy are much more detailed and precise than those for TUPE transfers. Where there are redundancies connected to a TUPE transfer both sets of rules must be met. The details are in *section 188* of the *Trade Union and Labour Relations (Consolidation) Act 1992*, as amended.

The employer must consult appropriate representatives prior to the dismissal. The appropriate representatives will be union representatives if the employer recognises an independent trade union in respect of the employees affected by the redundancy. Otherwise, where there is no recognised union, the employer must consult employee representatives elected by the affected employees.

Alternatively, the employer can consult existing bodies that are authorised to be consulted and receive information on the proposed dismissals.

Where the employer has to conduct an election the following rules should be followed:

- the employer will make such arrangements as are reasonably practical to ensure that the elections are fair;
- the number of representatives will be decided by the employer but must be such as to represent the interests of all the affected groups, having regard to the number and classes of those employees;
- the employer will decide whether the representatives should represent all employees or particular classes;
- the term for which the representatives stand will be determined by the employer but must be long enough for the information to be given and consultation to take place;
- candidates must be affected employees on the date of the election;
- no affected employee should be unreasonably excluded as a candidate;
- all affected employees must be entitled to vote for employee representatives;
- employees can vote for as many candidates as there are representatives to represent them or, where there are representatives of particular classes, as many candidates as representatives for that class;
- the election, as far as is reasonably practicable, should be secret and the votes must be fairly and accurately counted;
- if an elected representative ceases to be an employee a new representative will be elected in accordance with these rules.

The consultation is not restricted to those who are likely to be dismissed but includes anyone who might be affected by the redundancies, such as retained employees whose work or responsibilities will change. The length of the consultation period is based on the number of persons the employer proposes to dismiss from the establishment concerned. The length of consultation depends on the number of persons it is proposed to dismiss. The rules are as follows:

- nineteen or less dismissed within 90 days – no consultation;
- twenty to 99 dismissed within 90 days – consultation must begin in good time and last for at least 30 days; and

- one-hundred or more dismissed within 90 days – consultation must be in good time and last for at least 90 days.

Case study

MSF v Refuge Assurance plc and United Friendly Assurance [2002] IRLR 324 EAT.

Facts

Before August 1996, Refuge Assurance PLC (Refuge) and United Friendly Insurance PLC (United) were separate companies. They each had field staff operating out of a network of branch offices. Each member of the field staff was assigned to a particular branch office. The employees of Refuge and United included numerous members of the Manufacturing, Science and Finance union (MSF). In May to July that year, talks took place between Refuge and United with a view to a merger. Approximate numbers of staff were discussed between them.

If adopted, the merger would lead to a great reduction in jobs over the next two or three years, but the jobs to be lost were not identified. By August, the merger had been agreed and MSF were given short notice of a press announcement. It was confirmed that there would be a reduction in employees of about a quarter. By September, MSF had complained about the failure of the companies to consult with it earlier and about the manner in which the announcement of the merger had been made.

Findings

It was decided the UK construction of the consultation rules that required a proposal to dismiss employees necessitated there be a firm proposal for the legal obligations to bite. The Collective Redundancies Directive 1975 (75/129/EEC) refers to 'contemplates' which is an earlier stage in the process. UK law does not comply with EEC Directive 75/129. But this Directive will apply in the public sector where employers should consult when dismissals are 'contemplated'.

The *MSF* case also decided that each branch of an insurance company was an establishment so, as there was no single branch involved when 20 or more employees were to be made redundant, the redundancies were spread too thinly across the organisation to necessitate consultation. ➡

If the decision is a 'thing done' then any subsequent consultation does not meet the requirements of the law.

Case study

Middlesborough BC v TGWU and anor [2002] IRLR 332.

Facts

MBC was one of four unitary authorities created on the abolition of Cleveland County Council in April 1996. From the start, the council had serious financial problems. In December 1997, the council appointed a new managing director who, together with four corporate directors, would form the corporate management team (CMT). CMT proposed to address the council's mounting deficit through savings made by staff reductions. Word leaked out. When notices for redundancies were issued, the union's representatives felt there was insufficient time for them to respond. The union alleged the whole idea of consultation was, in the particular circumstances, a sham and that a predetermined position and intention to make up to 150 redundancies had already been taken.

Findings

The EAT upheld the union's contention and made a finding of fact that the employer failed to consult representatives of two trade unions that it recognised, in respect of more than 100 employees that it was proposing to make redundant, within 90 day about ways of avoiding the dismissals. The employer's (CMT) belief that there was no alternative to redundancies did not preclude the tribunal's clear finding that such consultation that did take place about avoiding the dismissals was a sham.

Written information [12.23]

Consultation commences when the representatives receive written notification and must be with a view to reaching agreement. The representatives must be provided with the following written information:

- details of the reasons for the redundancy;

- number and description of those to be dismissed plus the actual number employed in those categories;

- method of selection and the procedure and timing of dismissals;

- calculation of benefit;

- avoidance of dismissals;

- reduction of dismissals; and

- mitigating the effect of dismissals.

The fact that the employer does not have the information because the decision was taken by another organisation is not a defence to failure to consult.

Dealing with employee representatives [12.24]

The employer must reply to any written representation that the appropriate representative may make. Employee representatives are given protection against detrimental treatment for participating in the election of representatives and against dismissal where that is the sole or main reason for dismissal. He will also be entitled to paid time off not only for his duties but now also for training and preparation. Trade union representatives already have similar rights.

Failure to conduct elections or consult in accordance with the legal requirements will allow the representatives and employees to bring a claim for a protective award and obtain up to 90 days' pay. Pay is currently capped at £290 per week. This sum is reviewed annually in February in line with the RPI. The tribunals tend to give an award equivalent to the period for which the employer failed to consult.

The TUPE regulations provide that it is the union or representatives who should bring claims where the claim relates to them. But, in relation to election failures or other cases, a claim can be brought by an affected employee or group of affected employees.

Informing the Secretary of State [12.25]

The Secretary of State must be informed of all redundancies when it is intended to dismiss 20 or more employees. The Secretary of State must also be informed that the collective consultation has begun.

Key points and new developments [12.26]

- The 1981 TUPE regulations did not deal expressly with redundancy. *Regulation 7* of the 2006 TUPE regulations provides that a dismissal for which the sole or principal reason is not the transfer itself, but is a reason connected with the transfer that is an ETO reason, is to be regarded as having been by reason of redundancy.

- The normal redundancy rules will apply to dismissals caused by TUPE except where TUPE impacts on those rules.

- Employees can only claim redundancy benefit where they have been dismissed.

- Employees who are dismissed by the outgoing employer but start work with the incoming employer have not been dismissed but have transferred to the incoming employer under *regulation 4* of the 2006 TUPE regulations, thus making their apparent dismissal a nullity.

- Redundancy dismissals will usually be for an economic or organisational reason and so will be for an ETO reason, but they are still redundancy dismissals for redundancy purposes.

- Even if there is an ETO reason, the redundancy dismissal will be an unfair dismissal unless there is an objective selection process and a proper procedure, including individual consultation, is followed.

- The pool for selection should include all employees doing similar work and not be automatically restricted to the transferred staff.

- It is necessary to follow the collective redundancy consultation procedure as well as the TUPE procedure but these can be combined.

- The sanction for breach by the employer is a protective award of up to 90 days' pay to each affected employee. Pay is currently capped at £290 per week.

Questions and answers   **[12.27]**

Question

If I consult the workplace representatives as required under TUPE, do I also have to consult under the collective redundancy requirements of the *ERA 1996*?

Answer

If it is your intention to make employees redundant wholly or mainly because of a TUPE transfer you will have to comply with both sets of consultation rules, but it should be a simple process to combine them (see **12.13**). ➡

Question

We have just taken over a new contract under a TUPE transfer. The work is very over-manned and we intend to make 50% of the staff redundant. Can we restrict our selection to the staff that transferred to us?

Answer

Not necessarily. You have to include in your selection pool other staff doing similar, though not identical, work. This may necessitate your putting some of your existing staff into the pool.

Question

We have acquired employees under a TUPE transfer and we now need to make staff redundant. Our employees are only entitled to statutory redundancy pay but the transferred employees insist they are entitled to more generous redundancy terms because this is what their previous employer always paid. Is this correct?

Answer

There is a chance that they may be right. You should first check the contract of employment to see if there is an express incorporation of the alleged enhanced terms. Look to see if the contract or written particulars refer to other terms in a handbook or collective agreements because if the handbook or collective agreement deals with redundancy then those terms have been expressly incorporated. The other possibility is the previous employer had published the redundancy policy and automatically followed it consistently through several redundancies. That could make it contractual. But even when the policy is incorporated most employers retain the right to decide how much to pay, preventing the employee from relying on past generosity.

Question

Following a transfer of employees into our business we need to make several employees redundant. We are currently establishing selection criteria. We are having difficulty agreeing the criteria with the elected representatives. They will not agree to certain criteria, in particular attitude and willingness to undertake training. Can we enforce these two criteria?

➡

Answer

The resistance you are experiencing is understandable. You are entitled to choose your criteria for selection but the tribunal will expect such criteria to be objective. Subjective criteria, such as an individual's attitude, is almost impossible to apply it fairly without bias. For this reason criteria containing such subjective elements are likely to make the redundancy process flawed. To continue to use subjective criteria could well lead to a successful claim for unfair dismissal. Ensure the criteria you use are objective and measurable, for example length of service, qualifications, skills and experience.

Question

We have an employee who will not accept a position as an alternative to redundancy. We believe the position to be highly suitable albeit on a different site five miles from the current location. The employee says he cannot accept the new position because he has to check on his dependant grandmother at lunchtime. This, he claims, would be impossible from the new location. Does this make the position unsuitable?

Answer

Quite probably. Provided the reason given is truthful it is likely to be regarded as valid by a tribunal. The tribunal will look at the circumstances of any individual subjectively. In this case, the decision to decline the alternative position will be seen as reasonable and the employee will be entitled to statutory redundancy pay and any contractual entitlements.

Redundancy pay ready reckoner

Complete years of service

Age in years at date of redundancy	2	3	4	5	6	7	8	9	10	11	12	13	14	15	16	17	18	19	20
20	1	1	1	1	—														
21	1	1½	1½	1½	1½	—													
22	1	1½	2	2	2	2	—												
23	1½	2	2½	3	3	3	3	—											
24	2	2½	3	3½	4	4	4	4	—										
25	2	3	3½	4	4½	5	5	5	5	—									
26	2	3	4	4½	5	5½	6	6	6	6	—								
27	2	3	4	5	5½	6	6½	7	7	7	7	—							
28	2	3	4	5	6	6½	7	7½	8	8	8	8	—						
29	2	3	4	5	6	7	7½	8	8½	9	9	9	9	—					
30	2	3	4	5	6	7	8	8½	9	9½	10	10	10	10	—				
31	2	3	4	5	6	7	8	9	9½	10	10½	11	11	11	11	—			
32	2	3	4	5	6	7	8	9	10	10½	11	11½	12	12	12	12	—		
33	2	3	4	5	6	7	8	9	10	11	11½	12	12½	13	13	13	13	—	
34	2	3	4	5	6	7	8	9	10	11	12	12½	13	13½	14	14	14	14	—
35	2	3	4	5	6	7	8	9	10	11	12	13	13½	14	14½	15	15	15	15
36	2	3	4	5	6	7	8	9	10	11	12	13	14	14½	15	15½	16	16	16
37	2	3	4	5	6	7	8	9	10	11	12	13	14	15	15½	16	16½	17	17

Age in years at date of redundancy	Complete years of service																		
	2	3	4	5	6	7	8	9	10	11	12	13	14	15	16	17	18	19	20
38	2	3	4	5	6	7	8	9	10	11	12	13	14	15	16	16½	17	17½	18
39	2	3	4	5	6	7	8	9	10	11	12	13	14	15	16	17	17½	18	18½
40	2	3	4	5	6	7	8	9	10	11	12	13	14	15	16	17	18	18½	19
41	2	3	4	5	6	7	8	9	10	11	12	13	14	15	16	17	18	19	19½
42	2½	3½	4½	5½	6½	7½	8½	9½	10½	11½	12½	13½	14½	15½	16½	17½	18½	19½	20½
43	3	4	5	6	7	8	9	10	11	12	13	14	15	16	17	18	19	20	21
44	3	4½	5½	6½	7½	8½	9½	10½	11½	12½	13½	14½	15½	16½	17½	18½	19½	20½	21½
45	3	4½	6	7	8	9	10	11	12	13	14	15	16	17	18	19	20	21	22
46	3	4½	6	7½	8½	9½	10½	11½	12½	13½	14½	15½	16½	17½	18½	19½	20½	21½	22½
47	3	4½	6	7½	9	10	11	12	13	14	15	16	17	18	19	20	21	22	23
48	3	4½	6	7½	9	10½	11½	12½	13½	14½	15½	16½	17½	18½	19½	20½	21½	22½	23½
49	3	4½	6	7½	9	10½	12	13	14	15	16	17	18	19	20	21	22	23	24
50	3	4½	6	7½	9	10½	12	13½	14½	15½	16½	17½	18½	19½	20½	21½	22½	23½	24½
51	3	4½	6	7½	9	10½	12	13½	15	16	17	18	19	20	21	22	23	24	25
52	3	4½	6	7½	9	10½	12	13½	15	16½	17½	18½	19½	20½	21½	22½	23½	24½	25½
53	3	4½	6	7½	9	10½	12	13½	15	16½	18	19	20	21	22	23	24	25	26
54	3	4½	6	7½	9	10½	12	13½	15	16½	18	19½	20½	21½	22½	23½	24½	25½	26½
55	3	4½	6	7½	9	10½	12	13½	15	16½	18	19½	21	22	23	24	25	26	27
56	3	4½	6	7½	9	10½	12	13½	15	16½	18	19½	21	22½	23½	24½	25½	26½	27½

Complete years of service

Age in years at date of redundancy	2	3	4	5	6	7	8	9	10	11	12	13	14	15	16	17	18	19	20
57	3	4½	6	7½	9	10½	12	13½	15	16½	18	19½	21	22½	24	25	26	27	28
58	3	4½	6	7½	9	10½	12	13½	15	16½	18	19½	21	22½	24	25½	26½	27½	28½
59	3	4½	6	7½	9	10½	12	13½	15	16½	18	19½	21	22½	24	25½	27	28	29
60	3	4½	6	7½	9	10½	12	13½	15	16½	18	19½	21	22½	24	25½	27	28½	29½
61	3	4½	6	7½	9	10½	12	13½	15	16½	18	19½	21	22½	24	25½	27	28½	30
62	3	4½	6	7½	9	10½	12	13½	15	16½	18	19½	21	22½	24	25½	27	28½	30
63	3	4½	6	7½	9	10½	12	13½	15	16½	18	19½	21	22½	24	25½	27	28½	30
64	3	4½	6	7½	9	10½	12	13½	15	16½	18	19½	21	22½	24	25½	27	28½	30

13. Collective Agreements

Enforceability [13.1]

In the UK, collective agreements are rarely enforceable between the contracting employers and trade unions. In addition, there is no legal rule giving employees an automatic right to any collectively agreed benefits. So a provision requiring the transfer of collective agreements from the transferring to the acquiring employer has little effect.

Whilst this may be the current position in the UK, in some EU member states certain collective agreements have considerably greater power and are backed by the force of law. They may be binding on the signatory employers and trade unions, and union members and employees covered by them are frequently entitled to enforce their terms in the courts. Where collective agreements are such powerful determinants of employment terms, the only way to ensure that transferring employees does not suffer detrimental changes after a TUPE transfer is to provide that the collective agreements transfer too.

As a result, Article 3(2) of the EU Acquired Rights Directive 1977 (77/187/EEC) ('the Directive') specifically provides that:

'the transferee shall continue to observe the terms and conditions agreed in any collective agreement on the same terms as applicable to the transferor under that agreement, until the date of termination or expiry of the collective agreement or the entry into force or application of another collective agreement.'

Member states are given an option of putting a time limit on the application of transferred agreements, but they must be observed for at least one year.

Incorporation of the Directive by the UK [13.2]

The UK has incorporated, although not exactly, Article 3(2) in *regulation 5* of the *Transfer of Undertakings (Protection of Employment) Regulations 2006* (TUPE). So, where a collective agreement, which is made with a trade union recognised by the employer, exists before the transfer, it will have effect after the transfer:

'as if it had been made by or on behalf of the transferee with that trade union, and accordingly anything done by or in connection with it . . .after the transfer shall be deemed to have been done by or in relation to the transferee.'

Unlike other parts of employment law, this agreement does not have to be made with an independent trade union. That said, in the UK collective agreements have very little legal effect and as a result Article 3(2) and *regulation 5* have had virtually no impact.

Collective agreements in the UK [13.3]

Collective agreements are usually made between an employer, employers or an employer's association on one side and on the other a trade union or unions. As there is no definition of a collective agreement at common law it is not known whether an agreement made with representatives of the workforce could be a collective agreement. The reported common law cases all involve agreements with trade unions but they do not deal with the question of whether it is essential that one party should be a trade union. Instead, they concentrate on the issue of intention to create legal relations.

It is possible that the body electing the representatives could itself be a trade union if it has a constitution, whether formal or informal, and its main objective is to regulate the relationship with the employer. By way of example, in *Midland Cold Storage Ltd v Turner [1972] ICR 230 NIRC*, a joint shop stewards' committee was held to be a trade union. However, in *Frost v Clarke & Smith Manufacturing Ltd [1973] IRLR 216 NIRC*, a consultative works committee was held not to be a trade union.

Enforceable contract [13.4]

For an agreement to become an enforceable contract in addition to the requirements of an offer, acceptance of the offer and consideration (causa in Scotland), the parties must have an intention to create legal relations. The intention to create legal relations is as perceived using the 'officious bystander' test (objective), not the parties' actual intentions.

At common law there was a presumption that there was no intention to create legal relations in collective agreements (*Young v Canadian Northern Railway Company [1931] AC 83 HL*), although this could always be rebutted.

In *Burke v Royal Liverpool Hospital NHS Trust [1997] ICR 730 EAT*, the Employment Appeal Tribunal (EAT) confirmed that a collective agreement required an offer, acceptance and consideration in the same way as in other contracts, but that legal language was not needed and custom and practice played an important part. Crucially, the lack of an intention to create legal relations made collective agreements unenforceable. In *Ford v AUEF and TGWU [1969] 2 QB 303*, Ford failed in its attempt to obtain an injunction to prevent breach of a collective agreement because there was no intention to be legally bound.

Statutory change [13.5]

A change to the common law position was introduced by *section 34* of the *Industrial Relations Act 1971* (*IRA 1971*) under which written collective agreements were legally binding unless the agreement provided otherwise. It became standard practice to insert a 'TINALEA clause' (this is not a legally enforceable agreement) in all collective agreements and although it is no longer so vital, the practice continues to this day. When the *IRA 1971* was repealed the common law presumption prevailed and became enshrined in legislation.

Today, certain types of collective agreement (as described in *sections 178* and *179* of the *Trade Union and Labour Relations (Consolidation) Act 1992* (*TULR(C)A 1992*)) can be legally enforceable if they are in writing and the agreement states the agreement, or part of the agreement, will be legally binding. The collective agreements concerned are those relating to:

- terms and conditions of employment or the physical conditions of work;

- engagement or non-engagement, or termination or suspension of employment or the duties of employment of one or more workers;

- allocation of work;

- discipline;

- trade union membership;

- facilities for trade union officials; and

- machinery for consultation, negotiations and other procedures.

In practice, the standard TINALEA clause is usually inserted preventing legal enforceability.

Transfer of collective agreements [13.6]

To transfer under TUPE a collective agreement must comply with the requirements of *section 178* of the *TULR(C)A 1992* above. But, under *section 178*, there can be two separate types of agreement. These are agreements between the employer and the union that govern the relationship between them (procedural agreements), and collective agreements concerned with terms and conditions of employment or the relationship between the employer and his employees (substantive agreements). Some collective agreements contain both procedural and substantive elements. The distinction is important but neither the Directive nor TUPE make any distinction between the two types of collective agreement.

Transfer of procedural and substantive agreements   [13.7]

Generally, although procedural agreements transfer under *regulation 5* of the 2006 TUPE regulations, the transfer will have little effect as it is most unlikely that the agreement is legally binding.

Substantive collective agreements that regulate terms and conditions of employment have no effect on employment contracts unless they have been incorporated into the contract. This is normally achieved by an express term such as 'your terms and conditions are such as may be agreed from time to time with the union'. This is a suitably wide term that will enable future collective agreements to be incorporated automatically.

If the collective agreement is incorporated then the terms of the agreement transfer because they are contract terms and do so under *regulation 4* rather than *regulation 5*. If collective agreements are not then, because the employees are not parties to agreements, the employees cannot enforce them or have them enforced against them unless the agreement is incorporated into their contracts. For example, in *Lee v GEC Plessey Telecomunications [1993] IRLR 383*, a collective agreement withdrawing a redundancy scheme did not change the employees' entitlement to the redundancy benefit because they were not parties to the collective agreement.

Case study

Facts

In *Ackinclose and ors v Gateshead Metropolitan Borough Council [2005] IRLR 79 EAT*, A and her colleagues were employed part time in the Council's school meal service. In 1995 their employment transferred to the private sector via a company called Castle View. Later in 2000 the contract reverted back to the Council. In 1997, whilst working in the private sector, changes took place to the national bargaining arrangements in local government. The White Book was replaced by the Green Book, a new collective agreement covering both manual and white-collar local authority employees. Under the Green Book agreement there were advantages to certain employees in respect of a reduction in hours of work for the same level of pay. Castle View did not apply the benefit to the claimants during their employment in the private sector. When employment reverted back to the Council the Green Book principles were applied. A and her colleagues brought a claim for unlawful deductions from wages arguing the Green Book terms should have applied to their time in the private sector by operation of TUPE. ➡

> *Findings*
>
> The EAT held that the contracts which transferred to Castle View incorporated only the White Book and the employees could not claim the benefit of the replacement collective agreement – the Green Book.

Checklist for the acquiring employer [13.8]

For an acquiring employer it is vital to know whether collective agreements are incorporated into the employment contract and also whether the incorporation is wide enough to encompass future changes. Incorporation can occur in various ways. Acquiring employers should check the following:

- Is there express incorporation in an employment contract?

- Is incorporation implied from custom and practice? (In the past this has been difficult to prove, but in recent cases the courts and tribunals have shown a greater willingness to accept this argument.)

- Has a union negotiator been acting as an agent for his members? (If acting as an agent, what is agreed may become incorporated into the contract of employment).

- Has the agreement been mentioned in written particulars? If it has, it is evidence that the employer considers the agreement to be incorporated.

- Was the collective agreement offered to the employees? If it was, it may have been accepted and become incorporated into the contract.

Limited incorporation [13.9]

The courts have interpreted clauses incorporating collective agreements into employment contracts as only incorporating the substantive terms affecting employees' terms and conditions. This will include any procedure relating to the employer/employee relationship, such as a disciplinary procedure, but not a bargaining or negotiating procedure.

New style collective agreements [13.10]

In recent legislation, collective agreements have been used in a completely new way. The legislation concerned sets out rules governing any particular right or activity. It allows the rules to be changed by a collective agreement entered into with a recognised independent trade union or by a workforce agreement. Changes can be made in this way to rights under:

- The *Working Time Regulations 1998* (*SI 1998/1833*);

- The *Maternity and Parental Leave etc. Regulations 1999 (SI 1999/3312)*;

- The *Part-time Workers (Prevention of Less Favourable Treatment) Regulations 2000 (SI 2000/1551)*; and

- The *Fixed Term Employees (Prevention of Less Favourable Treatment) Regulations 2002 (SI 2002/2034)*.

Here the agreement is not to contract terms but to changing statutory rights. For example, *regulation 8(4)* of the *Fixed Term Regulations 2002* provides that:

> 'a collective agreement or workforce agreement may modify the application of paragraphs (1) to (3) of this regulation in relation to any employee, or specified description of employees, substituting for either or both of the conditions set out in paragraph (2), one or more different conditions . . .'.

Collective agreements made under the auspices of these regulations should transfer under *regulation 5* of the 2006 TUPE regulations and be enforceable against the acquiring employer.

Workforce agreements [13.11]

The interesting question is whether workforce agreements made under the stated regulations in **13.10** will transfer? A distinction needs to be made between a 'collective agreement' and a 'workforce agreement'. A collective agreement in the strict sense involves an agreement between one or more employers or employers' associations on the one side and one or more trade unions on the other. A workforce agreement is, in effect, a sort of collective agreement that does not involve a union as such. It is an agreement between an employer and his workers that satisfies certain conditions.

A workforce agreement must satisfy five conditions:

1. It must be in writing.

2. It must be for a fixed term of not more than five years.

3. It must cover all the relevant employees.

4. It must be signed by the duly elected representatives of the employees (or the majority of the employees where there are less than 20 of them).

5. Before the agreement is made available for signature, copies of the text must have been provided to all the employees concerned together, if necessary, with an intelligible explanation of its meaning.

The particular significance of a workforce agreement, as defined above, lies in the fact that such an agreement may supplement or modify various enactments.

A workforce agreement may vary a worker's rights without his individual consent and without the guarantees implied by trade union negotiations. The workforce agreement goes a step further than TUPE. It is the result of non-union negotiations (not merely non-union consultations) and it may bargain away workers' rights, thus reducing minimum standards without the safeguard of approval by a trade union.

The TUPE regulations clearly see workforce agreements as different from collective agreements. Under TUPE, a workforce agreement is made between the employer and elected representatives of the workforce, or an elected representative body or, where there are 20 or fewer employees, with the agreement of the majority of the workforce.

Transfer of workforce agreements [13.12]

Could a workforce agreement be a collective agreement at common law and so transfer under *regulation 5* of the 2006 TUPE regulations? This requires an answer to the question whether collective agreements can only be made with trade unions. Bearing in mind that the objective of TUPE is to preserve employees' rights, it is possible that for the purpose of TUPE workforce agreements will be treated as collective agreements. If neither of these potential solutions are adopted we reach the conclusion that collective agreements made under the stated regulations in **13.10** transfer and workforce agreements do not. This would appear an absurdity.

But workforce agreements are not made with independent recognised trade unions and so are not collective agreements under *section 178* of the *TULR(C)A 1992*. This suggests collective agreements adjusting the stated regulations will transfer and workforce agreements will not. This is not just a point of theoretical interest. The employer who breaches the various regulations incurs penalties. Indeed, under the *Working Time Regulations 1998* he might even be committing criminal offences. In practice, it is vital to know whether the terms in the regulations or the adjusted terms of the workforce agreement apply. If the workforce agreement does not apply but the employer follows its terms, then he will be in breach of the regulations. Until this matter is clarified the safe solution might be for the new employer to enter into a new identical workforce agreement.

Key points and new developments [13.13]

- Collective agreements transfer to the acquiring employer.

- Collective agreements are normally unenforceable in the UK because the parties have no intention to create legal relations.

- Collective agreements may be incorporated into individual contracts and so transfer as a contract term to the acquiring employer.

- If regulations or legislation allow changes to be made to statutory rights by collective agreement such collective agreements should transfer.

- The position of workforce agreements that change statutory rights is unclear.

Questions and answers [13.14]

Question

We are in the process of contracting out our maintenance agreement. As we have had a recognised union for our maintenance and engineering workers for over 25 years our relationship with our employees is almost entirely set out in collective agreements. The transferring employees are very concerned about the effect of the transfer on these agreements.

Answer

Collective agreements will transfer under *regulation 5* of the 2006 TUPE regulations. The drawback from your employees' point of view is that collective agreements are not binding between the union and the employer. So, although the agreements transfer, they will not be enforceable.

Collective agreements which affect employment terms, such as wages, hours or disciplinary and grievance procedures, are often incorporated into individual employment contracts. These terms will transfer under *regulation 4* of the 2006 TUPE regulations that provides the transferring employees transfer on their existing employment terms.

Question

We are in the process of acquiring a business where the workforce is unionised. Collective agreements exist. What should we look out for in trying to determine whether any terms are incorporated into the employment contract?

Answer

This is not always easy to spot. You are right to be wary. Obviously, look first to whether any documentation exists indicating express incorpora-➡

tion. Next, look to custom and practice and whether a term has been incorporated impliedly. More subtle incorporation can be achieved, according to case law, by union members acting as a negotiating agent, a collective agreement being offered and accepted by employees and other employment documentation (such as the written particulars of employment) being regarded as evidence of incorporation where it refers to a collective agreement.

Question

Having recently taken over a business we have inherited a particular group of workers. This group claim they have agreed, by way of a workforce agreement, to vary certain statutory requirements under the *Working Time Regulations 1998*. Am I safe to rely on this agreement as being effective?

Answer

In short, probably not. First, it will only be a valid workforce agreement if it complies with the five required conditions (see **13.11** above). If it does, the agreement is capable of varying statutory rights. Whether it amounts to a collective agreement capable of being transferred under *regulation 5* of the 2006 TUPE regulations is questionable and not settled in law. The definition of collective agreement at common law could be interpreted widely to include workforce agreements where a trade union is not involved, or TUPE construed widely to incorporate workforce agreements within the definition of a collective agreement. Neither of these constructions is certain and it would, therefore, be best practice to enter into a new and identical workforce agreement to avoid being in breach of the *Working Time Regulations*.

14. Union Recognition Agreements

Conditions for application [14.1]

Union recognition agreements are another example of the *Transfer of Undertakings (Protection of Employment) Regulations 2006 (SI 2006/246)* (TUPE) falling short of the requirements in the EU Acquired Rights Directive 1977 (77/187/EEC) ('the Directive'). The law provides indirectly, and imperfectly, that an employer will be taken automatically to have recognised a trade union where there is a transfer of an undertaking or part thereof.

The obligation under *regulation 6* of the 2006 TUPE regulations will only be applied in certain conditions. The conditions are:

- a relevant undertaking or part thereof is transferred;
- the undertaking (or part) maintains a distinct identity in the hands of the transferee;
- a union was recognised by the transferor in respect of a category of employees transferred with the undertaking; and
- the union is independent.

Where these conditions are satisfied the union is deemed recognised by the transferee to the same extent as it was recognised by the transferor. However, this legal obligation is not as straightforward as it might appear.

Representation rights [14.2]

The Directive seeks to ensure that the representation rights of the transferring employees are preserved, unless national law provides for the reappointment of representatives or the reconstitution of the representation arrangements. Article 5 provides that:

> 'If the business preserves its autonomy, the status and function, as laid down by the laws, regulations or administrative provisions of member states, of the representatives or the representation of the employees affected by the transfer . . .shall be preserved.'

Although there is nothing to prevent an employer establishing a system for the election of permanent employee representatives or a form of company council, UK law only requires the existence of representatives on an ad hoc basis to deal with particular events, such as redundancy and TUPE consultation. Therefore, not having a mandatory representation requirement, the UK applied Article 5 to the representation of employees through union recognition agreements but limited it to recognition agreements entered into with independent trades unions. This resulted in *regulation 6(2)* of the 2006 TUPE regulations:

'Where, before such transfer an independent trade union is recognised to any extent by the transferor in respect of employees of any description who in consequence of the transfer become employees of the transferee, then, after the transfer:

(a) the union shall be deemed to have been recognised by the transferee to the same extent in respect of employees of that description so employed; and

(b) any agreement for recognition shall be varied or rescinded accordingly.'

It had been a standard practice for the UK to replace 'representation' or 'representative' in any EU document with 'recognised independent trade union' and 'a representative of such a union' until, in *Commission of the European Communities v United Kingdom of Great Britain and Northern Ireland [1994] IRLR 392 ECJ*, the European Court decided this did not correctly transpose the EU requirements into UK law.

Case study

Commission of the European Communities v United Kingdom of Great Britain and Northern Ireland.

Facts

The case itself concerned the duty of employers to inform and consult with employee representatives under the Collective Redundancies Directive 1975 (75/129/EEC) and the Acquired Rights Directive 1977.

Findings

The UK had failed to discharge its obligations under the Acquired Rights Directive 1977 to inform and consult employee representatives.

The UK responded immediately with the *Collective Redundancies and Transfer of Undertakings (Protection of Employment) (Amendment) Regulations 1995 (SI 1995/2587)*, amending existing domestic legislation to provide for information and consultation to take place with elected representatives whenever the employer had not recognised an independent trade union. Oddly, although *regulation 10* of the 1981 TUPE regulations was duly amended to extend the consultation duty to elected representatives, *regulation 9* of the 1981 regulations (now *regulation 6* of the 2006 regulations) on the transfer of representatives and representation was not.

As a result, under TUPE, only recognition agreements with independent trades unions transfer. Other representation arrangements, such as works councils or recognition agreements with unions that are not independent, do not.

Recognition agreements [14.3]

There is no definition of a recognition agreement at common law. It is assumed that it is an agreement made between an employer(s) and a trade union(s) to regulate the relationship between the union(s) and employer(s) or between the employer(s) and their workers. However, there is a definition for statutory purposes, in particular in relation to time off for union matters, under *section 178(3)* of the *Trade Union and Labour Relations (Consolidation) Act 1992*. This is the definition used in TUPE. *Section 178* of the Act defines a recognition agreement as the recognition of the union by the employer to any extent for the purpose of collective bargaining on any of the following matters:

- terms and conditions of employment or the physical conditions of work;

- engagement or non-engagement, or termination or suspension of employment or the duties of employment of one or more workers;

- allocation of work;

- discipline;

- trade union membership;

- facilities for trade union officials; and

- consultation, negotiations and procedures.

For recognition it is essential that the employer and union *bargain*. It is not enough to provide information or to consult, although bargaining over the format of the consultation procedure would be recognition.

For a recognition agreement to fall within *section 178*, the union must be independent. Whether, in fact, a union is genuinely independent is certified by the Certification Officer (*section 5*). To gain independent status the union must demonstrate freedom from employer influence and show that it has financial independence.

Only recognition agreements that relate to bargaining with independent trade unions transfer under *regulation 6* of the 2006 TUPE regulations. However, theoretically, in the public sector where employers are bound by the Directive as well as by TUPE, representatives and representation arrangements as described in the Directive could also transfer.

Distinct identity   [14.4]

Not every recognition agreement will transfer. The recognition agreement will only transfer if, after the transfer, the transferred undertaking or part of an undertaking maintains a distinct identity from the rest of the employer's undertaking (2006 TUPE regulations, *regulation 6(1)*). The Directive is even more demanding requiring that the undertaking should preserve 'its autonomy'.

Whether the identity is retained is a question of fact. If the undertaking is absorbed into the new employer's business the distinct identity will be lost.

Effect of the transfer   [14.5]

As collective agreements, and therefore recognition agreements, are not legally binding, *regulation 6* of the 2006 TUPE regulations has had little practical impact. As detailed in **CHAPTER 13 – COLLECTIVE AGREEMENTS**, collective agreements are rarely legally enforceable. The agreement would have to be in writing and state that it was intended to be legally binding. What the TUPE regulations give with the one hand (*regulation 6(1)(a)*), they appear to take away with the other (*regulation 6(1)(b)*). The acquiring employer is free to terminate the recognition agreement (unless it has been awarded under the compulsory recognition provisions of the *Employment Relations Act 1999* (*ERA 1999*) – discussed below (**14.6**)).

On a literal interpretation, the provision allows the transferee to vary or rescind forthwith the recognition agreement he is deemed to have entered with the transferor's union upon completion of the transfer of the undertaking. The Employment Appeal Tribunal (EAT) in *Whent v Cartledge Ltd [1997] IRLR 153 EAT* simply assumed a transferee was entitled forthwith to rescind the deemed recognition agreement. The EAT in this case failed to consider the effect, if any, of *regulation 9* of the 1981 TUPE regulations (now *regulation 6* of the 2006 regulations).

Even though the agreement has no legal force the employer usually gives notice to terminate the recognition; either the period specified in the agreement itself or a reasonable period. If notice is given the recognition will continue until notice expires. During this period the union and its members are entitled to all the statutory rights attached to recognition. The ones most likely to apply are paid time off to the union officials to carry out their trade union duties and unpaid time off for members for trade union activities.

Statutory changes [14.6]

There has been a change whereby the *ERA 1999* introduced compulsory recognition. This allows an independent trade union to seek an award of recognition from the Central Arbitration Committee (CAC). Once an award is made the employer and union have to agree a bargaining procedure. If they fail to do so one will be drawn up by the CAC and imposed upon them. The imposed bargaining procedure is a rare example of a legally enforceable arrangement regulating the relationship of employer and union. Under the *ERA 1999* it is a legally enforceable agreement. The employer who is in breach and does not take action to remedy the situation will be in contempt of court.

Unfortunately, the *ERA 1999* has not considered the problem of a TUPE transfer and an award of compulsory recognition.

If the whole of the bargaining unit transfers the recognition agreement will transfer. But the situation is quite unclear when only part of the bargaining unit transfers. In this situation, both the transferring and the acquiring employer will be affected. The law in this area is unsettled. It is not known how the law is to be applied to this situation.

Possible interpretations [14.7]

One possible solution is for the bargaining unit for the compulsory recognition to split into two units and so apply to both employers. Article 6 of the Directive does not seem to prevent this, but it is not known how the *ERA 1999* will be interpreted in these circumstances.

Alternatively, the transfer of a part of the bargaining unit brings to an end the recognition agreement for both employers. Again, there is no guidance on whether this is a reasonable interpretation of the law.

Finally, in the exploration of possible interpretations, the agreement could continue to apply to the employer against whom it was ordered (the transferring employer) but not to the new employer. In respect of all three alternative interpretations, it remains to be seen how the courts will react when cases of similar fact are put before them.

The union abandons its role [14.8]

All of the above assumes that the trade union will positively want to conduct collective bargaining with the transferee employer. If it does not, the transferee cannot compel the union to come to the negotiating table. If the union abandons its role, it may be held that any recognition agreement has lapsed.

Case study

Prison Officers' Association and Wackenhut (UK) Ltd Escort Services (TURI/108/01, 26 September 2001)CAC.

Facts

The GMB was recognised by Group 4. Group 4 transferred part of its undertaking to Wackenhut. The GMB persistently failed to respond to Wackenhut's invitations to negotiate. The Prison Officers' Association then applied for statutory recognition by Wackenhut.

Findings

There was no subsisting recognition agreement to bar that claim. The previous agreement with the GMB was held to have lapsed.

Variation [14.9]

The practical difficulty is that a compulsory recognition agreement remains in force even if there is a change in the circumstances, although the employer (or the union) can apply to the CAC for a variation in the bargaining unit or for complete de-recognition.

A variation can be sought under the provisions of the *ERA 1999* where there is:

- a change in the organisation or structure of the business; or

- a change in the activities pursued by the employer; or

- a substantial change in the number of workers employed in the unit.

Both employers should be able to rely on one of these if seeking a variation.

When deciding whether a new bargaining unit would be appropriate as a replacement for the original one, the CAC's overriding consideration should be the compatibility of the unit with managerial effectiveness. But it can also look at a range of other factors, including:

- national and local and bargaining arrangements;
- the need to avoid fragmentation of bargaining;
- the characteristics of those workers in the unit and those outside it; and
- the location of the workers.

The parties may themselves reach agreement on a change in the bargaining unit, but this too must be accepted by the CAC.

De-recognition applications under the *ERA 1999* can be made where the employees' support for the recognition may be in question. It follows that applications can be made where:

- there are less than 21 employees in the unit (there can be no compulsory recognition unless there are more than 20 employees in the unit); and
- de-recognition is requested by one party.

If the CAC accept the request, and it has to believe there is support for de-recognition in the workforce before doing so, then the support of the employees will be tested by a ballot or by checking whether more than 50% of the workers in the unit are union members.

In practice, employers with established collective bargaining arrangements will want to continue them without fragmentation and, where there is an established union in place, the union representing the transferred staff usually gives way. Employers who do not want to recognise unions have also been able to de-recognise whenever a transferred unit has a recognition agreement. It is this latter strategy that is put at risk by compulsory recognition.

New laws [14.10]

The present situation will be forced to change. Article 5 of the new Acquired Rights Directive 1998 (98/50/EC) ('1998 Directive') repeats the requirement for continued representation where the transferred undertaking retains its autonomy. Importantly, it goes on to deal with transfers where autonomy is not preserved, requiring member states to provide measures to ensure that staff who were represented before the transfer continue to be properly represented until such time as the reconstitution of the representation system takes place, or representatives are reappointed in accordance with national law or practice. This, of course, can only apply where there are prior representation arrangements. Eventually, even the UK may have these.

The EU Directive on Information and Consultation 2002 (2002/14/EC), which establishes a general framework for employee information and consultation in the European Community, requires the establishment of a framework within which employers can share information and consult with their employees through employee representatives. It does not require elected representatives or a company council, but some organisations will adopt that format. If they do, then representation rights will transfer.

As detailed in **11.20**, the *Information and Consultation of Employees Regulations 2004* came into force on 6 April 2005 for undertakings employing 150 or more employees. The regulations implement the *EC Information and Consultation Directive* and apply to undertakings with 100 or more employees from 6 April 2007 and to those with 50 or more employees from 6 April 2008. The European Commission estimates that, once fully implemented by EU member states, the Directive will cover 50% of EU employers.

Key points and new developments [14.11]

- The 1998 Directive provides that where, prior to the transfer, employees in a transferring undertaking had representation rights then, so long as the undertaking preserved its autonomy after the transfer, those representation rights transferred.

- Under the 1998 Directive the representation arrangement could be changed.

- Under TUPE, representation arrangements do not transfer but recognition agreements made with independent trade unions do so as long as the undertaking remains identifiable after the transfer.

- Until 1999, recognition agreements were not legally binding so it was easy when a recognition agreement transferred for the new employer to de-recognise the union.

- The *ERA 1999* has introduced compulsory recognition. It is not clear how this applies in a TUPE transfer.

- The 1998 Directive extends the right to continued representation to transferring undertakings that do not retain their autonomy after transfer.

Questions and answers [14.12]

Question

We do not recognise any unions but we are acquiring some staff under a TUPE transfer that are covered by a union recognition agreement. Do we have to recognise the union? ➡

Answer

If the recognition agreement is with an independent trade union and if the transferring unit remains a distinct identity from the rest of your organisation then yes, the recognition agreement transfers and you will have to recognise the union.

But, assuming the recognition agreement is not a compulsory one awarded by the CAC, you can always de-recognise the union. If the recognition agreement contains a notice clause then comply with the provisions and give the appropriate period of notice to facilitate de-recognition. If there is no notice clause then it is usual to give a reasonable period of notice. This is so even though the agreement is not legally binding.

Question

If there is a compulsory recognition agreement will it transfer under TUPE?

Answer

It is not easy to answer this question. The recognition award will specify the bargaining unit. If the whole unit transfers then the acquiring employer will be bound. The bargaining unit can only be changed or the unit de-recognised through an application to the CAC.

It is not clear what happens if only part of the bargaining unit transfers. The unit may become two units with each being a compulsory recognition unit, or only the original named employer may be bound, or it may be the end of the unit. Only the CAC can end or change a compulsory recognition award.

Question

We have recently acquired part of a business that had an existing union recognition agreement. It would be convenient for us to continue this agreement. We have invited the union concerned to negotiate but have heard very little from it. The union appears to have little interest in continuing the agreement Can we force the union to continue the recognition agreement post transfer? ➡

Answer

According to case law you cannot compel the union to negotiate with you. It may well be the union has intentionally abandoned its role. It is worth clarifying whether this is its intention. If it has abandoned its role, you are free to promote an alternative within the workforce concerned.

Question

Is it true that the EU Directive on Information and Consultation 2002 will change the face of collective consultation and that many more agreements will exist and be capable of transferring?

Answer

It is too early to judge what the full impact will be. The *Information and Consultation of Employees Regulations 2004* came into force on 6 April 2005 for undertakings employing 150 or more employees and apply to undertakings with 100 or more employees from 6 April 2007 and to those with 50 or more employees from 6 April 2008.

The general obligation is on employers to share information and, in certain circumstances, to consult with representatives of their employees about certain business and commercial decisions before such decisions are made. Initially, the new obligations apply to businesses with more than 100 employees. It is not intended the obligations will apply to businesses with fewer than 50 employees. This Directive does not require elected representatives or a company council, but some organisations will adopt that format. If they do, then representation rights will transfer.

15. Insolvency and Related Matters

Insolvency and TUPE [15.1]

It is not the intention in this chapter to deal with the details of insolvency law and the winding up of companies, but rather with the effect of insolvency on (*Transfer of Undertakings (Protection of Employment) Regulations 2006 (SI 2006/246)*) TUPE transfers.

The extent of the Directive [15.2]

The EU Acquired Rights Directive 1977 (77/187/EEC) ('the Directive') does not deal specifically with transfers connected with insolvencies, but the European Court has accepted that insolvency transfers do not lie entirely without its scope. In *Abels v Bedriffs-vereniging voor de Metaal-industrie en de Electro-technische-industrie [1987] CMLR 406 ECJ*, the European Court commented that had the Directive been intended to apply to insolvencies, an express provision would have been provided. In deciding the Directive does not apply where the transferor has been adjudged to be insolvent, it still concluded that the Directive could apply in the course of other proceedings falling short of insolvency, for example the Dutch 'surseance van betaling' under which the company had been granted judicial leave to suspend payment of debts before being put into liquidation.

In *D'Urso v Ercole Marrelli Elettromeccanica Generale SpA [1992] IRLR ECJ*, the court drew a distinction between insolvencies and procedures that permit the business to trade under a receiver with the objective of ensuring its viability. It thought that in those situations the employees should have the same rights as other employees and that the Directive should apply. Finally, in *Jules Dethier Equipment SA v Dassy [1998] IRLR 266 ECJ*, the court stated that the procedure should apply where the substance and form was to allow the business to trade with a view to securing its future. So the Directive will not apply in the case of business closure insolvency but will apply if the business is being run with the object of ensuring its future.

Accordingly, in *Charlton v Charlton Thermosystems (Romsey) Ltd [1995] IRLR 79, [1995] ICR 56 EAT*, there was held to be a relevant transfer for the purpose of the TUPE regulations in a case where a company 'died' as a result of being struck off by the Registrar of Companies for failure to file accounts, and its former directors thereupon assumed control of its business.

Transfer following insolvency [15.3]

There are several reported cases where, following the insolvency of a business, the European Court decided that a transfer of an undertaking had occurred. These were not transfers taking place as part of insolvency or analagous proceedings, but were based on events following the insolvency. In *P Bork International v Foreningen af Arbejdsledere [1989] IRLR 41 ECJ*, the new employer did not buy the business but following an insolvency he bought the insolvent company's assets and carried on a similar business. The court held that this was a transfer of an undertaking.

The UK position [15.4]

In the UK, when a company is wound up or placed in administration, whether enforced by financial circumstances or by choice, a receiver or administrator will be appointed to run the business. Frequently, part of the business can be salvaged and may be transferred to a new owner. This raises three separate questions:

1. The effect of the appointment of an administrator or receiver on the employment contract.

2. The personal liability of the administrator or receiver.

3. Whether there is a TUPE transfer to the receiver or administrator.

Appointment of an administrator or receiver [15.5]

If the administrator or administrative receiver is appointed under the *Insolvency Act 1986 (IA 1986)*, they are agents of the company and so there is no change in the employment contract. The employee remains in the employment of the company and there is no transfer of the business to the administrator. The duty of the administrator is to run the company and where appropriate to sell the business or part of it for the benefit of the company.

The liquidator in a voluntary liquidation is in the same position. He too is an agent of the company but his purpose is to run the company only so far as this is necessary to complete the winding up.

A liquidator appointed by the court is different. He acts under instructions from the court and his appointment does end the contract of employment of each and every employee in the business.

Personal liability [15.6]

If an administrator or receiver adopts the contracts of employment, he will become personally responsible for some employment liabilities from that date (*Insolvency (No. 2) Act 1994*), and must ensure these employment liabilities are met from the company funds before his own. If the administrator continues to employ staff 14 days after his appointment, the contracts will be deemed adopted by the administrator even if the administrator says he has no intention of adopting them. This was the decision of the House of Lords in *Powdrill and Atkinson v Watson [1995] IRLR 269 HL*. The employment liabilities for which the administrator or liquidator becomes personally responsible include wages, salaries and pension contributions. Other employment liabilities do not receive this preferential treatment and remain the responsibility of the company.

The receiver is responsible for the employment liabilities after he takes over the running of the business.

TUPE transfer [15.7]

As long as the administrator or liquidator is acting as the agent of the company there can be no TUPE transfer to him. But the position of a court appointed liquidator is different. There may well be a TUPE transfer to him if he continues to run the business. If he runs the business before selling it, or part of it, he would be the transferring employer under TUPE and there would be two TUPE transfers; one to him and one to the ultimate purchaser. Contrast this with the situations where the administrator or liquidator is an agent of the company. Here there is only one transfer from the company itself to the purchaser.

Series transfers and hiving down [15.8]

Insolvency practitioners obviously favour fast sales and it hardly needs saying that the fewer the liabilities the faster the sale and the higher the price for the business. The business is far more attractive if it can be transferred free of employee liabilities. One favoured technique to achieve this was the so-called practice of 'hiving down'.

There are various ways of hiving down but however the device is structured there are common elements. Briefly, the assets are transferred to another company, usually a new subsidiary of the existing original insolvent owner. The shares in that new subsidiary company or the business now owned by the subsidiary company are then sold to the ultimate purchaser. The final step is for the ultimate purchaser to offer employment (as new employees) on his terms and conditions only to those employees he wishes to employ.

The business debts and excess staff remain the responsibility of the original employer. Staff employed by the ultimate purchaser have no continuity of employment, no employment liabilities and are not entitled to the same terms and conditions as they previously enjoyed. Often the employees were only aware of this process when the ultimate purchaser made his offers of employment to the selected few and the others were made redundant.

Example

An administrator decides that the machine tooling department of Company A is viable and could be sold. He sets up M&T Co and transfers most of Company A's machine tooling plant and other assets to M&T Co, leaving the staff still employed by Company A. Company B then buys the shares in M&T Co. At this point, M&T Co ceases to be a wholly owned subsidiary of Company A. The liability for the staff of Company A does not pass to M&T Co.

Even when this device was used prior to TUPE it was not viewed with favour by the courts.

The effect of TUPE on hiving down   [15.9]

TUPE has considerably restricted the use of hiving down. *Regulation 3(6)(a)* of the 2006 TUPE regulations provides that the transfer of an undertaking may be effected by more than one transaction, thus combining all the various stages of the transaction into one and allowing the employees employed at every stage to take advantage of TUPE. This makes it difficult to use hiving down to shed employee liabilities.

In order to prove that the transfer was effected by more than one transaction, and so bring it within *regulation 3*, it is necessary to show that each of the series of transactions were related to the transfer. The fact the action was taken around the time of the transfer is not conclusive proof of this.

Case study

Longden and Paisley v Ferrari Ltd and Kennedy International Ltd [1994] IRLR 157 EAT.

Facts

Ferrari was in the hands of administrative receivers and planning to dismiss all the staff. Kennedy was considering purchasing Ferrari and, in ➡

---

order to preserve the business during negotiations, provided money to keep the business going. Kennedy also indicated the staff it thought essential to keep the business alive. The next day Mrs Longden, who was not on the essential list, was dismissed. Eight days later Kennedy purchased an option on Ferrari and five days after that it purchased the business by an asset sale from the receivers.

Findings

The Employment Appeal Tribunal held that this was not a series of transactions effecting the transfer to Kennedy. It was 'effected' by the one simple transaction of an asset sale. Mrs Longden's dismissal was not related to the sale but to Ferrari's financial situation.

Preserving hiving down [15.10]

In its defence, hiving down had proved to be a useful tool in insolvencies. Hence, there was an attempt to preserve it in *regulation 4* of the 1981 TUPE regulations while limiting its use to receivers and administrators appointed under *Part II* of the *IA 1986* and the liquidator in a creditor's winding-up petition. The provisions are extremely complicated, are rarely used and may not work.

Regulation 4 of the 1981 regulations postponed the date of the transfer until either the transferee company ceases to be a wholly owned subsidiary of the transferor company, or the relevant business is sold by the transferee company to another person. When this final step occurred, the postponement ended and all the earlier steps would then take place almost simultaneously with the final stage in the process.

Example

Company A (the transferor company) is in administration. The administrator believes the research and development department is viable and can be sold so he transfers the research department to R&D Co, a wholly owned subsidiary (the transferee company) of Company A. Company B (the third party) then buys the business from R&D Co. At this point two transfers occur simultaneously; the postponed transfer from Company A and the sale to Company B. Any employees employed at that time by Company A would transfer to Company B.

Regulation 4 of the 1981 TUPE regulations
in practice [15.11]

The usefulness of *regulation 4* of the 1981 TUPE regulations was virtually destroyed by a decision of the House of Lords.

Case study

Litster v Forth Dry Dock and Engineering Co Ltd [1989] IRLR 161 HL.

Facts

The case involved a business that had gone into receivership. The receivers had successfully negotiated the transfer of the business utilising a newly formed subsidiary. About an hour before the execution of the transfer, the entire workforce was dismissed at the request of the transferees. Some 48 hours later, the new company recruited some of the dismissed employees but on terms and conditions of employment that were less attractive than those they previously enjoyed.

Findings

The House of Lords set out the following process to decide if liability for a dismissed employee transfers to the acquiring employer:

- It must first be decided whether the dismissal was for a reason connected with the transfer. This would make it automatically unfair under *regulation 8* of the 1981 TUPE regulations.

- Then there must be a check to see if there is an economic, technical or organisational (ETO) reason requiring a change in the nature of the workforce which would justify the dismissal and remove the unfairness.

- In the absence of an ETO reason, the employee will have been employed immediately before the transfer and liability will transfer to the incoming employer.

- If there is an ETO reason, then any existing liability will remain with the outgoing employer.

An employee dismissed during the series of transactions forming the transfer will be dismissed for a transfer-related reason. Had he not been dismissed he would still have been employed at the point of transfer and so would have transferred to the acquiring employer. So, if any employee is➡

---

dismissed during any stage of the hiving down process, he will (or rather any liabilities relating to him) still transfer to the ultimate acquiring employer unless the dismissal is unconnected with the transfer or is for an ETO reason. Combining *regulation 4* of the 1981 regulations and *Litster*, employees still employed at the transfer will transfer under *regulation 4* and the liability for those dismissed during the process will transfer under *Litster*.

Case study

A further nail in the coffin of *regulation 4* came in *Maxwell Fleet and Facilities Management Ltd [2000] IRLR 368 Ch D.*

Facts

Maxwell was in administration and had dismissed 41 employees. Fleet Distribution and Management Ltd was willing to buy the business but only after it had been hived down to a subsidiary. To facilitate this, the administrators obtained an off-the-shelf company, Dancequote, and became its two subscriber shareholders. First, it dismissed all the remaining staff. Then it transferred the assets and business of Maxwell to Dancequote as a going concern with Dancequote agreeing that it would not employ any Maxwell staff. Dancequote agreed to sell the business and assets to Fleet on similar terms so Fleet obtained the business as a going concern without the staff. This all took place on one day. Finally, most of the staff accepted employment with Fleet to do similar work to that performed for Maxwell. The employees had put in claims for sums due to them amounting to £355,910.63 based on the dismissal and the transfer. Who had to meet these payments?

Findings

The court decided it was Fleet.

The parties agreed the transfer was indeed a TUPE transfer and so the point in dispute was whether *regulation 4* of the 1981 regulations applied, as Fleet claimed. It certainly looks like a classic *regulation 4* hiving down, a clear series of transactions to achieve a transfer. The business was transferred to Dancequote but the employees were not. When Dancequote sold the business to Fleet this was the final stage in the transactions and at this point there was a transfer under TUPE. But Dancequote employed no staff so none could transfer. Nor did Dancequote have any employment liabilities that could transfer. ➡

The court accepted that no employee could transfer but found that the employment liabilities did transfer from Maxwell to Fleet. It first considered *regulation 4* in the light of the purpose expressed in the Directive and concluded that *regulation 4* was a proper way to apply the Directive in the UK. It allowed the application of *regulations 3* and *5* to be postponed to the final stage in the transfer process in order to protect employees, otherwise employees might be transferred to a shell company part way through the process and be left with little meaningful protection. Instead, the transfer was postponed to the point where part of the business could be sold and their employment preserved. The purpose of the Directive was to protect employment and not to create a way by which employers could avoid their liabilities. So *regulation 4* could only apply in a genuine hiving down where the intention was to secure employment and not to avoid liabilities. The court looked at the substance not the form. This was not a case of a genuine hiving down. In substance this was a single transfer occurring on one day. Liabilities transferred to Fleet.

Transactions over time [15.12]

In *Maxwell* the transactions all took place on one day. Would the answer have been different if they had been spread over time?

Case study

Celtic Ltd v Astley and ors ECJ, 26.5.05 (C-478/03).

Facts

The Government set up Training and Enterprise Councils (TECs) to take over the Department of Employment's training activities in 1989. They were to be staffed by civil servants on three-year secondment contracts. The civil servants would be redeployed in the civil service at the end of their secondment. Arrangements were then made for TECs to employ their own staff and at this stage, nearly five years after the take over, Astley resigned to join TECs. The issue before the ECJ was the commencement date of Astley's continuity of employment. If he transferred under TUPE all his civil service continuity would be included. If he did not, then only his actual service with TECs would count.

Findings

The ECJ held a transfer of an undertaking does not take place in stages. It can only occur on a particular date, namely when the transferee assumes ➡

responsibility for carrying on the business unit transferred. Workers employed on that date will be entitled to the employment protection conferred by the *Acquired Rights Directive* (see **5.2**).

Clearly, *regulation 4* of the 1981 TUPE regulations presented more obstacles than solutions. The situation required change.

New law in insolvency situations [15.13]

The new *Acquired Rights Directive 1998* (98/50/EC) ('1998 Directive') deals specifically with bankruptcies and analogous insolvencies. It contains many new provisions:

- The transfer of rights (Article 3 of the 1998 Directive and TUPE 2006, *regulation 4*) and protection against dismissal (Article 4 and TUPE 2006, *regulation 7*) will not apply to transfers of undertakings where the transferor is the subject of bankruptcy or analogous insolvency proceedings where the intention is to liquidate the assets, and which are being supervised by a public authority or an authorised insolvency practitioner. However, member states can choose to apply the 1998 Directive to these situations should they so wish.

- When Article 3 and 4 apply, either because there is no intention to liquidate the assets or because the member state has extended the application to proceedings where the intention is to liquidate the assets, member states may provide that:

  — employment debts and liabilities will not transfer to the transferee so long as the employee will be able to take advantage of the state guarantee of payments in accordance with the Directive on Protection of Employees in the Event of Insolvency 1980 (80/987/EEC);

  — the transferor (or person exercising his functions), the transferee and representatives of employees may agree alterations to the employees' terms and conditions where this would safeguard employment and ensure the survival of the business;

  — the transfer has to be supervised by a public authority or an approved insolvency practitioner; and

  — there is also an option for member states to apply the power to vary terms to situations of serious economic crisis.

The new 2006 TUPE regulations [15.14]

The new regulations provide that:

- The transferor's pre-existing debts toward the employees do not pass to the transferee (*regulation 8*); and/or

- Employers and employee representatives may exceptionally agree changes to terms and conditions of employment by reason of the transfer itself, provided that this is in accordance with national law and practice and with a view to ensuring the survival of the business and thereby preserving jobs (*regulation 9*).

By these two measures the Government aims to promote a 'rescue culture' where insolvent businesses may be sold as going concerns.

Regulation 8 defines 'relevant employees' as including those who have passed from the transferor to the transferee and those who would have done so but for the fact they were unfairly dismissed by the transferor by reason of the transfer itself or a non-ETO reason connected with the transfer. The net effect of *regulation 8* is to ensure that, where the transfer is in one of the types of insolvency proceedings described (and it is widely drafted), those who transferred to the transferee and those who were unfairly dismissed by the transferor are entitled to receive payments from the Secretary of State in respect of relevant debts incurred by the transferor, just as if they had been dismissed by the transferor in circumstances where the dismissal would have been potentially fair.

The liability for any other debts owed by the insolvent transferor to relevant employees will still pass to the transferee.

Regulation 9 defines a 'permitted variation' to mean a variation that would normally be rendered unlawful under the regulations (because the sole or principal reason for it is either the transfer itself or a reason connected with the transfer that is not an ETO reason) and that is designed to safeguard employment opportunities by ensuring the survival of the organised grouping of employees involved in the relevant transfer.

Protection of payments in insolvency [15.15]

When an employer is insolvent or bankrupt, payments due to the employee are protected in two ways. First, under the *IA 1986* the past four months' wages (including sick pay, maternity pay, guarantee pay, suspension pay, paid time off for trade union duties, paid time off for antenatal care and seeking work in redundancy situations) and protective awards are preferential debts to a maximum sum of £800. Second, to comply with EEC Directive 80/987, *section 182* of the *ERA 1996* allows an employee whose employer is unable to pay (he does not have to be bankrupt or insolvent) to claim from the NIF:

- up to eight weeks' arrears of pay;

- wages during statutory notice;

- a maximum of six weeks' holiday pay accrued in the last twelve months;

- unfair dismissal basic award;

- a reasonable sum as reimbursement for any fee or premium paid by an apprentice or articled clerk; and

- redundancy pay (under *section 166* of the *ERA 1996*).

Key points and new developments   [15.16]

- The European Court has decided that although the 1998 Directive does not apply to transfers taking place within the insolvency process, it does apply where the objective is to secure employment through the transfer of a viable unit.

- In the UK, when a company is in financial difficulties it is placed in the hands of an administrator or liquidator.

- In the UK, when a liquidator or administrator takes control of a company as agent of that company there is no transfer to the liquidator or administrator. But where the liquidating receiver is appointed by the court there is a transfer.

- A transfer cannot be made by a series of transactions.

- The device of hiving down is limited to receivers, liquidators and administrators. But its effectiveness has largely been destroyed by the House of Lords' decision in *Litster v Forth Dry Dock and Engineering Co Ltd*.

- Hiving down cannot be used as a device to avoid the transfer of liabilities.

- The 1998 Directive will not apply to transfers occurring within bankruptcy or insolvency proceedings but will apply where the objective is to preserve employment in a viable unit.

- The 1998 Directive also contains provisions for the variation of terms in transfers in bankruptcy and insolvency and situations of economic crisis.

- The 1998 Directive permits the transfer of employees without the transfer of the full debts owing to them where those debts are secured in accordance with the EEC Directive 80/987.

- The new 2006 TUPE regulations have taken full advantage of the 1998 Directive provisions and came into force on 6 April 2006.

Questions and answers [15.17]

Question

We are thinking of buying the viable part of an unsound business. It is quite likely that there will be a creditor's liquidation. What problems would we face if we took the business on?

Answer

You will have some protection afforded to you under the new 2006 TUPE regulations as they provide the transferor's pre-existing debts toward the employees do not pass to the transferee (*regulation 8* – see **15.14** above). That said, full due diligence remains a prudent requirement.

Question

Our company has recently acquired a part of an insolvent business from a receiver. The receiver was appointed by the court and continued to run the business in order to sell the viable parts. We now need to make some of the staff redundant. Do we need to take into account service before the receiver was appointed?

Answer

When a receiver is appointed by the court all the employment contracts come to an automatic end. The receiver is not acting as agent for the company, but has continued to operate the company. So it is quite likely there was a transfer of an undertaking to the receiver and then, of course, from the receiver to you. This would mean the employees' continuity of employment would extend back to their commencement of continuity of employment with the insolvent company.

Question

We have recently bought some assets of a business that went into liquidation. Are there circumstances where a transfer can follow the insolvency of a business? ➡

Answer

Yes, a transfer can follow the insolvency of a business, for example where following the insolvency the new employer buys the assets of the business and carries on a similar business.

Question

How long does an administrator or receiver have before being deemed to have adopted the contracts of employment of the employees of a business and thereby becomes personally liable for some employment liabilities?

Answer

If the administrator continues to employ staff 14 days after his appointment, the contracts will be deemed adopted by the administrator even if the administrator says he has no intention of adopting them. The employment liabilities for which the administrator or liquidator become personally responsible include wages, salaries and pension contributions.

Question

Can I avoid a transfer under the TUPE regulations and the attaching liabilities by making a series of transfers and, in effect, hiving down the business?

Answer

First, TUPE has considerably restricted the use of hiving down. *Regulation 3(6)* of the 2006 TUPE regulations provides that the transfer of an undertaking may be effected by more than one transaction. Second, in *Litster v Forth Dry Dock and Engineering Co Ltd*, the House of Lords held that an employee dismissed during the series of transactions forming the transfer will be dismissed for a transfer-related reason.

Question

Will there still be a relevant transfer for the purposes of the TUPE regulations if it takes effect over a period of time? ➡

Answer

No. According to the ECJ in *Celtic Ltd v Astley and ors*, a transfer of an undertaking does not take place in stages. It can only occur on a particular date, namely when the transferee assumes responsibility for carrying on the business unit transferred.

16. Special Cases

Workers – a wide definition [16.1]

Whereas at one time employers had the option of engaging employees or using the services of the self-employed, the situation has become more complicated. Now there are a growing band of workers who fit into neither the employed or self-employed category but have some of the attributes of both. They may have the commitment and continuous working relationship of the employee with greater freedom over some aspects of the relationship, but lack the independence of the truly self-employed. These individuals who fall halfway between employment and self-employment are generally referred to as 'self-employed but not genuinely running their own business'. They have become an important group because some recent legislation applies to 'workers' rather than 'employees' and 'workers' encompasses both employees and the self-employed that do not run their own business.

The application of TUPE [16.2]

Despite the above trend with new legislation, TUPE (*Transfer of Undertakings (Protection of Employment) Regulations 2006 (SI 2006/246)*) only applies to individuals who work under a contract of service or apprenticeship. That is to say it only applies to employees. Persons working under contracts for the provision of services are expressly excluded (*regulation 2*). So the self-employed persons, whether genuinely running their own business or not, will not transfer under TUPE.

Before deciding that a person is self-employed and therefore will not transfer under TUPE, it is important to look at the substance of the contract rather than just the form. Contracts expressed to be of self-employment can sometimes be found by the courts and tribunals to be contracts of employment. This can be illustrated by the self-employed construction workers cases where the employees' contract stated they were self-employed but they only worked for one employer. In *Lee v (1) Chung (2) Shun Shing Construction & Engineering Co Ltd [990] IRLR236 PC*, the worker was an employee and in *Byrne Brothers (Formwork) Ltd v Baird [2002] IRLR 96 EAT*, the workers were self-employed but not genuinely running their own business. Each case depends on the wording of the contract and the surrounding facts so a thorough investigation is essential.

'Employee' will not include agency or temporary staff unless they have become the employee of the transferring employer.

TUPE protection and working abroad [16.3]

The application of the EU Acquired Rights Directive 1977 (77/187/EEC) ('the Directive') is limited to the territorial scope of the European Economic Area (EEA). TUPE only applies to undertakings, or parts of undertakings, that were situated in the UK immediately before the transfer. However, undertakings situated in the UK can have employees who are working abroad. These are the employees with whom this section is concerned.

Until 1999, most UK employment protection legislation was restricted to persons employed wholly or mainly in the United Kingdom of Great Britain and Northern Ireland, or to those who ordinarily work in the UK. But following a Directive on workers posted abroad (Posted Workers Directive 1996 (96/71/EC)), it was necessary to amend this. So the provisions in the *Employment Rights Act 1996* and discrimination legislation limiting the application of the legislation to those persons working in the UK were repealed. The 2006 TUPE regulations brought this area of employment law in line with other employment rights legislation. Whether or not an employee working abroad is able to bring a claim under the regulations will in future depend on the normal principles of international law.

Ships and seafarers [16.4]

Matters relating to the transfer of ships are often treated differently from the transfer of other property and TUPE is no exception. The Directive itself in Article 1(3) states quite bluntly that 'this Directive shall not apply to seagoing vessels.' This was repeated in a more ambiguous way in *regulation 2(2)* of the 1981 TUPE regulations that stated:

> 'references in these regulations to the transfer of part of an undertaking are references to a part which is being transferred as a business and, accordingly, do not include references to the transfer of a ship without more.'

The 2006 regulations contain no provision equivalent to *regulation 2(2)* of the 1981 regulations. It would appear the Government took the view that this provision was declaratory only and added nothing to the substance or effect of the regulations, since the sale of a ship (with its crew) could not itself constitute a relevant transfer in any event, unless it was sold as part of a business undertaking.

Where there is a transfer of a ship plus crew, in principle, the TUPE regulations would apply to protect the employment of the crew.

Death of a single employer [16.5]

It is clear the TUPE regulations are not intended to apply to the case of a transfer of an undertaking from the deceased to his personal representatives. The regulations operate to preserve those contracts of employment that would otherwise have been terminated by the transfer (*regulation 4(1)*). However, where an individual employer dies, the contracts of his employees are terminated by his death and not by the transfer of the ownership of the business to the personal representatives. Therefore, the regulations have no operation and the transfer does not preserve the contract of employment.

There is a possible conflict here between domestic law and community law, for example if an employee's employer has died and he reasonably expects, but is not offered, new or renewed employment with the personal representatives. In this case, the employee is, on the face of it, entitled to his redundancy payment from the deceased's estate but he cannot insist he should be given continued employment. Nor does he have a claim for unfair dismissal since frustration (the employer's death) is not a dismissal for the purposes of unfair dismissal. It is arguable in such circumstances that the employee, under the Directive, may deem his contract preserved as against the personal representatives; therefore any refusal to employ him is a constructive dismissal. This argument is plausible, uncertain and, as yet, untested.

Employer's liability insurance [16.6]

In *Bernadone v Pall Mall Services Group and Martin v Lancashire County Council [2000] IRLR 487*, the Court of Appeal held that not only could liability for an industrial accident in tort be transferred by *regulation 5* of the 1981 TUPE regulations, but so too could the insured employer's right to indemnity under an insurance policy. This right will transfer to the transferee. The court held the right was one 'arising from' or 'in connection with' the employee's contract of employment within the meaning of *regulation 5(2)(a)*. The insurer had received the premium in respect of the liability, therefore, there was no good reason why the regulation should be construed in such a way as to enable the insurers to keep the premium but avoid the liability.

The Government considered the Court of Appeal's judgment in the above cases was satisfactory from a legal point of view. Therefore, *regulation 17* of the 2006 regulations provides for the transferor and transferee to be jointly and severally liable for liabilities to employees for injury or disease arising from their pre-transfer employment.

Key points and new developments [16.7]

- Only employees and apprentices are covered by TUPE. The self-employed and agency workers are excluded.

- Whether or not an employee working abroad is able to bring a claim under the 2006 regulations will in future depend on the normal principles of international law.

- Employees working outside the UK have only limited protection. They cannot bring claims of automatic unfair dismissal or in respect of breaches of the information and consultation process.

- The Directive does not apply outside the EEA territorial waters. Further to the decision in *R v Secretary of State for Trade and Industry, ex parte Greenpeace Ltd (CO 1336/00)*, TUPE regulations do apply to the continental shelf.

- The transfer of seagoing ships is not necessarily excluded from TUPE. Much will depend on whether the sale of a ship (with its crew) was sold as part of a business undertaking.

Questions and answers [16.8]

Question

We are about to buy a business as a going concern. It has a number of individuals working within its IT department that have contracts expressing them to be self-employed contractors. Are we safe to assume TUPE will not apply to them?

Answer

Before deciding that a person is self-employed and therefore will not transfer under TUPE, it is important to look at the substance of the contract rather than just the form. Contracts expressed to be of self-employment can be found by the courts and tribunals to be contracts of employment. Look at the real relationship between the parties, not the labels that have been attached to them. They may be classified as workers that are self-employed but not genuinely running their own business. Conversely, they may be regarded as employees. Each case will turn on its own facts. ➡

Question

To what extent is an employee working outside the UK protected by TUPE?

Answer

The 1981 TUPE regulations only applied in full when the employee ordinarily worked in the UK. The 2006 TUPE regulations brought this area of employment law in line with other employment rights legislation. Whether or not an employee working abroad is able to bring a claim under the regulations will in future depend on the normal principles of international law.

Question

If a seagoing ship is transferred can the crew rely on TUPE to protect their employment?

Answer

Possibly. The 2006 regulations contain no provision equivalent to *regulation 2(2)* of the 1981 regulations. It would appear the Government took the view that this provision was declaratory only and added nothing to the substance or effect of the regulations, since the sale of a ship (with its crew) could not itself constitute a relevant transfer in any event, unless it was sold as part of a business undertaking.

Where there is a transfer of a ship plus crew, in principle, the TUPE regulations would apply to protect the employment of the crew.

TRANSFER OF UNDERTAKINGS (PROTECTION OF EMPLOYMENT) REGULATIONS 2006, SI 2006/246

1   Citation, commencement and extent

(1) These Regulations may be cited as the Transfer of Undertakings (Protection of Employment) Regulations 2006.

(2) These Regulations shall come into force on 6 April 2006.

(3) These Regulations shall extend to Northern Ireland, except where otherwise provided.

2   Interpretation

(1) In these Regulations—
'assigned' means assigned other than on a temporary basis;
'collective agreement', 'collective bargaining' and 'trade union' have the same meanings respectively as in the 1992 Act;
'contract of employment' means any agreement between an employee and his employer determining the terms and conditions of his employment;
references to 'contractor' in regulation 3 shall include a sub-contractor;
'employee' means any individual who works for another person whether under a contract of service or apprenticeship or otherwise but does not include anyone who provides services under a contract for services and references to a person's employer shall be construed accordingly;
'insolvency practitioner' has the meaning given to the expression by Part XIII of the Insolvency Act 1986;
references to 'organised grouping of employees' shall include a single employee;
'recognised' has the meaning given to the expression by section 178(3) of the 1992 Act;
'relevant transfer' means a transfer or a service provision change to which these Regulations apply in accordance with regulation 3 and 'transferor' and 'transferee' shall be construed accordingly and in the case of a service provision change falling within regulation 3(1)(b), 'the transferor' means the person who carried out the activities prior to the service provision change and 'the transferee' means the person who carries out the activities as a result of the service provision change;'the 1992 Act' means the Trade Union and Labour Relations (Consolidation) Act 1992;'the 1996 Act' means the Employment Rights Act 1996;'the 1996 Tribunals Act' means the Employment Tribunals Act 1996;'the 1981 Regulations' means the Transfer of Undertakings (Protection of Employment) Regulations 1981.

(2) For the purposes of these Regulations the representative of a trade union recognised by an employer is an official or other person authorised to carry on collective bargaining with that employer by that trade union.

(3) In the application of these Regulations to Northern Ireland the Regulations shall have effect as set out in Schedule 1.

3   A relevant transfer

(1) These Regulations apply to—
(a)   a transfer of an undertaking, business or part of an undertaking or business situated immediately before the transfer in the United Kingdom to another person where there is a transfer of an economic entity which retains its identity;
(b) · a service provision change, that is a situation in which—
  (i)   activities cease to be carried out by a person ('a client') on his own behalf and are carried out instead by another person on the client's behalf ('a contractor');
  (ii)   activities cease to be carried out by a contractor on a client's behalf (whether or not those activities had previously been carried out by the client on his own behalf) and are carried out instead by another person ('a subsequent contractor') on the client's behalf; or
  (iii) activities cease to be carried out by a contractor or a subsequent contractor on a client's behalf (whether or not those activities had previously been carried out by the client on his own behalf) and are carried out instead by the client on his own behalf,
        and in which the conditions set out in paragraph (3) are satisfied.

(2) In this regulation 'economic entity' means an organised grouping of resources which has the objective of pursuing an economic activity, whether or not that activity is central or ancillary.

(3) The conditions referred to in paragraph (1)(b) are that—
(a)   immediately before the service provision change—
  (i)   there is an organised grouping of employees situated in Great Britain which has as its principal purpose the carrying out of the activities concerned on behalf of the client;
  (ii)   the client intends that the activities will, following the service provision change, be carried out by the transferee other than in connection with a single specific event or task of short-term duration; and
(b)   the activities concerned do not consist wholly or mainly of the supply of goods for the client's use.

(4) Subject to paragraph (1), these Regulations apply to—
(a)   public and private undertakings engaged in economic activities whether or not they are operating for gain;
(b)   a transfer or service provision change howsoever effected notwithstanding—
  (i)   that the transfer of an undertaking, business or part of an undertaking or business is governed or effected by the law of a country or territory outside the United Kingdom or that the service provision change is governed or effected by the law of a country or territory outside Great Britain;
  (ii)   that the employment of persons employed in the undertaking, business or part transferred or, in the case of a service provision change, persons employed in the organised grouping of employees, is governed by any such law;

(c) a transfer of an undertaking, business or part of an undertaking or business (which may also be a service provision change) where persons employed in the undertaking, business or part transferred ordinarily work outside the United Kingdom.

(5) An administrative reorganisation of public administrative authorities or the transfer of administrative functions between public administrative authorities is not a relevant transfer.

(6) A relevant transfer—
(a) may be effected by a series of two or more transactions; and
(b) may take place whether or not any property is transferred to the transferee by the transferor.

(7) Where, in consequence (whether directly or indirectly) of the transfer of an undertaking, business or part of an undertaking or business which was situated immediately before the transfer in the United Kingdom, a ship within the meaning of the Merchant Shipping Act 1995 registered in the United Kingdom ceases to be so registered, these Regulations shall not affect the right conferred by section 29 of that Act (right of seamen to be discharged when ship ceases to be registered in the United Kingdom) on a seaman employed in the ship.

4   Effect of relevant transfer on contracts of employment

(1) Except where objection is made under paragraph (7), a relevant transfer shall not operate so as to terminate the contract of employment of any person employed by the transferor and assigned to the organised grouping of resources or employees that is subject to the relevant transfer, which would otherwise be terminated by the transfer, but any such contract shall have effect after the transfer as if originally made between the person so employed and the transferee.

(2) Without prejudice to paragraph (1), but subject to paragraph (6), and regulations 8 and 15(9), on the completion of a relevant transfer—
(a) all the transferor's rights, powers, duties and liabilities under or in connection with any such contract shall be transferred by virtue of this regulation to the transferee; and
(b) any act or omission before the transfer is completed, of or in relation to the transferor in respect of that contract or a person assigned to that organised grouping of resources or employees, shall be deemed to have been an act or omission of or in relation to the transferee.

(3) Any reference in paragraph (1) to a person employed by the transferor and assigned to the organised grouping of resources or employees that is subject to a relevant transfer, is a reference to a person so employed immediately before the transfer, or who would have been so employed if he had not been dismissed in the circumstances described in regulation 7(1), including, where the transfer is effected by a series of two or more transactions, a person so employed and assigned or who would have been so employed and assigned immediately before any of those transactions.

(4) Subject to regulation 9, in respect of a contract of employment that is, or will be, transferred by paragraph (1), any purported variation of the contract shall be void if the sole or principal reason for the variation is—
(a) the transfer itself; or

(b)   a reason connected with the transfer that is not an economic, technical or organisational reason entailing changes in the workforce.

(5)   Paragraph (4) shall not prevent the employer and his employee, whose contract of employment is, or will be, transferred by paragraph (1), from agreeing a variation of that contract if the sole or principal reason for the variation is—

(a)   a reason connected with the transfer that is an economic, technical or organisational reason entailing changes in the workforce; or

(b)   a reason unconnected with the transfer.

(6)   Paragraph (2) shall not transfer or otherwise affect the liability of any person to be prosecuted for, convicted of and sentenced for any offence.

(7)   Paragraphs (1) and (2) shall not operate to transfer the contract of employment and the rights, powers, duties and liabilities under or in connection with it of an employee who informs the transferor or the transferee that he objects to becoming employed by the transferee.

(8)   Subject to paragraphs (9) and (11), where an employee so objects, the relevant transfer shall operate so as to terminate his contract of employment with the transferor but he shall not be treated, for any purpose, as having been dismissed by the transferor.

(9)   Subject to regulation 9, where a relevant transfer involves or would involve a substantial change in working conditions to the material detriment of a person whose contract of employment is or would be transferred under paragraph (1), such an employee may treat the contract of employment as having been terminated, and the employee shall be treated for any purpose as having been dismissed by the employer.

(10)   No damages shall be payable by an employer as a result of a dismissal falling within paragraph (9) in respect of any failure by the employer to pay wages to an employee in respect of a notice period which the employee has failed to work.

(11)   Paragraphs (1), (7), (8) and (9) are without prejudice to any right of an employee arising apart from these Regulations to terminate his contract of employment without notice in acceptance of a repudiatory breach of contract by his employer.

5   Effect of relevant transfer on collective agreements

Where at the time of a relevant transfer there exists a collective agreement made by or on behalf of the transferor with a trade union recognised by the transferor in respect of any employee whose contract of employment is preserved by regulation 4(1) above, then—

(a)   without prejudice to sections 179 and 180 of the 1992 Act (collective agreements presumed to be unenforceable in specified circumstances) that agreement, in its application in relation to the employee, shall, after the transfer, have effect as if made by or on behalf of the transferee with that trade union, and accordingly anything done under or in connection with it, in its application in relation to the employee, by or in relation to the transferor before the transfer, shall, after the transfer, be deemed to have been done by or in relation to the transferee; and

(b)   any order made in respect of that agreement, in its application in relation to the employee, shall, after the transfer, have effect as if the transferee were a party to the agreement.

6 Effect of relevant transfer on trade union recognition

(1) This regulation applies where after a relevant transfer the transferred organised grouping of resources or employees maintains an identity distinct from the remainder of the transferee's undertaking.

(2) Where before such a transfer an independent trade union is recognised to any extent by the transferor in respect of employees of any description who in consequence of the transfer become employees of the transferee, then, after the transfer—
(a) the trade union shall be deemed to have been recognised by the transferee to the same extent in respect of employees of that description so employed; and
(b) any agreement for recognition may be varied or rescinded accordingly.

7 Dismissal of employee because of relevant transfer

(1) Where either before or after a relevant transfer, any employee of the transferor or transferee is dismissed, that employee shall be treated for the purposes of Part X of the 1996 Act (unfair dismissal) as unfairly dismissed if the sole or principal reason for his dismissal is—
(a) the transfer itself; or
(b) a reason connected with the transfer that is not an economic, technical or organisational reason entailing changes in the workforce.

(2) This paragraph applies where the sole or principal reason for the dismissal is a reason connected with the transfer that is an economic, technical or organisational reason entailing changes in the workforce of either the transferor or the transferee before or after a relevant transfer.

(3) Where paragraph (2) applies—
(a) paragraph (1) shall not apply;
(b) without prejudice to the application of section 98(4) of the 1996 Act (test of fair dismissal), the dismissal shall, for the purposes of sections 98(1) and 135 of that Act (reason for dismissal), be regarded as having been for redundancy where section 98(2)(c) of that Act applies, or otherwise for a substantial reason of a kind such as to justify the dismissal of an employee holding the position which that employee held.

(4) The provisions of this regulation apply irrespective of whether the employee in question is assigned to the organised grouping of resources or employees that is, or will be, transferred.

(5) Paragraph (1) shall not apply in relation to the dismissal of any employee which was required by reason of the application of section 5 of the Aliens Restriction (Amendment) Act 1919 to his employment.

(6) Paragraph (1) shall not apply in relation to a dismissal of an employee if the application of section 94 of the 1996 Act to the dismissal of the employee is excluded by or under any provision of the 1996 Act, the 1996 Tribunals Act or the 1992 Act.

8 Insolvency

(1) If at the time of a relevant transfer the transferor is subject to relevant insolvency proceedings paragraphs (2) to (6) apply.

(2) In this regulation 'relevant employee' means an employee of the transferor—

(a) whose contract of employment transfers to the transferee by virtue of the operation of these Regulations; or
(b) whose employment with the transferor is terminated before the time of the relevant transfer in the circumstances described in regulation 7(1).

(3) The relevant statutory scheme specified in paragraph (4)(b) (including that sub-paragraph as applied by paragraph 5 of Schedule 1) shall apply in the case of a relevant employee irrespective of the fact that the qualifying requirement that the employee's employment has been terminated is not met and for those purposes the date of the transfer shall be treated as the date of the termination and the transferor shall be treated as the employer.

(4) In this regulation the 'relevant statutory schemes' are—
(a) Chapter VI of Part XI of the 1996 Act;
(b) Part XII of the 1996 Act.

(5) Regulation 4 shall not operate to transfer liability for the sums payable to the relevant employee under the relevant statutory schemes.

(6) In this regulation 'relevant insolvency proceedings' means insolvency proceedings which have been opened in relation to the transferor not with a view to the liquidation of the assets of the transferor and which are under the supervision of an insolvency practitioner.

(7) Regulations 4 and 7 do not apply to any relevant transfer where the transferor is the subject of bankruptcy proceedings or any analogous insolvency proceedings which have been instituted with a view to the liquidation of the assets of the transferor and are under the supervision of an insolvency practitioner.

9 Variations of contract where transferors are subject to relevant insolvency proceedings

(1) If at the time of a relevant transfer the transferor is subject to relevant insolvency proceedings these Regulations shall not prevent the transferor or transferee (or an insolvency practitioner) and appropriate representatives of assigned employees agreeing to permitted variations.

(2) For the purposes of this regulation 'appropriate representatives' are—
(a) if the employees are of a description in respect of which an independent trade union is recognised by their employer, representatives of the trade union; or
(b) in any other case, whichever of the following employee representatives the employer chooses—
  (i) employee representatives appointed or elected by the assigned employees (whether they make the appointment or election alone or with others) otherwise than for the purposes of this regulation, who (having regard to the purposes for, and the method by which they were appointed or elected) have authority from those employees to agree permitted variations to contracts of employment on their behalf;
  (ii) employee representatives elected by assigned employees (whether they make the appointment or election alone or with others) for these particular purposes, in an election satisfying requirements identical to those contained in regulation 14 except those in regulation 14(1)(d).

(3) An individual may be an appropriate representative for the purposes of both this regulation and regulation 13 provided that where the representative is not a trade

union representative he is either elected by or has authority from assigned employees (within the meaning of this regulation) and affected employees (as described in regulation 13(1)).

(4) In section 168 of the 1992 Act (time off for carrying out trade union duties) in subsection (1), after paragraph (c) there is inserted—

', or

(d) negotiations with a view to entering into an agreement under regulation 9 of the Transfer of Undertakings (Protection of Employment) Regulations 2006 that applies to employees of the employer, or

(e) the performance on behalf of employees of the employer of functions related to or connected with the making of an agreement under that regulation.'.

(5) Where assigned employees are represented by non-trade union representatives—

(a) the agreement recording a permitted variation must be in writing and signed by each of the representatives who have made it or, where that is not reasonably practicable, by a duly authorised agent of that representative; and

(b) the employer must, before the agreement is made available for signature, provide all employees to whom it is intended to apply on the date on which it is to come into effect with copies of the text of the agreement and such guidance as those employees might reasonably require in order to understand it fully.

(6) A permitted variation shall take effect as a term or condition of the assigned employee's contract of employment in place, where relevant, of any term or condition which it varies.

(7) In this regulation—

'assigned employees' means those employees assigned to the organised grouping of resources or employees that is the subject of a relevant transfer;'permitted variation' is a variation to the contract of employment of an assigned employee where—

(a) the sole or principal reason for it is the transfer itself or a reason connected with the transfer that is not an economic, technical or organisational reason entailing changes in the workforce; and

(b) it is designed to safeguard employment opportunities by ensuring the survival of the undertaking, business or part of the undertaking or business that is the subject of the relevant transfer;

'relevant insolvency proceedings' has the meaning given to the expression by regulation 8(6).

10   Pensions

(1) Regulations 4 and 5 shall not apply—

(a) to so much of a contract of employment or collective agreement as relates to an occupational pension scheme within the meaning of the Pension Schemes Act 1993; or

(b) to any rights, powers, duties or liabilities under or in connection with any such contract or subsisting by virtue of any such agreement and relating to such a scheme or otherwise arising in connection with that person's employment and relating to such a scheme.

(2) For the purposes of paragraphs (1) and (3), any provisions of an occupational pension scheme which do not relate to benefits for old age, invalidity or survivors shall not be treated as being part of the scheme.

(3) An employee whose contract of employment is transferred in the circumstances described in regulation 4(1) shall not be entitled to bring a claim against the transferor for—

(a) breach of contract; or

(b) constructive unfair dismissal under section 95(1)(c) of the 1996 Act,

arising out of a loss or reduction in his rights under an occupational pension scheme in consequence of the transfer, save insofar as the alleged breach of contract or dismissal (as the case may be) occurred prior to the date on which these Regulations took effect.

11 Notification of Employee Liability Information

(1) The transferor shall notify to the transferee the employee liability information of any person employed by him who is assigned to the organised grouping of resources or employees that is the subject of a relevant transfer—

(a) in writing; or

(b) by making it available to him in a readily accessible form.

(2) In this regulation and in regulation 12 'employee liability information' means—

(a) the identity and age of the employee;

(b) those particulars of employment that an employer is obliged to give to an employee pursuant to section 1 of the 1996 Act;

(c) information of any—

(i) disciplinary procedure taken against an employee;

(ii) grievance procedure taken by an employee,

within the previous two years, in circumstances where the Employment Act 2002 (Dispute Resolution) Regulations 2004 apply;

(d) information of any court or tribunal case, claim or action—

(i) brought by an employee against the transferor, within the previous two years;

(ii) that the transferor has reasonable grounds to believe that an employee may bring against the transferee, arising out of the employee's employment with the transferor; and

(e) information of any collective agreement which will have effect after the transfer, in its application in relation to the employee, pursuant to regulation 5(a).

(3) Employee liability information shall contain information as at a specified date not more than fourteen days before the date on which the information is notified to the transferee.

(4) The duty to provide employee liability information in paragraph (1) shall include a duty to provide employee liability information of any person who would have been employed by the transferor and assigned to the organised grouping of resources or employees that is the subject of a relevant transfer immediately before the transfer if he had not been dismissed in the circumstances described in regulation 7(1), including, where the transfer is effected by a series of two or more transactions, a person so employed and assigned or who would have been so employed and assigned immediately before any of those transactions.

(5) Following notification of the employee liability information in accordance with this regulation, the transferor shall notify the transferee in writing of any change in the employee liability information.

(6) A notification under this regulation shall be given not less than fourteen days before the relevant transfer or, if special circumstances make this not reasonably practicable, as soon as reasonably practicable thereafter.

(7) A notification under this regulation may be given—
(a) in more than one instalment;
(b) indirectly, through a third party.

12   Remedy for failure to notify employee liability information

(1) On or after a relevant transfer, the transferee may present a complaint to an employment tribunal that the transferor has failed to comply with any provision of regulation 11.

(2) An employment tribunal shall not consider a complaint under this regulation unless it is presented—
(a) before the end of the period of three months beginning with the date of the relevant transfer;
(b) within such further period as the tribunal considers reasonable in a case where it is satisfied that it was not reasonably practicable for the complaint to be presented before the end of that period of three months.

(3) Where an employment tribunal finds a complaint under paragraph (1) well-founded, the tribunal—
(a) shall make a declaration to that effect; and
(b) may make an award of compensation to be paid by the transferor to the transferee.

(4) The amount of the compensation shall be such as the tribunal considers just and equitable in all the circumstances, subject to paragraph (5), having particular regard to—
(a) any loss sustained by the transferee which is attributable to the matters complained of; and
(b) the terms of any contract between the transferor and the transferee relating to the transfer under which the transferor may be liable to pay any sum to the transferee in respect of a failure to notify the transferee of employee liability information.

(5) Subject to paragraph (6), the amount of compensation awarded under paragraph (3) shall be not less than £500 per employee in respect of whom the transferor has failed to comply with a provision of regulation 11, unless the tribunal considers it just and equitable, in all the circumstances, to award a lesser sum.

(6) In ascertaining the loss referred to in paragraph (4)(a) the tribunal shall apply the same rule concerning the duty of a person to mitigate his loss as applies to any damages recoverable under the common law of England and Wales, Northern Ireland or Scotland, as applicable.

(7) Section 18 of the 1996 Tribunals Act (conciliation) shall apply to the right conferred by this regulation and to proceedings under this regulation as it applies to the rights conferred by that Act and the employment tribunal proceedings mentioned in that Act.

13   Duty to inform and consult representatives

(1) In this regulation and regulations 14 and 15 references to affected employees, in relation to a relevant transfer, are to any employees of the transferor or the transferee

(whether or not assigned to the organised grouping of resources or employees that is the subject of a relevant transfer) who may be affected by the transfer or may be affected by measures taken in connection with it; and references to the employer shall be construed accordingly.

(2) Long enough before a relevant transfer to enable the employer of any affected employees to consult the appropriate representatives of any affected employees, the employer shall inform those representatives of—
(a) the fact that the transfer is to take place, the date or proposed date of the transfer and the reasons for it;
(b) the legal, economic and social implications of the transfer for any affected employees;
(c) the measures which he envisages he will, in connection with the transfer, take in relation to any affected employees or, if he envisages that no measures will be so taken, that fact; and
(d) if the employer is the transferor, the measures, in connection with the transfer, which he envisages the transferee will take in relation to any affected employees who will become employees of the transferee after the transfer by virtue of regulation 4 or, if he envisages that no measures will be so taken, that fact.

(3) For the purposes of this regulation the appropriate representatives of any affected employees are—
(a) if the employees are of a description in respect of which an independent trade union is recognised by their employer, representatives of the trade union; or
(b) in any other case, whichever of the following employee representatives the employer chooses—
    (i) employee representatives appointed or elected by the affected employees otherwise than for the purposes of this regulation, who (having regard to the purposes for, and the method by which they were appointed or elected) have authority from those employees to receive information and to be consulted about the transfer on their behalf;
    (ii) employee representatives elected by any affected employees, for the purposes of this regulation, in an election satisfying the requirements of regulation 14(1).

(4) The transferee shall give the transferor such information at such a time as will enable the transferor to perform the duty imposed on him by virtue of paragraph (2)(d).

(5) The information which is to be given to the appropriate representatives shall be given to each of them by being delivered to them, or sent by post to an address notified by them to the employer, or (in the case of representatives of a trade union) sent by post to the trade union at the address of its head or main office.

(6) An employer of an affected employee who envisages that he will take measures in relation to an affected employee, in connection with the relevant transfer, shall consult the appropriate representatives of that employee with a view to seeking their agreement to the intended measures.

(7) In the course of those consultations the employer shall—
(a) consider any representations made by the appropriate representatives; and
(b) reply to those representations and, if he rejects any of those representations, state his reasons.

(8) The employer shall allow the appropriate representatives access to any affected employees and shall afford to those representatives such accommodation and other facilities as may be appropriate.

(9) If in any case there are special circumstances which render it not reasonably practicable for an employer to perform a duty imposed on him by any of paragraphs (2) to (7), he shall take all such steps towards performing that duty as are reasonably practicable in the circumstances.

(10) Where—
(a) the employer has invited any of the affected employee to elect employee representatives; and
(b) the invitation was issued long enough before the time when the employer is required to give information under paragraph (2) to allow them to elect representatives by that time,
     the employer shall be treated as complying with the requirements of this regulation in relation to those employees if he complies with those requirements as soon as is reasonably practicable after the election of the representatives.

(11) If, after the employer has invited any affected employees to elect representatives, they fail to do so within a reasonable time, he shall give to any affected employees the information set out in paragraph (2).

(12) The duties imposed on an employer by this regulation shall apply irrespective of whether the decision resulting in the relevant transfer is taken by the employer or a person controlling the employer.

14   Election of employee representatives

(1) The requirements for the election of employee representatives under regulation 13(3) are that—
(a) the employer shall make such arrangements as are reasonably practicable to ensure that the election is fair;
(b) the employer shall determine the number of representatives to be elected so that there are sufficient representatives to represent the interests of all affected employees having regard to the number and classes of those employees;
(c) the employer shall determine whether the affected employees should be represented either by representatives of all the affected employees or by representatives of particular classes of those employees;
(d) before the election the employer shall determine the term of office as employee representatives so that it is of sufficient length to enable information to be given and consultations under regulation 13 to be completed;
(e) the candidates for election as employee representatives are affected employees on the date of the election;
(f) no affected employee is unreasonably excluded from standing for election;
(g) all affected employees on the date of the election are entitled to vote for employee representatives;
(h) the employees entitled to vote may vote for as many candidates as there are representatives to be elected to represent them or, if there are to be representatives for particular classes of employees, may vote for as many candidates as there are representatives to be elected to represent their particular class of employee;
(i) the election is conducted so as to secure that—

(i)   so far as is reasonably practicable, those voting do so in secret; and

(ii) the votes given at the election are accurately counted.

(2) Where, after an election of employee representatives satisfying the requirements of paragraph (1) has been held, one of those elected ceases to act as an employee representative and as a result any affected employees are no longer represented, those employees shall elect another representative by an election satisfying the requirements of paragraph (1)(a), (e), (f) and (i).

15   Failure to inform or consult

(1) Where an employer has failed to comply with a requirement of regulation 13 or regulation 14, a complaint may be presented to an employment tribunal on that ground—

(a) in the case of a failure relating to the election of employee representatives, by any of his employees who are affected employees;

(b) in the case of any other failure relating to employee representatives, by any of the employee representatives to whom the failure related;

(c) in the case of failure relating to representatives of a trade union, by the trade union; and

(d) in any other case, by any of his employees who are affected employees.

(2) If on a complaint under paragraph (1) a question arises whether or not it was reasonably practicable for an employer to perform a particular duty or as to what steps he took towards performing it, it shall be for him to show—

(a) that there were special circumstances which rendered it not reasonably practicable for him to perform the duty; and

(b) that he took all such steps towards its performance as were reasonably practicable in those circumstances.

(3) If on a complaint under paragraph (1) a question arises as to whether or not an employee representative was an appropriate representative for the purposes of regulation 13, it shall be for the employer to show that the employee representative had the necessary authority to represent the affected employees.

(4) On a complaint under paragraph (1)(a) it shall be for the employer to show that the requirements in regulation 14 have been satisfied.

(5) On a complaint against a transferor that he had failed to perform the duty imposed upon him by virtue of regulation 13(2)(d) or, so far as relating thereto, regulation 13(9), he may not show that it was not reasonably practicable for him to perform the duty in question for the reason that the transferee had failed to give him the requisite information at the requisite time in accordance with regulation 13(4) unless he gives the transferee notice of his intention to show that fact; and the giving of the notice shall make the transferee a party to the proceedings.

(6) In relation to any complaint under paragraph (1), a failure on the part of a person controlling (directly or indirectly) the employer to provide information to the employer shall not constitute special circumstances rendering it not reasonably practicable for the employer to comply with such a requirement.

(7) Where the tribunal finds a complaint against a transferee under paragraph (1) well-founded it shall make a declaration to that effect and may order the transferee to pay appropriate compensation to such descriptions of affected employees as may be specified in the award.

(8) Where the tribunal finds a complaint against a transferor under paragraph (1) well-founded it shall make a declaration to that effect and may—

(a) order the transferor, subject to paragraph (9), to pay appropriate compensation to such descriptions of affected employees as may be specified in the award; or

(b) if the complaint is that the transferor did not perform the duty mentioned in paragraph (5) and the transferor (after giving due notice) shows the facts so mentioned, order the transferee to pay appropriate compensation to such descriptions of affected employees as may be specified in the award.

(9) The transferee shall be jointly and severally liable with the transferor in respect of compensation payable under sub-paragraph (8)(a) or paragraph (11).

(10) An employee may present a complaint to an employment tribunal on the ground that he is an employee of a description to which an order under paragraph (7) or (8) relates and that—

(a) in respect of an order under paragraph (7), the transferee has failed, wholly or in part, to pay him compensation in pursuance of the order;

(b) in respect of an order under paragraph (8), the transferor or transferee, as applicable, has failed, wholly or in part, to pay him compensation in pursuance of the order.

(11) Where the tribunal finds a complaint under paragraph (10) well-founded it shall order the transferor or transferee as applicable to pay the complainant the amount of compensation which it finds is due to him.

(12) An employment tribunal shall not consider a complaint under paragraph (1) or (10) unless it is presented to the tribunal before the end of the period of three months beginning with—

(a) in respect of a complaint under paragraph (1), the date on which the relevant transfer is completed; or

(b) in respect of a complaint under paragraph (10), the date of the tribunal's order under paragraph (7) or (8),

or within such further period as the tribunal considers reasonable in a case where it is satisfied that it was not reasonably practicable for the complaint to be presented before the end of the period of three months.

16 Failure to inform or consult: supplemental

(1) Section 205(1) of the 1996 Act (complaint to be sole remedy for breach of relevant rights) and section 18 of the 1996 Tribunals Act (conciliation) shall apply to the rights conferred by regulation 15 and to proceedings under this regulation as they apply to the rights conferred by those Acts and the employment tribunal proceedings mentioned in those Acts.

(2) An appeal shall lie and shall lie only to the Employment Appeal Tribunal on a question of law arising from any decision of, or arising in any proceedings before, an employment tribunal under or by virtue of these Regulations; and section 11(1) of the Tribunals and Inquiries Act 1992 (appeals from certain tribunals to the High Court) shall not apply in relation to any such proceedings.

(3) 'Appropriate compensation' in regulation 15 means such sum not exceeding thirteen weeks' pay for the employee in question as the tribunal considers just and equitable having regard to the seriousness of the failure of the employer to comply with his duty.

(4) Sections 220 to 228 of the 1996 Act shall apply for calculating the amount of a week's pay for any employee for the purposes of paragraph (3) and, for the purposes of that calculation, the calculation date shall be—

(a) in the case of an employee who is dismissed by reason of redundancy (within the meaning of sections 139 and 155 of the 1996 Act) the date which is the calculation date for the purposes of any entitlement of his to a redundancy payment (within the meaning of those sections) or which would be that calculation date if he were so entitled;

(b) in the case of an employee who is dismissed for any other reason, the effective date of termination (within the meaning of sections 95(1) and (2) and 97 of the 1996 Act) of his contract of employment;

(c) in any other case, the date of the relevant transfer.

17 Employers' Liability Compulsory Insurance

(1) Paragraph (2) applies where—

(a) by virtue of section 3(1)(a) or (b) of the Employers' Liability (Compulsory Insurance) Act 1969 ('the 1969 Act'), the transferor is not required by that Act to effect any insurance; or

(b) by virtue of section 3(1)(c) of the 1969 Act, the transferor is exempted from the requirement of that Act to effect insurance.

(2) Where this paragraph applies, on completion of a relevant transfer the transferor and the transferee shall be jointly and severally liable in respect of any liability referred to in section 1(1) of the 1969 Act, in so far as such liability relates to the employee's employment with the transferor.

18 Restriction on contracting out

Section 203 of the 1996 Act (restrictions on contracting out) shall apply in relation to these Regulations as if they were contained in that Act, save for that section shall not apply in so far as these Regulations provide for an agreement (whether a contract of employment or not) to exclude or limit the operation of these Regulations.

19 Amendment to the 1996 Act

In section 104 of the 1996 Act (assertion of statutory right) in subsection (4)—

(a) the word 'and' at the end of paragraph (c) is omitted; and

(b) after paragraph (d), there is inserted—
', and
(e)   the rights conferred by the Transfer of Undertakings (Protection of Employment) Regulations 2006.'.

20 Repeals, revocations and amendments

(1) Subject to regulation 21, the 1981 Regulations are revoked.

(2) Section 33 of, and paragraph 4 of Schedule 9 to, the Trade Union Reform and Employment Rights Act 1993 are repealed.

(3) Schedule 2 (consequential amendments) shall have effect.

21 Transitional provisions and savings

(1) These Regulations shall apply in relation to—

(a) a relevant transfer that takes place on or after 6 April 2006;

(b) a transfer or service provision change, not falling within sub-paragraph (a), that takes place on or after 6 April 2006 and is regarded by virtue of any enactment as a relevant transfer.

(2) The 1981 Regulations shall continue to apply in relation to—
(a) a relevant transfer (within the meaning of the 1981 Regulations) that took place before 6 April 2006;
(b) a transfer, not falling within sub-paragraph (a), that took place before 6 April 2006 and is regarded by virtue of any enactment as a relevant transfer (within the meaning of the 1981 Regulations).

(3) In respect of a relevant transfer that takes place on or after 6 April 2006, any action taken by a transferor or transferee to discharge a duty that applied to them under regulation 10 or 10A of the 1981 Regulations shall be deemed to satisfy the corresponding obligation imposed by regulations 13 and 14 of these Regulations, insofar as that action would have discharged those obligations had the action taken place on or after 6 April 2006.

(4) The duty on a transferor to provide a transferee with employee liability information shall not apply in the case of a relevant transfer that takes place on or before 19 April 2006.

(5) Regulations 13, 14, 15 and 16 shall not apply in the case of a service provision change that is not also a transfer of an undertaking, business or part of an undertaking or business that takes place on or before 4 May 2006.

(6) The repeal of paragraph 4 of Schedule 9 to the Trade Union Reform and Employment Rights Act 1993 does not affect the continued operation of that paragraph so far as it remains capable of having effect.

SCHEDULE 1
APPLICATION OF THE REGULATIONS TO NORTHERN IRELAND

Regulation 2

These Regulations shall apply to Northern Ireland, subject to the modifications in this Schedule.

Sub-paragraph (1)(b) of regulation 3 and any other provision of these Regulations insofar as it relates to that sub-paragraph shall not apply to Northern Ireland.

Any reference in these Regulations—
(a) to an employment tribunal shall be construed as a reference to an Industrial Tribunal; and
(b) to the Employment Appeal Tribunal shall be construed as a reference to the Court of Appeal.

For the words from 'Paragraph (1)' to 'the 1992 Act' in regulation 7(6) there is substituted—
'Paragraph (1) shall not apply in relation to a dismissal of an employee if the application of Article 126 of the Employment Rights (Northern Ireland) Order 1996 to the dismissal of the employee is excluded by or under any provision of that Order, the Industrial Tribunals (Northern Ireland) Order 1996 or the 1992 Act insofar as it

extends to Northern Ireland, the Industrial Relations (Northern Ireland) Order 1992 or the Trade Union and Labour Relations (Northern Ireland) Order 1995'.

For the words from 'In this Regulation' to 'Part XII of the 1996 Act' in regulation 8(4) there is substituted—
'In this Regulation the 'relevant statutory schemes' are—

   (a)   Chapter VI of Part XII of the Employment Rights (Northern Ireland) Order 1996 ('the 1996 Order');

   (b)   Part XIV of the 1996 Order'.

For paragraph (4) of regulation 9 there is substituted—
'In article 92 of the 1996 Order (time off for carrying out trade union duties) in paragraph (1), for the full stop at the end of sub-subparagraph (c) there is inserted—

   '(d)   negotiations with a view to entering into an agreement under regulation 9 of the Transfer of Undertakings (Protection of Employment) Regulations 2006 that applies to employees of the employer, or

   (e)   the performance on behalf of employees of the employer of functions related to or connected with the making of an agreement under that regulation.'.'

For the words from 'Paragraph (2)' to 'the employee's employment with the transferor' in regulation 17 there is substituted—
'Paragraph (2) applies where—

   (a)   by virtue of article 7(a), 7(aa) or 7(b) of the Employers' Liability (Defective Equipment and Compulsory Insurance) (Northern Ireland) Order 1972 ('the 1972 Order'), the transferor is not required by that Order to effect any insurance; or

   (b)   by virtue of article 7(c) of the 1972 Order, the transferor is exempted from the requirement of that Order to effect insurance.

(2)   this paragraph applies, on completion of a relevant transfer the transferor and the transferee shall be jointly and severally liable in respect of any liability referred to in article 5(1) of the 1972 Order, in so far as such liability relates to the employee's employment with the transferor'.

In regulation 2 for 'the 1992 Act' there is substituted 'the Industrial Relations (Northern Ireland) Order 1992' and for 'Part XIII of the Insolvency Act 1986' there is substituted 'Part XII of the Insolvency (NI) Order 1989'.

In regulation 5 for 'sections 179 and 180 of the 1992 Act' there is substituted 'Article 26 of the Industrial Relations (NI) Order 1992 No807 (NI 5)'.

(1) In regulation 10 for 'the Pensions Schemes Act 1993' there is substituted 'the Social Security Pensions (Northern Ireland) Order 1975'.

(2) In regulation 11 for 'the Employment Act 2002 (Dispute Resolution) Regulations 2004' there is substituted 'the Employment (Northern Ireland) Order 2003 (Dispute Resolution) Regulations (NI) 2004'.

(3) In regulation 12 for 'Section 18 of the 1996 Tribunals Act' there is substituted 'Article 20 of the Industrial Tribunals (NI) Order 1996 No 1921 (NI 18)'.

(4) In regulation 16—

(a)   for 'Section 18 of the 1996 Tribunals Act' there is substituted 'Article 20 of the Industrial Tribunals (NI) Order 1996 No 1921 (NI 18)'; and

(b) for any reference to 'those Acts' there is substituted a reference to 'those Orders'.

For a reference to a provision of the 1996 Act in column one of Table 1 there is substituted the corresponding reference to the Employment Rights (Northern Ireland) Order 1996 in column two of Table 1—

Table 1	
Column 1	*Column 2*
Provision of the Employment Rights Act 1996	**Equivalent Provision in the Employment Rights (Northern Ireland) Order 1996**
Part X	Part XI
Section 98(4)	Article 130(4)
Section 98(1)	Article 130(1)
Section 135	Article 170(I)
Section 98(2)(c)	Article 130(2)(c)
Section 95(1)(c)	Article 127(1)(c)
Section 1	Article 33
Section 205(1)	Article 247(I)
Sections 220–228	Articles 16–24
Section 139	Article 174
Section 155	Article 190
Section 95(1)	Article 127(1)
Section 95(2)	Article 127(2)
Section 97	Article 129
Section 203	Article 245
Section 104	Article 135

Any expression used in this Schedule which is defined in the Interpretation Act (Northern Ireland) 1954 shall have the meaning assigned by that Act.

SCHEDULE 2
CONSEQUENTIAL AMENDMENTS

Regulation 20

1 References to the 1981 Regulations

In the following provisions, for 'Transfer of Undertakings (Protection of Employment) Regulations 1981' or 'Transfer of Undertakings (Protection of Employment) Regulations 1981 (SI 1981/1794)' there is substituted 'Transfer of Undertakings (Protection of Employment) Regulations 2006'—
(a) section 2(2) of the Property Services Agency and Crown Suppliers Act 1990;

(b) paragraph 8 of Schedule 1 to the New Roads and Street Works Act 1991;

(c) paragraph 5 of Schedule 1 to the Ports Act 1991;

(d) section 9(1) of the Export and Investment Guarantees Act 1991;

(e) section 168(1)(c) of the Trade Union and Labour Relations (Consolidation) Act 1992;

(f) paragraph 8 of Schedule 2 to the Roads (Northern Ireland) Order 1993;

(g) paragraph 6 of Schedule 1 to the Ports (Northern Ireland) Order 1994;

(h) section 129(1)(b) of the Education Act 2002;

(i) section 102(8) of the Local Government Act 2003;

(j) sections 3(6)(a) and 32(6)(b) of, and paragraph 12(1) of Schedule 3 to, the Horserace Betting and Olympic Lottery Act 2004;

(k) section 90(4) of the Clean Neighbourhoods and Environment Act 2005;

(l) section 39(5) of the Equality Act 2006.

2 Industrial Training Act 1982

(1) Section 3B of the Industrial Training Act 1982 (transfer of staff employed by industrial training boards) is amended as follows.

(2) In subsection (2), for 'Transfer of Undertakings (Protection of Employment) Regulations 1981' there is substituted 'Transfer of Undertakings (Protection of Employment) Regulations 2006'.

(3) In subsection (3)(a), for 'within the meaning of those Regulations' there is substituted 'to which those Regulations apply'.

3 Ordnance Factories and Military Services Act 1984

(1) Paragraph 2 of Schedule 2 to the Ordnance Factories and Military Services Act 1984 (application of 1981 Regulations to ordnance factories transfer schemes) is amended as follows.

(2) In sub-paragraph (1), for the words from 'for' to the end there is substituted 'for a transfer that is a relevant transfer for the purposes of the 2006 regulations'.

(3) In sub-paragraphs (2) and (6), for '1981 regulations', in both places where it occurs, there is substituted '2006 regulations'.

(4) In sub-paragraph (3) for the words from 'the 1981 regulations' to the end there is substituted 'the 2006 regulations as if, immediately before the appointed day, they were employed in the entity subject to the transfer'.

(5) In sub-paragraph (4)(b)—

(a) for 'with the undertaking or part' there is substituted 'with the entity subject to the transfer', and

(b) for the words from 'the 1981 regulations' to 'or part' there is substituted 'the 2006 regulations as if he were employed in the entity subject to the transfer'.

(6) In sub-paragraph (7), for the definition of 'the 1981 regulations' there is substituted—

"the 2006 regulations' means the Transfer of Undertakings (Protection of Employment) Regulations 2006.'

4 Dockyard Services Act 1986

(1) Section 1 of the Dockyard Services Act 1986 (transfer of persons engaged in dockyard services) is amended as follows.

(2) In subsection (4)—

(a) for the words from the beginning to 'Regulations 1981' there is substituted 'The Transfer of Undertakings (Protection of Employment) Regulations 2006',

(b) for the words from 'an undertaking' to 'those Regulations' there is substituted 'an undertaking to whose transfer those Regulations apply', and

(c) for the words from 'a part' to 'a business' there is substituted 'a part of that undertaking to whose transfer those Regulations apply'.

(3) In subsection (5)—

(a) for the words from the beginning to 'Regulations 1981' there is substituted 'The Transfer of Undertakings (Protection of Employment) Regulations 2006',

(b) for 'regulation 10', in both places where it occurs, there is substituted 'regulation 13', and

(c) for 'regulation 11' there is substituted 'regulations 15 and 16'.

5 Dartford–thurrock Crossing Act 1988

(1) Schedule 5 to the Dartford-Thurrock Crossing Act 1988 (transfers of staff) is amended as follows.

(2) In paragraphs 3(1) and 4, for 'the Employment Transfer Regulations', in both places where it occurs, there is substituted 'the Transfer of Undertakings (Protection of Employment) Regulations 2006'.

(3) In paragraph 4, for 'Regulation 7' there is substituted 'Regulation 10'.

(4) In paragraph 6—

(a) in sub-paragraph (2), for 'this Schedule', in both places where it occurs, there is substituted 'Part 1 of this Schedule', and

(b) after that sub-paragraph there is inserted—

'(3)   Expressions used in Part 2 of this Schedule to which a meaning is given by the Transfer of Undertakings (Protection of Employment) Regulations 2006 have the same meaning in Part 2 of this Schedule.'

6 Atomic Weapons Establishment Act 1991

(1) Section 2 of the Atomic Weapons Establishment Act 1991 (provisions applying to the transfer of certain employees) is amended as follows.

(2) In subsection (1)—

(a) for the words from the beginning to 'Regulations 1981' there is substituted 'The Transfer of Undertakings (Protection of Employment) Regulations 2006', and

(b) for the words from 'an undertaking' to 'those Regulations' there is substituted 'an undertaking to whose transfer those Regulations apply'.

(3) In subsection (2), for the words from 'a part' to 'a business' there is substituted 'a part of that undertaking to whose transfer those Regulations apply'.

7 Railways Act 1993

In section 151 of the Railways Act 1993 (general interpretation), in subsection (6), for the words from 'the Transfer' to the end there is substituted 'the Transfer of Undertakings (Protection of Employment) Regulations 2006, in their application in relation to a relevant transfer within the meaning of those regulations'.

8 Employment Tribunals Act 1996

In section 4 of the Employment Tribunals Act 1996 (composition of a tribunal), in subsection (3)(ca), for the words from 'regulation 11(5)' to 'Regulations 1981' there is substituted 'regulation 15(10) of the Transfer of Undertakings (Protection of Employment) Regulations 2006'.

9 Industrial Tribunals (Northern Ireland) Order 1996

In Article 6 of the Industrial Tribunals (Northern Ireland) Order 1996 (composition of a tribunal), in paragraph (3)(ab), for the words from 'regulation 11(5)' to 'Regulations 1981' there is substituted 'regulation 15(10) of the Transfer of Undertakings (Protection of Employment) Regulations 2006'.

10 Employment Rights Act 1996

In each of the following provisions of the Employment Rights Act 1996, for the words from 'Regulations 10' to 'Regulations 1981' there is substituted 'regulations 9, 13 and 15 of the Transfer of Undertakings (Protection of Employment) Regulations 2006'—
(a) section 47(1)(a) and (1A);
(b) section 61(1)(a);
(c) section 103(1)(a) and (2).

11 Employment Rights (Northern Ireland) Order 1996

In each of the following provisions of the Employment Rights (Northern Ireland) Order 1996 for the words from 'Regulations 10' to 'Regulations 1981' there is substituted 'regulations 9, 13 and 15 of the Transfer of Undertakings (Protection of Employment) Regulations 2006'—
(a) Article 70(1)(a) and (1A);
(b) Article 89(1)(a);
(c) Article 134(1)(a) and (2).

12 Income Tax (Earnings and Pensions) Act 2003

(1) The Income Tax (Earnings and Pensions) Act 2003 is amended as follows.

(2) In section 498 (no charge on shares ceasing to be subject to share incentive plan in certain circumstances), in subsection (2)(c), for the words from 'a transfer' to the end there is substituted 'a relevant transfer within the meaning of the Transfer of Undertakings (Protection of Employment) Regulations 2006'.

(3) In Schedule 2 (approved share incentive plans), in paragraph 32(2)(c), for the words from 'a transfer' to the end there is substituted 'a relevant transfer within the meaning of the Transfer of Undertakings (Protection of Employment) Regulations 2006'.

13 Pensions Act 2004

(1) Section 257 of the Pensions Act 2004 (conditions for pension protection) is amended as follows.

(2) In subsection (1), for paragraph (a) there is substituted—
'(a) there is a relevant transfer within the meaning of the TUPE regulations,'.

(3) Subsection (6) is omitted.

(4) In subsection (8), in the definition of the 'TUPE Regulations', for the words from 'Transfer' to the end there is substituted 'Transfer of Undertakings (Protection of Employment) Regulations 2006'.

14   Energy Act 2004

(1) Paragraph 10 of Schedule 5 to the Energy Act 2004 (supplementary provisions about nuclear transfer schemes) is amended as follows.

(2) In sub-paragraphs (1), (2) and (3), in each place where it occurs, for '1981 regulations' there is substituted '2006 regulations'.

(3) In sub-paragraph (1)—
(a)   after 'an undertaking', in both places where it occurs, there is inserted 'or business', and
(b)   for 'that undertaking or part' there is substituted 'that undertaking or business or that part of an undertaking or business'.

(4) After sub-paragraph (1), there is inserted—
'(1A)The 2006 regulations apply to a service provision change—
     (a)   in accordance with a nuclear transfer scheme, or
     (b)   in accordance with a modification agreement,
         as if (in so far as that would not otherwise be the case) the references in those regulations to the transferor were references to the person by whom the activities affected by the service provision change were carried out immediately before the coming into force of the service provision change.'

(5) In sub-paragraph (2), after 'a transfer' there is inserted ' (or service provision change)'.

(6) In sub-paragraph (3), after 'transfer', in both places where it occurs, there is inserted ' (or service provision change)'.

(7) In sub-paragraph (4), for the definition of 'undertaking' there is substituted—
'references to a service provision change are references to a service provision change falling within regulation 3(1)(b) of the 2006 regulations.'

Index

Pensions – *contd*
  developments – *contd*
    generally,   7.12
  due diligence,   7.11
  employees' rights and liabilities,
    and,   6.2
  introduction,   7.1
  key points,   7.12
  negligent statements,   7.6
  occupational pension schemes,   7.5
  private sector, and,   7.10
  public sector, and,   7.9
  questions and answers,   7.14
  reform proposals,   7.8
  statutory provisions,   7.2
  transfer of staff, and,   5.15
  transferred pension
    arrangements
    generally,   7.3
    guidelines,   7.4
  TUPE Regulations 1981, and,   7.1–
                                                7.2

Performance-related pay
  employees' rights and liabilities,
    and,   6.12
Peripheral activities
  developments,   2.15
  generally,   2.13
Policies and procedures
  generally,   6.19
  identification of contractual
    terms,   6.6
Private finance initiative
  transfer of staff, and,   5.15
Privatisation
  'relevant transfer', and,   3.14
Protection of rights
  employees' rights and liabilities,
    and,   6.1
Protective award
  collective consultation, and,   11.19
  insolvency, and,   15.15
Public private partnerships
  transfer of staff, and,   5.15
Public sector
  pensions, and,   7.9
  'relevant transfer', and,   3.4

Public sector – *contd*
  'undertaking', and
    developments,   2.15
    generally,   2.9
Reasonableness
  automatically unfair dismissal,
    and,   8.8
Recognition agreements
  Acquired Rights Directive
    1998, and,   14.10
  common law, at,   14.3
  conditions,   14.1
  definition,   14.3
  developments,   14.11
  distinct identity of transferred
    entity,   14.4
  effect of transfer,   14.5
  introduction,   14.1
  key points,   14.11
  representation rights,   14.2
  questions and answers,   14.12
  statutory changes,   14.6–14.8
  TUPE Regulations 1981, and,   14.1
  variation,   14.9
Reduction of workforce
  change required even without
    sale,   8.21
  contract conditions,   8.23
  improvement to chances of
    sale,   8.22
  introduction,   8.20
Redundancy
  Acquired Rights Directive
    1977, and,   12.1
  acquiring employer's
    considerations,   12.14
  automatically unfair dismissal,
    and,   8.25
  changes to terms and
    conditions, and,   9.10
  collective consultation
    comparison table,   12.13
    introduction,   12.12
    rules,   12.22
  consultation,   12.10
  contractual arrangements,   12.11